Feldgrau 1915-16

The War and Peace Time Uniforms of the German Army

The Official Regulations of 1915-16

Edited by Charles Woolley

Schiffer Military History
Atglen, PA

Special thanks to the Anne S.K. Brown Military Collection, Brown University, Providence, RI and its head curator Peter Harrington for access to the materials presented in this book.

Translated from the German by David Johnston.

Book design by Stephanie Daugherty.

Library of Congress Control Number: 2011935461

Printed in China.
ISBN: 978-0-7643-3958-5

We are interested in hearing from authors with book ideas on related topics.

Published by Schiffer Publishing Ltd.
4880 Lower Valley Road
Atglen, PA 19310
Phone: (610) 593-1777
FAX: (610) 593-2002
E-mail: Info@schifferbooks.com.
Visit our web site at: www.schifferbooks.com
Please write for a free catalog.
This book may be purchased from the publisher.
Please include $5.00 postage.
Try your bookstore first.

In Europe, Schiffer books are distributed by:
Bushwood Books
6 Marksbury Avenue
Kew Gardens
Surrey TW9 4JF, England
Phone: 44 (0) 20 8392-8585
FAX: 44 (0) 20 8392-9876
E-mail: Info@bushwoodbooks.co.uk.
Visit our website at: www.bushwoodbooks.co.uk
Try your bookstore first.

Introduction

In a few short years from 1907 to 1915, the uniforms of the German Army went through dramatic changes. After 1907 the Prussian blue which had been the standard of the army for many years was transformed into the new 'feldgrau', or field gray, which was designed to make troops in the field less conspicuous in the new mode of warfare. The next change came in 1915 and is the subject of this volume. This was the introduction of the new field gray wartime and the accompanying peacetime uniforms.

This volume actually combines three contemporary volumes in one. Each is highly illustrated in color and refer only to the 1915 wartime and peacetime uniforms. The text which accompanies "Deutchlands Armee in feldgrauer Kriegs-und-Friedens-Uniform" by Oberleutnant a. D. Freiherr v. d. Osten-Sacken u. v. Rhein explains the changes in depth and quotes the official regulations. The explanations and verbatim official regulations have been translated for the first time into English which should be helpful to the non-German speaking students of the Model 1915 issue uniforms. Feldgrau in Krieg und Frieden, Berlin 1916, by Hrsg. Von Otto Weiss is in two sections.

The first section, or I. Teil, illustrates in depth, mostly by schematics, the variations of all the various regiments dress for enlisted men by branch; i.e., Infanterie, Jäger, Husaren, etc. The second section, or II. Teil, portrays in the same fashion the uniforms for officers and military officials. In both sections front and rear line drawings of the basic uniforms appear with a short text in German. No attempt has been made to translate these captions as they are appropriate in the original German to the images shown. Weiss states his source of information is from the official "Kabinettsordre vom 21. September 1915", but does not quote directly from them. Weiss' schematic method of detailing with the variations in the uniforms is clear, concise and simple to follow.

The third volume, Die Feldgrau Friedens-und Kriegs-Bekleiding der K. Bayerischen Armee, by Helm, Ströbel and Bayer, printed by J.C. Huber, Munich 1916, is relatively rare and to the Editor's knowledge has not been reprinted in any form. The Bavarian army was traditionally somewhat different in their uniforms and insignia from the Prussian and other states. During the blue period of dress, the Bavarian blue material was of a lighter hue than the Prussian blue which had been adopted by all the other states. When feldgrau became standard all Bavarians continued to use the rampant lion on their buttons rather than the Imperial crown. The lion also appeared on the NCO rank buttons worn on the collar. Blue and white diamond tressing worn on the uniform collars of both enlisted and officer grades was also unique to Bavaria. In essence there was an individual nationalism enjoyed by the Bavarians which they were loath to surrender. The Bavarian cavalry consisted of two Schweres Reiter, two Ulan and eight Chevaulegers regiments who were issued peacetime uniforms of the same cut as the Ulanka of the Prussian Ulan regiments. Colored Paraderabatte were issued in the individual regimental distinctive colors to be worn by all cavalry units when in full dress.

No text was included in the Bavarian volume, but the cover indicates that the contents were approved by K. Bayer-Kriegministerums. To assist the Bavarian researcher, the translation of the Supreme Cabinet Order of the King of Bavaria, No.33730 dated Munich 1 April 1916, precedes the Bavarian section of the book.

As the centennial of World War I approaches, a renewed interest in the uniforms and equipment of the Great War has blossomed.

Several researched and well-illustrated books have been recently published. For further research of 1914-1918 uniforms, as well as the individual equipment, the following are highly recommended.

Imperial German Field Uniforms and Equipment, 1907-1918. Three volumes by Johan Somers, Schiffer Publishing Ltd., 2005.

Uniforms and Equipment of the Imperial German Army, 1900-1918, by Charles Woolley. Schiffer Publishing Ltd., 1999.

The German Army in the First World War, Uniforms and Equipment, 1914-1918, by Jürgen Kraus, Verlag Militaria. 2004, Stefan Rest, Publisher, Vienna, Austria.

Die feldgraue Uniformierung des deutschen Heers, 1909-1918. Two volumes by Jürgen Kraus, Biblio Verlag, Osnabrück, 1999.

Equipped with any of these additional volumes, the student of Imperial Feldgrau uniforms, the collector or military modeler will be well informed on this somewhat complicated subject.

The reproduction of these three volumes is through the courtesy of The Anne S.K. Brown Military Collection, Brown University, Providence, Rhode Island, and Peter Harrington, the Collection's curator.

Deutschlands Armee

in feldgrauer

Kriegs- und Friedens-Uniform

Mit 32 farbigen Tafeln und Text-Abbildungen

gezeichnet von

Militärmaler Paul Casberg

Mit den amtlichen Bestimmungen und einem erläuternden Text

von

Oberstleutnant a. D. Freiherr v. d. Osten-Sacken u. v. Rhein

Preis: 6 Mark 50 Pfennig

P. M. Weber, Verlag, Berlin SW. 68

Buchdruckerei Gustav Schenck Nachflg. P. M. Weber, Berlin SW. 68.

Foreword

The Supreme Cabinet Order issued by His Majesty the Kaiser and King on 21 September 1915 and the War Ministry's implementing regulations of 27 September 1915 have brought about a complete upheaval in the areas of service dress worn by our army and have also affected some of its equipment. Now that similar regulations have been issued by the sovereigns of the remaining contingents of the Reich Army and the affected war ministries, henceforth the entire German Army will wear field-gray uniforms in war and peace. The greatest transformation ever to take place in the history of army service dress has thus become an accomplished fact.

No matter how simple and clear the regulations are, in the beginning there obviously had to be much ignorance and lack of clarity, for the areas into which the changes extended were vast and widely-branching. As well, the simplification of uniforms meant that they had become so similar that even a militarily-trained eye was often unable to spot the remaining differences. The publisher therefore felt it necessary to produce a uniforms book which would fill the need for an indispensable hand- and textbook for every member of our army, while at the same time providing every German with precise information about the uniforms worn by our army, a requirement which is doubly great given the military spirit of our people.

In order to meet these different requirements, it does not suffice just to illustrate some of the different uniforms using figure plates. The latter must be accompanied by schematic depictions of every uniform and patterns of the main items of clothing if the book is to meet all requirements. But is also appears necessary to add the Supreme Order and war-ministerial regulations concerning the introduction of the new dress and equipment. Finally, the publisher also considers it advisable to add to the book descriptive text covering the development of uniforms and the reasons for the introduction of new uniforms and equipment, which also complement the illustrations. The now completed book, which represents a magnificent work in its overall layout and content, is, apart from smaller publications, the first of its kind and the most complete. It is the publisher's intention to deal with such corrections and additions as may become necessary through amendment slips or by issuing revised editions. The publisher is grateful for suggestions and requests for the subsequent form of this textbook. In this way it hopes to always keep the book up to date and enable it to successfully fill the role of indispensable handbook for every officer and official and at the same time serve as a textbook for soldiers and non-soldiers.

Berlin, October 1916 — P.M. Weber, Publisher

Our Field Grays

I. Prehistory

Uniform actually means uniformity. For in fact the uniform was originally introduced for the purpose of creating uniformity and homogeneity in soldiers' dress. This purpose was soon to be partly lost, however, for it could only be maintained within individual units. The growth of the army demanded ever-new identification badges to differentiate the newly created units. And so the widest variety of insignia was introduced, and their spread soon forced the original sense of the word "uniform" into the background. Hundreds of different uniforms appeared in the old German Empire with its many small vstates. Each of the larger states wanted to have its own army with every possible class of weapon and soldier, and not even the smallest were prepared to forego the maintenance of an armed force. When the Imperial Army was mobilized, these small contingents were combined into extremely mixed regiments. As well, all the different uniforms underwent an endless process of study and change. Those who wish to gain a picture of this should take up the "Soldier's Friend", whose pictures and excellent drawings by Knötel allow us to follow the changes that took place in this area. The study of uniforms had become something of a science.

It is reserved for the most recent times to do away with such a nuisance. Even though in the past the armies of smaller states were for most part incorporated into those of the larger military powers, the differences that existed were still very great and inappropriate for the case of war, as we will see. Therefore the sense of the word "uniform", whose actual meaning had become irrelevant with the passage of time, regained some of its importance. Under the pressure of conditions, a natural and therefore in the main also unchangeable basis for the subsequent development of the entire field of uniforms was created. Our army put on the field-gray jacket in place of the blue one.

Feldgrau. It sounds like a powerful magic word. And yet a gentle feeling of nostalgia emanates from it. Who can forget all the battles fought by our army, rich in victories and honor, in the blue coat it wore from the first day of its existence until the present, who can forget the hundreds of thousands of young men in blue who sealed their loyalty unto death in these battles and gave their lives for king and country? But taking off the old coat did not mean that our army had also shed its demonstrated spirit. It has proved convincingly in one war that the sons wearing the new coat are capable of fighting and dying just as heroically as their fathers once did in the old. So our army's tremendous feats have completely reconciled us with the change brought about by the perfection of firearms. We can trust with firm confidence that the field-gray coat will always show itself to be a victorious and honorable article of dress, just as the old blue one did.

And our army has not been the only one that has had to pay its toll to the demands of the times. All the great armies have had to do the same. They all had to part with their historical uniforms. Standing armies were created in the period after the Thirty Years War, and the first uniforms, loose and comfortable, were introduced soon afterwards, first among the foot soldiery but then also in the cavalry, which already possessed a degree of uniformity on account of its equipment – armor or leather collars and high boots. From the start the armies favored two bright colors that would enable their troops to be identified from a distance. In the Catholic countries, such as Austria and France, a preference was shown for the color white, while Protestant countries like Denmark and England preferred red. Our army and that of the Russians, which only later found a place among European armies, went their own way. While Russia selected green as the basic color for its army, we introduced dark blue, later named Prussian blue, for the mass of the foot soldiery. On the other hand we, too, chose white as the color for the cavalry regiments (later cuirassiers) and the dragoons. Later, between 1742 and 1745, this was replaced by light blue. The different colors worn by the guards disappeared under the soldier king, who disbanded his father's magnificent and colorfully-dressed guard units. The only distinguishing feature of his famous tall boys was the wearing of red underclothes instead of the usual white or pale yellow. Uniforms changed greatly under the king; they became much simpler and were given the close-fitting cut which has remained our army's own to the present day. The army regained some of its color when he expanded the nine troops of cavalry in Hungarian dress formed under his father to ninety (not counting ten troops of Bosnians) and bestowed individual colors upon all hussar regiments.

The first big change occurred in France. Like so many other things, the great revolution did away with the white coats, which were generally replaced by dark blue. Under the first Napoleon the picture soon became more colorful again. The dark blue base color was retained, though the dragoons wore green and some of the light cavalry regiments very bright colors. The red trousers of the French infantry were only introduced under Louis Philipp. After the war of 1866 the Austrians also discarded the white coats. In our army, where the exaggerated shortage of uniforms and the associated constraints on the troops had eased somewhat, there was at first no reason for such drastic changes. It had already been demonstrated, however, that the shiny helmet fittings were unpractical, and in 1866 these were changed to black in infantry units.

Towards the end of the century, however, the rapid progress in the development of firearms made in recent decades was providing a growing impetus to make uniforms less visible. While we had already made a start in that direction by introducing helmet covers, it was far from enough. It is doubtful that it was recognized at the time that not only the shiny accessories but also the basic uniform color needed to be changed. In any event, our first colonial unit, the Witzmann unit formed in the mid-1880s, was issued a khaki-colored uniform instead of the blue, the English having worn similar uniforms during their colonial undertakings. Then when the situation in China made necessary the formation of the East Asian Expeditionary Corps, this was also issued khaki uniforms. The military actions in China did not, however, provide the opportunity to amass the necessary experience. It was not until the Boer War, the war in Manchuria and the uprising in our Southwest African colony that this happened. These conflicts revealed the absolute necessity of selecting a basic uniform color that stood out from the terrain as little as possible. All armies now began large-scale experiments.

These experiments resulted in our introduction of the field-gray uniform as service dress in accordance with the Supreme Cabinet Order of 23/2/1907 and the implementing regulations issued by the War Ministry on 18/3/1907. The cut of the uniform was little changed, however. The coat had been made slightly wider and the stand-up collar was replaced by a folding or stand-and-fall collar, but in general it retained the certain stiffness that had always made our uniforms a little strange to the eye of our enemies, who misunderstood the purpose of smartness it is intended to foster. Equipment had already undergone numerous changes. With the help of budgetary changes and special measures authorized by the Reichstag, in the years that followed it was possible to define the new service dress for the entire German field army. The dark blue uniform, including all uniforms of the earlier style, was to be retained alongside the field-gray for parades, garrison guard duty, church services, court duty and as dress and formal attire. So a standard uniform, with only minor deviations, had been introduced at least for the event of war. The question as to whether the old blue uniform would be retained as a permanent fixture in peacetime had still not been decided when the World War broke out. According to a statement by the army administration, the reason was that sufficient experience was still lacking to determine whether the field gray cloth would live up to expectations.

II. Field Gray in War and Peace

The war brought the experience that had previously been missing. The French had proceeded less quickly with the introduction of their new field uniform, not conducting the process until the war was already under way. While the French in their bright red trousers were visible from a great distance, they were usually unable to see our field-gray infantry in the field until they were very close. The field-gray cloth also proved extremely durable, and so there was nothing left standing in the way of its ultimate retention as war service dress and acceptance for use in peacetime. A Supreme Cabinet Order signed by the Emperor and King on 21 September 1915 ordered the necessary changes to the uniforms worn by elements of the army under Prussian administration. The necessary implementing instructions were issued by the War Ministry on 27 September 1915. For the remaining contingents of the Reichsheer, the necessary cabinet orders from their contingent masters and associated implementation orders from the appropriate authorities followed quickly.

And so the final decision had been taken, and it could not have been postponed any longer. The war, which by then had been under way for more than a year, had completely consumed existing stores. The available stocks of field-gray uniforms could never have met the needs of the army, which had grown beyond all expectations. Parade uniforms and even the oldest types of peacetime uniform had to be used. Supplies of all types of cloth, including that used to make the old blue uniforms, were almost exhausted. The clothing offices, whose capacity had been increased so extraordinarily to enable them to meet not only the current demand for the entire army but also begin filling the emptied unit stockrooms, were forced to work day and night to ensure the availability of sufficient uniforms in the event additional units had to be raised quickly or a peace settlement was reached. An unnecessary delay in reaching the decision was also undesirable in the interests of the textile industry, for they could remain in the darkness no longer as to how they should organize. Quite extraordinary quantities of clothing had to be produced as quickly as possible. If the matter was delayed, the situation might arise that these stocks were not available in sufficient quantity when the need arose. And this was not the only consideration. If the decision was not made, even larger stocks of old cloth would have to be manufactured which later could no longer be used.

The previously-cited cabinet order also settled a second fundamental question. It, too, could be delayed no longer, for it had to take place simultaneously with the decision on the first question. It dealt with whether or not the previous cut of the uniform should be retained. Wartime experience had led to the conclusion that there was no need to change the trousers, coat and cap. Or that at least they could be easily modified to meet the requirements of war and peace. It wVas realized, however, that the demands on the tunic, the main item of clothing, were so different that it would be impossible to design a tunic that could meet both. In peacetime, in public and while traveling, the soldier must present himself in well-fitting things not lacking in style; the King's tunic requires a certain splendor. Anyone who has been a soldier knows how effective the uniform is as a means of creating and maintaining discipline, that foundation of military life. And not only that. The observer also knows how a smart uniform helps improve the impression made by a unit and a soldier's attachment to it, even after he has left the service. The significance of this bond, which affects both current and former members of a unit, to a people at arms like our own cannot be underestimated. In time of war, however, these considerations are far outweighed by others. The soldier's field tunic must allow him complete freedom of movement, especially under the current conditions. It must not restrict him, rather it must permit him to throw himself down, to crawl, to jump up, to run, to climb, to carry out the hardest toil and more. The man must be able to wear woolen underwear beneath the tunic in winter. All this means that the tunic must be roomy and comfortable with generously cut armholes. In the process it must be kept as simple and inconspicuous as possible. That was not the case with the previous field tunic, which for reasons of economy was something of a compromise between a peace- and wartime tunic. Out of these considerations it was decided to introduce two completely different tunics. This decision conformed completely to the experiences and practices of civilian life. No one wears his best "dress" coat while doing physical labor instead he chooses a special "work coat" which is both more comfortable and less expensive.

The former service coat serves as dress or peacetime tunic. Its cut is the same as the old one. As it is no longer worn in the field, it meets all the requirements for a peacetime tunic outlined above. The new service coat, which again has plain buttons, fittings etc, and pockets on the front flounce, will no longer be worn as excessively, and in place of the soft collar the historical Prussian standing collar has returned. This tunic once again gives full expression to Prussian rigidity, so infamous and ridiculed and yet so praiseworthy. Among the cuirassiers, too, the service tunic has replaced the jerkin, but they have retained the collar, the cuffs and brightly-colored rear flounces. The Attila and the Ulanka (the lancer's tunic) have been retained, though the latter has been fitted with shoulder straps instead of epaulettes. The basic color is field gray, and only the Jäger (light infantry) battalions wear gray-green tunics. The tunic trimmings, such as collars and cuffs, have retained their old historic colors, but once again the light infantry battalions are the exception, with red fittings replaced by pale green. The gold or silver piping of the officers and the braids of the enlisted men and NCOs are worn again in the earlier way in keeping with the standing collar. The enlisted men of the machine-gun battalions and the headquarters orderlies will henceforth wear the uniforms of the units to which they are attached or came from; their special uniforms were done away with for economic reasons. The Regiment der Gardes du Corps, the Guards Cuirassier Regiment, and the Lifeguard, 1st and 2nd Lifeguard and the Brunswick Hussars Regiments wear the white jerkin (and trousers) or the red and black Attila as gala and parade uniform. The gala uniform of the Regiment der Gardes du Corps and the officers of the Guards Cuirassier Regiment are also unchanged, as are the clothing (and equipment) of the Leibgendarmerie and Castle Guards Company. The hussars also continue to wear their fur caps with their gala and parade uniforms. The same applies to the mortarboard portions of the Ulans' helmets (Rabatten).

For the entire army the tunic serves as the work coat, worn exclusively in the field. On the front at hip level there are two pockets, and those worn by generals also have two breast pockets. It too is field gray and only the light infantry battalions, the mounted light infantry and the mounted police corps wear the gray-green version. All experience with the previous field tunic and the old Litewka [undress jacket with concealed buttons] was evaluated before deciding on its cut and fittings. Consequently the tunic was kept as simple as possible, the buttons are fitted invisibly, it is worn loose, has wide armholes, upturned cuffs which form so-called "sleeve pockets", and a gray-green folding collar, different than the basic color, on which the matte piping and braid as well as the border trimming, which was introduced in place of braid trimming, are applied in the same way as on the earlier field-gray field tunic.

No distinguishing badges are permitted to be worn on the tunic. In addition to the gorgets of the flag and standard bearers, the cuirassiers' breastplates, fur garters and epaulettes, this includes the rifleman's badge, shooting decorations, Kaiser Badges, badges for gunners, fencers and signalers, and badges commemorating attachment to training units or equivalent and similar institutions.

Even if it was necessary to make the entire army's war clothing as simple and uniform as possible, it is impossible to do away with all badges, for it is an absolute necessity that individual units be able to tell each other apart, at least close up. These badges must be simple and as similar as possible to those on the peacetime tunic in order to avoid mistakes that could easily have drastic consequences. Identification is achieved with shoulder straps or – among the Hussars – shoulder cords bearing unit function – or in the case of the cavalry, troop function – colors. The current colors are:

- **Infantry:** white on the Waffenrock, field gray with white piping on the Bluse,
- **Jäger:** pale green on the Waffenrock, gray-green with pale green piping on the Bluse,
- **Cuirassiers:** white with piping in the regimental color,
- **Dragoons:** cornflower blue with piping in the regimental color,
- **Hussars:** cords in the regimental color (Bodyguard Hussars, for example, red-yellow),
- **Ulans (lancers):** red with piping in the regimental color (9th and 13th Ulans, for example, red with white piping),
- **Jäger zu Pferde (mounted rifles):** pale green with piping in the regimental color,
- **Field Artillery** – whose historic color was red: red with a yellow artillery shell,
- **Foot Artillery:** gold-yellow with two crossed red artillery shells,
- **Pioneers:** black with red piping,
- **Traffic Control Troops:** pale gray,
- **Train:** Berlin blue (instead of previous pale blue).

With the exception of guard units, the NCO schools and similar formations, all units which do not bear titles or similar distinctions, such as, for example, Infantry Regiment No.53, which at present has been awarded a crown, numbers are worn on the shoulder straps. Even the cuirassiers and hussars now wear these. Consequently, now that the entire infantry with the exception of the light infantry and the entire field artillery wear white or red shoulder straps on the Waffenrock, corps colors are being abandoned. A remnant of this remains in the infantry, however, with the corps color worn as piping around the pocket flaps and cuffs.

The enlisted men's shoulder straps resemble the shoulder boards worn by the officers. The silvery shoulder boards have proved too conspicuous and therefore unusable in the field. As a result new, matte-finished officers' shoulder boards have been introduced. The old shoulder boards are now only worn during peacetime, and the epaulettes and epaulette holders have been discarded. As these have been used to differentiate between temporarily and permanently retired officers, special badges have been introduced for the two categories (see Badge Plate No.23). The cloth backing of the officer's shoulder board is the same color as the shoulder strap. Any sort of piping, such as the Guards Infantry, the entire cavalry and several other units have (see Appendix 2 of the War Ministry Implementing Regulations of 27/9/1915), also appears on the cloth backing as border striping. It remains to be mentioned that acting officers wear border trim around the shoulder strap, braid trim on the Waffenrock.

So the main item of war clothing is now completely standardized, apart from a slight deviation in color among the light infantry and Jäger zu Pferde. This offers great advantages, both for the employment of troops and for the equipping of new formations, for supply and for the replacement of clothing in wartime. There is no longer any need to maintain supplies of so many different coats, instead one type of tunic is sufficient for the entire army. It is both easier to make than the previous coats and for the most part just one type of cloth has to be procured. This is a significant gain, achieved through the introduction of the tunic.

Replacement of the dark blue color of the Prussian soldier's coat, and with it the different colors worn by the cuirassiers, dragoons and hussars, with field gray had become an absolute necessity. As previously stated, with the blue color a good piece of tradition vanished from the army, which had achieved all its victories in the old color. But it was an unavoidable sacrifice that had to be made to meet the changing requirements of warfare, a sacrifice that was no omen, for the army has retained its previous spirit. An effort was made to make this sacrifice as easy as possible for the army through the decision to allow the various branches and arms of the service to retain the style and color of their identifying badges. Units were also allowed to keep special decorations they had won and worn on the Waffenrock – and helmet. So the wearers of the new uniforms always remember the old in which their predecessors, often their ancestors, won their great victories on the Brandenburg-Prussian and Prussian-German battlefields. Their traditions live on in the army. The new peacetime uniform has also lost nothing in style. By now we have already become so accustomed to the field gray coat that we are almost surprised when we see the old blue one, and we already find it more becoming and modern than the colorful coats once worn by our cavalry.

The remaining pieces of the uniform have also become more standardized, consequently their introduction and replacement have also become much simpler.

As far as the trousers are concerned, the acceptance of the field gray uniform has also resulted in considerable simplification. Just two colors were retained for the long trousers as well as the riding and boot trousers, field gray for the major branches of the army and gray-green for the light infantry, the Jäger zu Pferde and the mounted police corps. A further simplification is now being introduced. The entire army is receiving trousers in a standard color. As they must go with both field gray and gray-green tunics, a neutral color, popularly referred to as stone-gray, was selected. The colored piping in the side seams of the cloth trousers and the border trim of the breeches worn by the hussars have been retained. The latter is its original color, meaning un-matted. The boot trousers worn by officers have piping only if provided with trim stripes. The generals and general staff officers of combat units do not wear trim stripes on their boot trousers. These are worn only in the homeland and in the rear areas. It should also be mentioned that the basic cloth of the dress trousers worn by all officers, with the exception of those of Regiment der Gardes du Corps and the Guards Cuirassier Regiment, is gray.

The color of the greatcoat has also been changed somewhat. The advent of positional warfare has made it impossible to predict when the war will end, and even the worst winter weather is incapable of interrupting the fighting. During much of the year, therefore, the greatcoat is an indispensable item of clothing for our troops. For this reason it has also been given the field-gray color. The greatcoats worn by the light infantry battalions and the Jäger zu Pferde are also field gray and not gray-green. The cut of the coat has also been changed slightly. The present war has revealed the unlined greatcoat previously worn by the foot soldiers to be too light, while the mounted troops have complained that the greatcoat is too long and heavy. A decision was made, therefore, to replace the previous foot and cavalry coats with a standard one for the entire army which is a cross between the two. This, too, is a significant simplification. The cut is unchanged. As with the tunic, the cuffs are turned up to form so-called "sleeve pockets". Proper side pockets are provided at hip level. The patches on the collar, which had to be removed in time of war, have now been completely eliminated. Instead, the coat – like the tunic – has a reseda-green collar that makes it stand out without being too conspicuous. The greatcoat's shoulder straps, which serve to differentiate between the various classes of arms and units, are the same as those of the Bluse.

The rather different color of the officer's greatcoat and its distinctive cut have proved extremely disadvantageous. The bright color and the two rows of buttons on the coat allow the officers to be identified at great distances. The officer's greatcoat with two rows of buttons is therefore being replaced by a field-gray coat with a single row of buttons, whose appearance is to be exactly the same as the coat worn by the enlisted men. While the equally conspicuous officer's cloak has not been eliminated because of its other advantages, it may no longer be worn in battle. It has now been moved to the list of permitted, but not absolutely necessary items. From now on it, too, will be field gray with a riding slit in the back.

The Feldmutze, or forage cap, has retained the basic gray colors used since the introduction of the field-gray uniform – field gray for the bulk of the army, gray-green for the light infantry battalions, Jäger zu Pferde and mounted police. In the field the colored trim stripes of the foot troops and cavalry are covered with gray bands. The service cap worn by officers with the field uniform has a folding gray leather visor and a leather chinstrap. The color of the peacetime or peaked cap is the same as the forage cap, however an exception has been made for the cuirassiers, dragoons and hussars in that they have been permitted to retain their old colorful caps. Henceforth, however, the visor of all caps is field gray. Like the enlisted men of the foot troops, those of the mounted troops now have visors on their own caps.

It remains to be said that the black neck stock was eliminated when the field-gray peacetime uniform was introduced. It was replaced by a gray

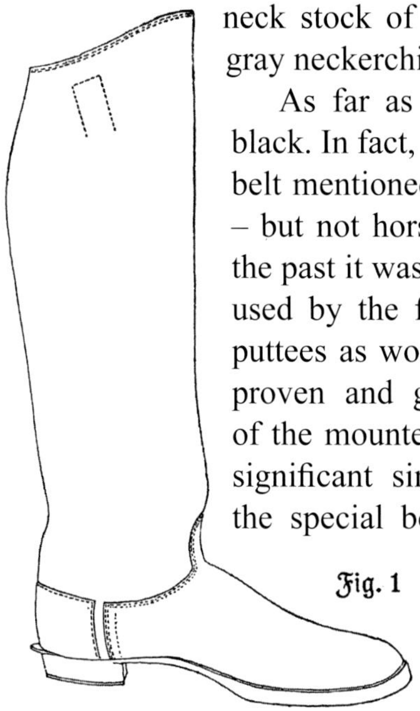

Fig. 1

neck stock of better cut, which also replaced the previous gray neckerchief of the field uniform.

As far as footwear is concerned, this continues to be black. In fact, apart from the newly-introduced officer's field belt mentioned below, all leather worn by officers and men – but not horses – will from now on be black, whereas in the past it was part white, part black or brown. The footwear used by the foot troops, ankle boots or laced shoes with puttees as worn by officers and various formations, is well proven and generally remains unchanged. The footwear of the mounted troops, on the other hand, has undergone a significant simplification, resulting in the elimination of the special boots worn by cuirassiers, hussars and Jäger zu Pferde. In future the so-called Standard Cavalry Boot will be worn (Fig.1). Its soft shaft is held upright by a light steel strip to keep it from sliding down and creasing. The boots worn by hussars have a trim stripe matching the trousers. The regulation requiring that unmounted personnel of the field artillery, with the exception of manual laborers, wear cavalry boots and consequently boot trousers in future, meets a desire long held by this arm for economic reasons. Concerning officers' footwear, a decision has been made that in all arms the laced shoes with puttees (Fig.2) are to be considered equivalent to the high boots and may also be worn with parade dress.

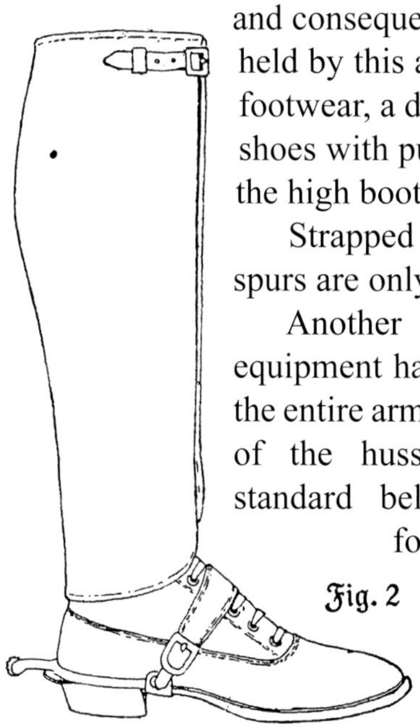

Fig. 2

Strapped spurs are prescribed as standard. Heel fixing spurs are only permitted to be worn with long trousers.

Another simplification of equipment has taken place in that the entire army, with the exception of the hussars, now wears a standard belt with the former foot troop belt buckle. When wearing the Attila [short jacket with braid], hussars wear the belt under the coat to protect the lacing, and the belt is fitted with a closing ring instead of a buckle. Conversely, the Ulans, who have lost the sash, will henceforth wear the standard belt over their Ulankas [lancer or Ulan tunic]. While in the field or on field exercises, the entire cavalry vnow wears the short bayonet on the standard belt or Leibriemen. The bayonet was introduced into general service because of its frequent use in dismounted combat, when the possibility of close combat must always be anticipated. The carbine hangs down on the left side of the horse so that it is immediately to hand when the rider dismounts. It is usually inserted into the carbine holster, while the Jäger zu Pferde have a considerably shorter model. In the field the man is supposed to carry the carbine with him at all times when dismounted; except in combat, it is to be worn on the back as shown in the plate depicting enlisted cavalrymen. No decision has yet been made as to whether the man should not perhaps also carry the carbine on his back while mounted. The cavalryman, with the exception of officers, is to have his saber with him at all times when mounted; it is carried on the right side with the exception of officers. Except in battle, the saber is worn on the Leibriemen when the rider is on foot. In the field some regiments no longer carry the sword at all, relying on the lance for horse-mounted combat; some regiments leave the lance pennants at home. The cavalryman now also wears the cartridge pouches on the front of the Leibriemen; so-called shoulder belts, which pass under the shoulder straps and join in the back, prevent the weight of the cartridge pouches from pulling the garrison belt down and bothering the man while riding. The new way of carrying ammunition has rendered the bandolier and cartridge pouches unnecessary. These are now no longer used by NCOs and enlisted men. A decision is pending as to whether officers, who also no longer wear them in the field, should retain them for wear with the Waffenrock in peacetime.

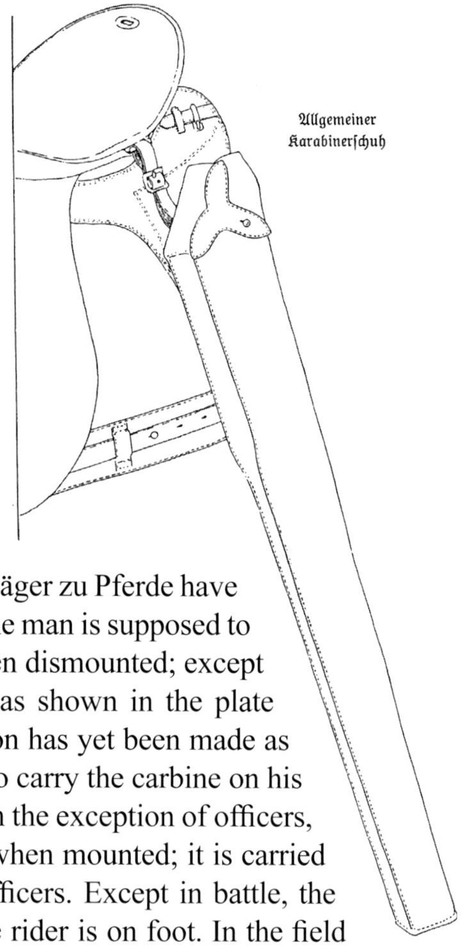

Allgemeiner Karabinerschuh

When the war began, officers still wore the silver Feldbinde instead of the Leibriemen; as it was too conspicuous, it was worn covered. It is being replaced by the leather field belt, on which are carried the field glasses, revolver holster, map pouch and short bayonet, of which the latter is now carried by most officers in the field. Initially the field belt was supposed to be black like the rest of the leather items, but in the end a decision was made in favor of brown, which provides an inconspicuous way of telling the officers from the men. Adjutants also wear the field belt in the war. Like other sashes, the adjutant's sash is now only worn with the Waffenrock, meaning in peacetime. The silver Feldbinde is still worn only by medical officers, who were awarded this just prior to the war. They are to wear it on all occasions when other officers wear the sash.

Like the silver Feldbinde, the wide ribbon bar with decorations has disappeared from the officer's field equipment as too conspicuous. It is now worn only with the Waffenrock, meaning in peacetime. While in the field officers are to wear a narrow ribbon bar without decorations.

As far as the helmet is concerned, it must first be noted that henceforth all dragoon regiments, with the sole exception of the 1st Guards Dragoon Regiment, will have nickel-silver fittings – and matching nickel buttons on the tunic. All helmets have been given removable spikes (or balls), the Tschapka [square-topped lance cap] a removable cover; spikes, balls and covers are not carried in the field, as all items that might make the wearer too conspicuous are to be avoided. For this reason the color green has been chosen for regiment and battalion numbers, which all units are to wear on their helmet covers in future, instead of the more conspicuous red. The field emblem on the shako, the hussar cap and the Tschapka is no longer worn with the field uniform. When fitted with cover, the helmet, shako, hussar cap and Tschapka are now generally worn with the chinstrap; scale chains have been retained only for the metal helmet, for the 1st Foot Guards Regiment and for officers, but also only for the case that the headgear is worn without a cover. For parade purposes the horsehair plumes worn by individual units in peacetime have been retained.

Not surprisingly, trench warfare has resulted in a large number of head wounds. In consequence, both we and our enemies have given much thought to a different type of headgear offering better protection for the main arm, the infantry. After much experimentation, we, along with the French and English, have adopted the steel helmet. Although no implementation order has yet been issued (August 1916), the equipping of our infantry with the new helmet, which could no longer be postponed, is proceeding apace. The helmet is extremely popular with the troops that have already received it. Even though it will not stop a rifle bullet, it does provide protection against shrapnel and smaller explosive rounds. It is, of course, considerably heavier than the old infantry helmet; its weight is about the same as the metal helmet worn by the cuirassiers and the Jäger zu Pferde. A type of sight can be fitted to the helmet for use by lookouts in the trenches, who can be killed by a bullet fired from close range as soon as they expose their heads, although this of course makes the helmet even heavier. One significant advantage of the new helmet is that the metal tears when pierced by a bullet instead of fragmenting. A unit wearing the new helmet may look rather foreign to us at first, but the eye soon becomes accustomed to the new look. The war has brought many other changes in the equipment worn by our troops which did not appeal to us at first but which were necessary. Moreover the new helmet, whose introduction had to be accelerated under the pressure of conditions, is still in the early stages of its development, and the possibility of improvement cannot be excluded. In the process it might perhaps lose the foreign impression it presently makes to our eye.

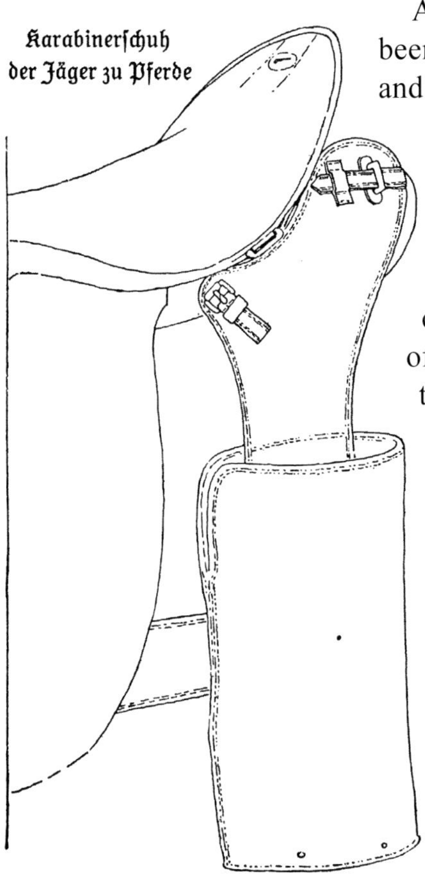

Karabinerschuh der Jäger zu Pferde

Among other items of equipment that have been changed are the backpack, the haversack and the bivouac sheet. Even before the war it had already been decided that the latter two would henceforth be gray instead of brown, and that the pack would follow. Mention is also made here that the haversack and canteen with drinking cup now form part of the field equipment of officers attached to foot units. Regarding the canteen it should be added that an ingenious and very simple mechanism has been added to prevent the stopper from freezing, which often caused it to break off.

Concerning the bivouac sheet, it remains to be mentioned that experience gained in the war has made it necessary to also provide the cavalry with these, although this process has yet to be completed. Stowage of the bivouac sheet on the horse's rear pack is illustrated in the plate depicting a Saxon Garde Reiter.

The horse equipment is otherwise unchanged. The brown color has been retained for the leathers. In the field – and likewise on maneuvers – officers' horses have the woolen horse blanket instead of the saddle blanket. It has yet to be decided whether the parade saddle cover and cavalry pistol cover will be retained in peacetime.

There is no need to come back to the officer's equipment. In general we are already familiar with it. The present war has confirmed the need for the officer's equipment to resemble as closely as possible that of the enlisted man, so that the enemy cannot identify him as such from a distance and shoot him. This realization has existed since the advent of rifled firearms, however not enough has been done about it. This danger is doubly great if, as is the case with us, officers in their enthusiasm lead their men from the front in order to inspire them through their example, instead of limiting themselves to urging them forward from the rear. Another reason for closely tailoring his equipment to that of the enlisted man is because the officer in the field is often forced to supplement his equipment from the spare items carried by his men. Offsetting these two points of view is the need for an officer to be clearly identifiable as such from a certain distance, on the one hand as a superior for disciplinary reasons, but also as a leader for tactical ones. In the latter respect it is particularly important that runners delivering orders are able to recognize the commanding officer as quickly as possible.

We have already seen how the new regulations seek to do justice to these points of view. In addition to the removal of all conspicuous badges, it has been expressly ordered that the cloth used in officers' field caps, coats and tunics must be identical to that worn by the enlisted men. A finer fabric may only be used for peacetime tunics and trousers, but it is strictly prescribed that officers' boot trousers must be exactly the same as the enlisted man's riding trousers in width and seat. In order to make it easier for officers to obtain regulation fabric, the War Ministry's implementing regulations state that cloth for coats, tunics and trousers may be procured by their units from the quartermaster's stores, which henceforth will stock lighter cloth for officers in addition to enlisted man's cloth. Officers can even obtain the items in question from the unit stores in completed condition by paying the cost price, however they are responsible for the necessary alterations. Field bags, canteens and drinking cups can also be obtained from unit stores. The experience of mobilization made the adoption of this measure appear to be absolutely necessary, for in many cases reserve officers lacked necessary items. This regulation was also issued to address the economic circumstances of the officers. This had not been given sufficient consideration for the earlier, often very expensive, uniforms.

It may also have been a crucial factor in the deletion of the overcoat and the interim Attila by the order of 21 September 1915. Instead of these, officers now wear the formerly gray Litewka, which has been given the name "kleine Rock" [small coat]; only the officers of the Lifeguard Hussars Regiment are permitted to wear a field gray interim Attila. The color and piping of the collar patches on the kleine Rock, usually called "Spiegel" (mirrors), are similar to those of the shoulder board bases and thus also the shoulder straps. The collar patches of medical and veterinary officers have remained unchanged. The piping of the kleine Rock down the front and around the collar and cuffs, previously a variety of colors, is now poppy-red for all officers and cornflower-blue for Beamte (officials). It should be noted that with the kleine Rock officers are permitted to wear a white collar visible to a height of 3mm under the neck stock, something that was strongly disapproved of in the past. The small coat may only be worn by officers and senior officials, but not by senior officer cadets, bandmasters, assistant paymasters, etc. Reserve officers do not need to possess it. For temporarily – and permanently – retired officers as well, it is only an authorized item. The ultimate demise of the overcoat, whose existence has often been threatened in the past, will be greeted with dismay in some quarters, for it was a very suitable item of clothing for older and especially for stouter officers.

Remaining to be mentioned is the introduction of a special uniform for the officers of the military cabinet. The field gray Waffenrock has poppy red piping. Collar and cuffs are the same color with special silver embroidery, while the trousers have poppy-red trim stripes.

Consideration must also be given here to the arms carried by the officers. When the army moved into the field, these consisted mainly of sabers and revolvers. Among the foot troops, however, it quickly became apparent that even the burnished saber made its bearer extremely conspicuous. The unexpectedly large number of close engagements also revealed the need to arm officers with a suitable weapon for such actions. The result was the introduction of the short bayonet for officers of foot units, which they now carry. Now, when there is to be an assault, an officer picks up the rifle of a killed or wounded soldier, making him even less distinguishable from his men than before, when the absence of a rifle made him identifiable. In infantry units the saber is still worn only by mounted officers, who leave it on the horse when they dismount. This practice has even established itself in the cavalry, which is now completely organized for combat on foot. Even artillery officers, who generally do not become involved in hand-to-hand combat, frequently carry the short bayonet in place of the saber. No ultimate regulations have yet taken effect with respect to this.

Changes to the uniforms of army administration officials (Beamte) corresponding to those contained in the cabinet order of the 21st and the implementing regulations of 27 September 1915 are contained in a special order and implementing regulations issued at the same time. The principles for the uniforming of officers and enlisted men are essentially the same for the Beamte. Details are contained in the implementation regulations on Pages 31 and 32. Mention will only be made of a few points. For example: as previously mentioned, senior officials are permitted to wear the kleine Rock with cornflower-blue piping and collar patches in the color and fabric of the Waffenrock collar, which are the same as before; the collar patch piping is the same color as the piping on the Waffenrock if this differs from the color of the patches. Those junior officials who previously wore a long overcoat (Überrock) instead of the Waffenrock, have now been given a field-gray Waffenrock with collar, Swedish cuffs and piping in the same color as the former overcoat. Instead of the saber tassel made of yellow silk, junior officials now wear one made of white silk, etc. As a special marking the officials now wear the prominent badge on their shoulder boards.

As for the troop contingents directly attached to the Prussian Army, only those of Hesse, Mecklenburg-Schwerin and Mecklenburg-Strelitz received direction from their contingent commanders for minor changes, limited to badges and identity markings. It must be mentioned that the nationality badges, etc, worn by the non-Prussian units presently being incorporated into the Prussian Army, such as the troops from Oldenburg, Brunswick, etc, have not been affected by the order of 21 September 1915 or the associated implementing regulations.

All that remains to be mentioned are the uniform changes of the Bavarian and Saxon Armies and the Württemberg Army Corps, which, because of alliance treaties and military conventions, have their own administration and separate war ministries. The changes adopted by all three contingents follow closely those for the Prussian Army and those differences that do exist are insignificant.

In Bavaria the introduction of the new uniforms was brought about by a supreme decision on 31 March 1916 and the implementing regulations of 1 April 1916. The following sentences will show that both were written somewhat differently than the Prussian regulations. See pages 33-41.

Henceforth the basic Waffenrock cloth for the entire army, including the light infantry, will be field gray. The basic cloth for trousers and caps will also be field gray. The Waffenrock has Swedish cuffs, in the cavalry only the Ulans retain Polish cuffs, which in future will also be worn by the Heavy Horse. The entire cavalry is receiving the Cheveauleger (light horse) coat with two rows of buttons, but the Ulans retain their former piping in the sleeve and back seams. For the shoulder straps the same color rules apply as in Prussia, but on the coats and blouses of the light infantry they are also green, not field gray with green edging. The cavalry's arm of service colors, which match the piping on the Waffenrock, are also somewhat different, as may be seen in Plate VI of the schematic illustrations. As well, cloth parade cap covers in the same colors form part of the parade uniform for the entire cavalry. It is mentioned here that the latter also includes a white belt. As a special marking, the Bavarian Army introduced narrow diamond-shaped lace trim on the collars of all new-style items of clothing. This is white-blue (officers silver-blue on the Waffenrock and kleiner Rock), while in the field it is gray (officers matte-silver base color).

The lace is applied to the top and front edges of the standing collar and around the outer edges of the stand and fall collar.

As for the long field-gray trousers, in all arms of service they had piping which matched the piping on the Waffenrock. The Bavarian Army's distinctive stripes on the long trousers of the cavalry and field artillery have been discarded. Riding and boot trousers worn by officers and men of all arms of service have no piping. Generals, who will henceforth wear the same embroidery as in Prussia but in silver, aides-de-camp, and officers of the war ministry and general staff retain their previous stripes, including on their breeches.

Coat, cape and blouse have a collar of the basic fabric, not trimmed fabric. The officer's coat has a single slit which allows the saber belt to pass through, as in future this will be worn outside the field-gray coat.

Helmets worn by the field and foot artillery and the ordnance and pyrotechnics personnel are henceforth to be fitted with a ball instead of a spike. The red and black plumes worn with the parade uniform by the artillery and train have been discarded.

In Saxony, the necessary uniform changes are governed by a supreme decree issued on 9 November 1915 and implementing regulations issued by the war ministry the same day. The regulations are closely patterned on the Prussian. All that needs to be mentioned is that the piping running along the bottom edge of the Waffenrock has been retained, that the Rifle Regiment has the same basic cloth as the light infantry battalions but with black trim material, and that the two heavy cavalry regiments have been given new Waffenröcke with white or black piping on the back seams. The Guards Cavalry Regiment still wears the cornflower-blue Waffenrock with Kirsenhose and previous riding boots as parade and gala uniform, however. Otherwise the regiment's gala uniform is also unchanged, while in other units the officers' gala trousers have been discarded. The officers of the 19th and 20th Hussar Regiments now wear silver cords on the Attila. Metal scales on the helmet without cover remain for the metal helmet, the two grenadier regiments and the officers.

In Wurttemberg a similar supreme decree with the necessary implementing regulations from the war ministry was issued on 10 October 1915. This contains no significant deviations from the Prussian regulations.

And so at last complete standardization in the uniforming of the army of the German Reich has now finally been achieved. The minor deviations that remain, mainly among the Bavarian and Saxon troops, are of no great significance. The entire German Army now wears a thoroughly standard field-gray uniform – during the war, as in the peace to come, that is after the old stocks are no longer permitted to be worn. One clue to the importance of standardization is offered by the example of the French in 1870, who directed their spies in Orléans to report as soon as Prussians wearing dark blue uniforms and spiked helmets arrived there to join the Bavarians, attired in light blue with their Raupenhelm helmets. Greater standardization will also reduce the instances of troops from the same army firing on each other. An even higher degree of standardization has been achieved through maximum simplification of the uniform, so that there are few significant differences between the various arms of service.

Even if one views the totality of the changes from this point of view, the following points stand out:

Every arm of service of the entire German Army now wears as wartime dress a type of blouse which differs only in the arm of service color on the shoulder straps. Only among the Prussian and Saxon light infantry and riflemen and the mounted rifle regiments is the color slightly different. Likewise there is now just one type of greatcoat, one neck stock, one type of cavalry boot, belt and belt buckle, one color for all leather items and footwear. All unnecessary items like the lancer's Leibbinde and the bandolier and cartridge pouches worn by the NCOs and men of the mounted units have been discarded. The prominent badges worn by flag bearers, etc., are now worn only with the new-style Waffenrock, meaning in peacetime. As well, the non-commissioned officer's lace bars have been replaced by less conspicuous braid.

In order to make officers less conspicuous, these changes include the introduction of field shoulder boards and replacement of the silver-colored Feldbinde by a leather field belt. Other changes, adopted for economic reasons, include the elimination of the greatcoat and the interim Attila, epaulettes and epaulette holders, and the recognition of ankle boots with puttees as equal to high boots.

In their totality, these changes represent a complete revision in the field of dress and equipment, something never experienced by the Prussian Army and not by the other contingents of the empire for a very long time. Of course these changes, made more difficult by the army's war footing, were not achieved overnight. Consequently, provisional regulations had to be issued. These were influenced by three main points of view:

1. rapid elimination of all conspicuous badges, etc.,
2. soonest possible introduction of the new identification badges (shoulder straps, officers' shoulder boards, collar patches) to avoid mistaken identity,
3. simplest possible transition.

Consequently the implementation orders issued by the Prussian War Ministry on 27 September 1915 – and by those of Bavaria, Saxony and Wurttemberg – essentially state the following:

The existing stocks of clothing and equipment are being worn unchanged. To be removed immediately, however, are the officers' silver belts without covering, adjutant's sash with field uniform, bandolier and pouches worn by NCOs and enlisted men, epaulettes and epaulette holders. Also to be immediately removed or eliminated are the field badges on the shakos, hussar caps and Tschapkas, and the particularly prominent badges worn by flag bearers. Shoulder boards of all kinds are to be replaced by the new type as soon as possible. The previously field- or gray-green Waffenröcke, Attilas and Ulankas will receive NCO braid instead of NCO lace, and after the existing shoulder straps have been used up they will be replaced by the new ones. Tschapkas and covers of all types are to be replaced with new ones as quickly as possible, but may still be worn in the homeland. Collar patches on previous field tunics and Litewkas – as well as the cloth backing – are to be changed as soon as possible as per the regulation for blouses, likewise the piping on the Litewka. The general's field tunic may continue to be worn as before. Any combination of old and new items of clothing is permissible, but dark blue Waffenröcke must not be worn with field-gray trousers, nor field-gray Waffenröcke with mixed dark blue trousers, with the terms "dark blue" or "mixed dark blue" understood to mean all items of clothing with the exception of the field-gray (gray-green) war clothing. Greatcoats, coats and capes of the previous type are to be fitted with collars of the basic fabric, and shiny buttons are to be replaced by new ones as on the coat.

Determination of the wearing times of all items of clothing was reserved until after peace has been reached.

During mobilization not all of the officers' equipment was up to the requirements of the situation, and in some places commanders issued orders independently. At its conclusion the supreme cabinet order of 21 September 1915 said of this:

> "Now that the army's clothing and equipment have been revised to incorporate the lessons learned in the war, I expect all special orders, permits and concessions issued by various headquarters to be rescinded.
>
> Deviations from the regulations and the introduction of special badges require my special authorization, even during the war."

With reference to this passage, the War Ministry stressed that the following items are contrary to regulations:

> for officers and men, puttees, provided they are not prescribed for specific formations,
>
> for non-commissioned officers and enlisted men, officers' caps, ankle boots with putties, brown gloves, NCO insignia in the form of chevrons or the like. The latter may, however, be worn by the fighting troops until the new braid becomes available.

There is a good reason why the closing sentence of the cabinet order makes reference to the possibility of further changes and reserves supreme authorization for them. In no aspect of human life, and least of all in any of the military, is there anything that is so perfect as to allow a halt in development. Even though all of the experience gained by the time the order was issued was taken into account, rapid advances in all areas of military technology mean that the war is constantly placing new demands on the army administration, whose fulfillment must be demanded by the army command. One only has to think about the matter of head protection. Thus the question of dress and equipment is not yet closed. All that has been achieved is to create a new basis for its further development. We must assume, however, that the right path has been taken and that our hope is justified that if we continue to follow it, it will lead to the objective. May our army enjoy the same success in the new field-gray uniform as it did in the old one. A magnificent, promising beginning has already been made.

Mantel und Bluse, Gold oder Silber matt

Für Generale

Waffenrock und Kleiner Rock

Generale

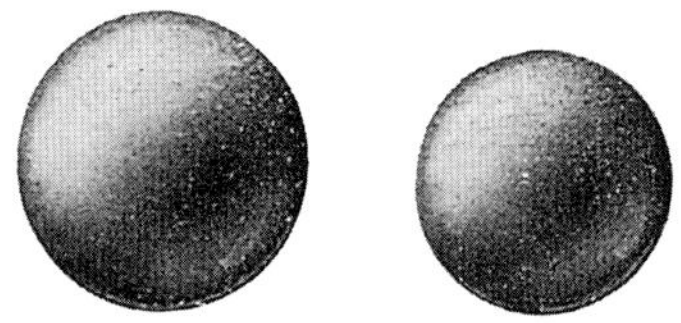

Waffenrock, gelb oder weiß blank

Für Offiziere und Mannschaften der deutschen Armee

Mantel und Bluse, gelb matt oder weiß matt

Für Offiziere der deutschen Armee

Mantel und Bluse, Tombak matt oder nickelfarbig matt

Für alle Mannschaften der deutschen Armee

Feldwebel Gefreiter Schießschule

Preußische Auszeichnungs-Knöpfe am Waffenrock, gelb oder weiß blank

Feldwebel Gefreiter Schießschule

Preuß. Ausz.-Knöpfe an der Bluse, Tombak matt oder nickelfarbig matt

Bayerische Auszeichnungs-Knöpfe der Bluse (Am Waffenrock blank)

Sächsische Auszeichnungs-Knöpfe der Bluse (Am Waffenrock blank)

Württembergische Auszeichnungs-Knöpfe der Bluse (Am Waffenrock blank)

Hessische Auszeichnungs-Knöpfe der Bluse (Am Waffenrock blank)

Mecklenb.-Schweriner Ausz.-Knöpfe der Bluse (Am Waffenrock blank)

Mecklenburg-Strelitzer Auszeichnungs-Knöpfe der Bluse (Am Waffenrock blank)

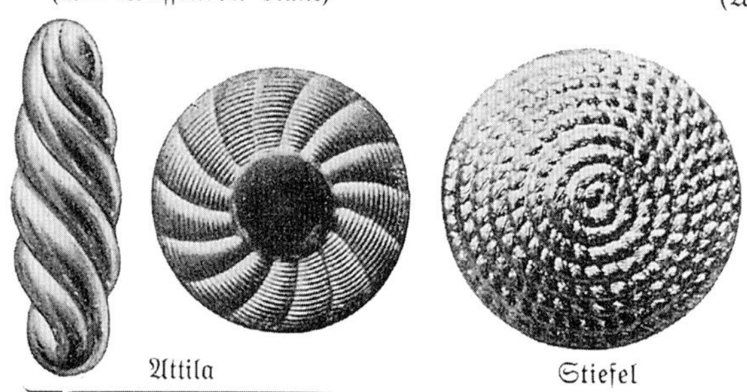

Attila Stiefel

Husaren-Offiziere, blank

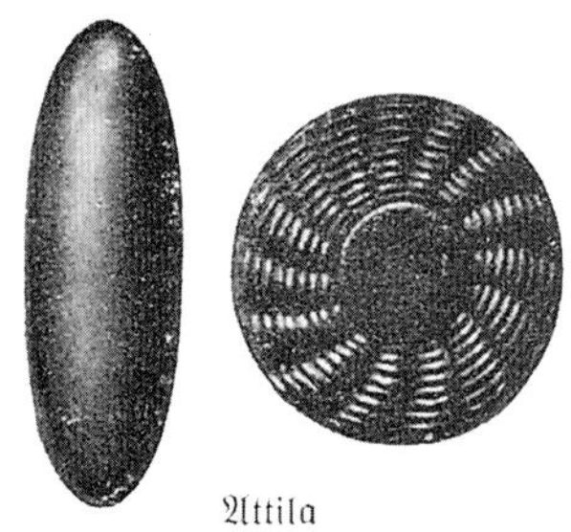

Attila

Husaren-Mannschaft, schwarz

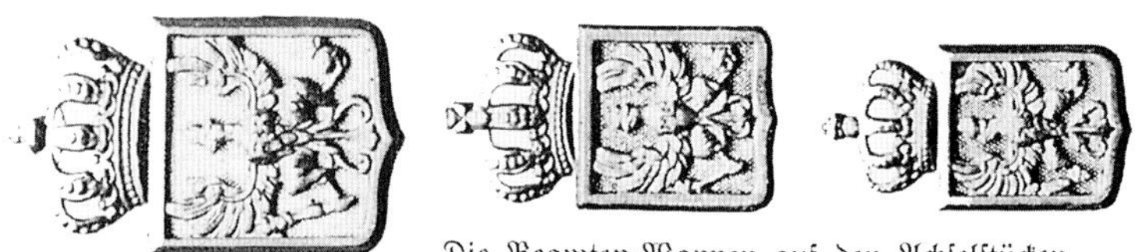

Die Beamten-Wappen auf den Achselstücken

Mütze

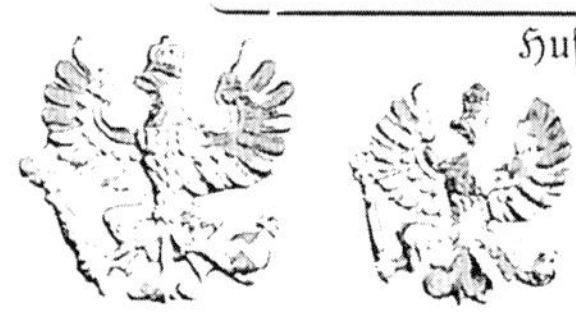

Desgl. an der Mütze für zu grüßende Beamte

Offiziers-Seitenhaken

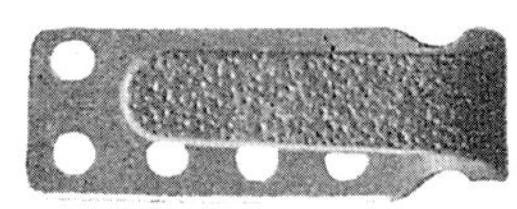

Mannschafts-Seitenhaken

Berlin, day 21, September 1915

Supreme Cabinet Order

by His Majesty the Emperor and King

of 21 September 1915 (No. 735) concerning changes to the uniforms of officers and men

Concerning the proposals submitted to me, I decree:

1. Henceforth the basic material of the Waffenrock (Attila, Ulanka) and the peaked cap shall be field-gray, for light infantry and riflemen, mounted rifles and the mounted police corps gray-green, specifically the darker gray-green authorized by me. There is no change, however, in the basic material of the peaked caps worn by cuirassiers, dragoons and hussars.

   Henceforth the cape is also field-gray; it will have a collar of coat trim material and a slit in the rear and will be issued only to authorized units.

2. The trim material of the light infantry is pale gray, that of the train potash-blue; the pale yellow and lemon yellow trim material is replaced by gold yellow, except for the exceptions in Appendices 1 and 2.

3. The previous colors of enlisted men's shoulder straps and sleeve patches as well as officers' shoulder boards are replaced by those depicted in Appendices 1* and 2.

4. The cuirassiers and hussars will wear their regiment number on their shoulder straps (shoulder cords), provided they have no title, the 1st Bodyguard Hussar Regiment No. 1 my name in the style approved by me.

5. The dragoons—with the exception of the 1st Guards Dragoon Regiment—will all receive nickel buttons and nickel-silver helmet fittings.

6. Lance-corporals and privates of all arms of service will henceforth wear a peak on their own caps.

7. The mounted rifles' Waffenrock will have the same cut as that of the dragoons, for officers with a slit for the sword; the buttons are shiny.

8. The special uniforms of the machine-gun battalions and headquarters orderlies are abolished.

9. I authorize the designs proposed to me:

   a. A field-gray coat, of identical cut for unmounted and mounted troops and with common trim material on the collar for all arms of service, instead of the previous coat and instead of the officer's coat and greatcoat, for generals with poppy-red lapel lining and piping.

   b. A field-gray (gray-green) blouse instead of the former field-gray Waffenrock (Attila, Ulanka), of the same cut and with common trim material on the collar for all arms of service, plus the embroidery, decorative bars and NCO braid instead of lace bars on this blouse.

   c. A Waffenrock for the cuirassiers instead of the former cape and Waffenrock.

   d. A new Attila for the Hussars to replace the current Attila.

   e. A field-gray officer's Litewka, henceforth called the "kleine Rock", instead of the previous gray one, together with the badges depicted in Appendix 3.

   f. For the foot artillery, enlisted men's shoulder straps and cords with a width of 4.5 cm with two crossed shells. Shoulder straps replace epaulettes for enlisted men of the lancers.

   g. A standard belt for enlisted men of all arms of service with a standard buckle instead of the existing garrison belt, under-belt, and saber belt with buckle or clasp, plus a dark brown, grained, leather field belt in place of the discarded field belt for officers.

      The Ulans' Leibbinde is abolished.

      Instead of the belt buckle, the hussars wear a closing ring with the belt worn under the coat.

      Instead of the Leibbinde, bandmasters wear the enlisted man's belt with the matte buckle from the Leibbinde.

   h. A gray neck stock instead of the neckerchief and the black and gray neck stocks. Officers may wear a white collar visible to a height of 3 mm beneath the neck stock with the kleine Rock.

   i. A standard cavalry boot instead of the former turndown boot, cavalry boot and hussar boot.

   k. The black ankle boots and puttees for officers.

   l. A field cap for officers and a field-gray peak for all peaked caps.

   m. Shoulder boards for temporarily- and permanently-retired officers.

10. Overcoat and interim Attila leave the inventory; the kleine Rock takes their place for officers. For temporarily- and permanently-retired officers and reserve status this is a permitted item only.

11. Not to be worn with the blouse:

    a.) badges for flag and standard bearers, rifleman badges, marksmanship awards, Kaiser badges and Kaiser shooting prizes, the badges for artillery gunners, fencers, Infantry Instruction Battalion, Military Riding Institute, shooting schools, NCO schools and pre-schools, and signalers;

    b.) flag and standard bearer's gorgets and cuirassiers' breastplates;

    c.) fur garters and swallow's nests.

12. The cut of officers' breeches will henceforth be identical in width and seat to the riding trousers for enlisted men, and piping in the seams only if it includes trim stripes.

    Hussars will have regimentally-patterned braid or lace on their breeches and riding trousers as on the earlier dark-blue trousers.

13. The non-mounted of the field artillery wear cavalry boots and breeches, the non-mounted of the machine-gun battalions infantry boots and long trousers.

14. Tricot may also be used in the Waffenröcke (Attila, Ulanka) and the officers' kleine Rock, corduroy may also be used in boot trousers; field caps, coats and blouses, on the other hand, must be of cloth whose appearance is fully compatible with the approved pattern for enlisted men.

15. All helmets and Tschapkas receive removable spikes (balls) or covers. Chin straps will generally be worn with covered helmets (shako, hussar's cap, Tschapka). For helmets etc without cover, scale chains for the metal helmet are approved only for my 1st Guards Regiment and for the officers.

16. The bandolier and cartridge pouches disappear from the equipment of NCOs and enlisted men. Officers are exempted from this order.

17. Leather articles (bark-tanned for all arms of service), shoes, as well as binocular cases, pistol holsters and map cases are to be worn blackened. The color of riding equipment has not changed.

18. Officers of all arms of service may on any occasion wear black ankle boots with putties instead of high boots.

19. Officers will generally wear strapped spurs of the type approved by me instead of heel-fixing spurs both with high boots and ankle boots with puttees.

20. The adjutant's sash will only be worn with the peacetime uniform; adjutants will wear the field belt with the field uniform like all other officers.

21. The existing ribbon bar will be replaced by

    a large ribbon bar (with medals) and

    a small ribbon bar (without medals).

22. Epaulettes and epaulette holders are discontinued. On the field uniform field, shoulder boards of the design approved by me will be worn on the blouse and coat.

23. To the field equipment of non-mounted officers with the foot troops will be added the haversack, canteen and drinking cup of the type for enlisted men.

24. As gala and parade uniform my Regiment der Gardes du Corps and the Guards Cuirassier Regiment will wear the white tunic and the Kirsenhosen, my Bodyguard Hussars Regiment the red, the 1st and 2nd Bodyguard Hussar Regiments No. 1 and 2 plus the Brunswick Hussars Regiment No. 17 will wear the black Attila. Otherwise the gala uniform of my Regiment der Gardes du Corps and that of the officers of the Guards Cuirassier Regiments remain unchanged, likewise the clothing and equipment of the Leibgendarmerie and Castle Guard Company.

The basic material of the gala trousers for all other officers is gray.

25. The Hussars will now only wear the pelisse with the parade and gala uniform.

26. Old style items must no longer be procured.
    Uniformity in officers' dress within the units is not to be pursued at any time during the wearing times.

27. Furthermore, in keeping with my directives the war ministry is to issue the details and regulations concerning the wearing of earlier items.

28. Now that the army's clothing and equipment have been revised to incorporate the lessons learned in the war, I expect all special orders, permits and concessions issued by various headquarters to be rescinded.

Deviations from the regulations and the introduction of special badges, even during the war, require my special authorization.

Grand Headquarters, the 21st of September 1915

Wilhelm

Un das Kriegsministerium — Wild v. Hohenborn

War Ministry
No. 1924/9. 15. B. 3. Grand Headquarters, 27 September 1915

Implementing Regulations

The following brings the preceding **Supreme Cabinet Order** to the attention of the army:

1. The changes ordered for the uniforms of officers or the regulations listed below are also generally applicable to medical and veterinary officers. Medical officers retain the Feldbinde for occasions at which the officers wear the sash.

2. The existing items of clothing and equipment are to continue to be worn unchanged, however the following are no longer to be worn: Feldbinden without wrapping, adjutant's sashes with field uniform, bandolier and cartridge pouches by NCOs and enlisted men, epaulettes and epaulette holders. Old-style shoulder boards are to be replaced by new-style ones as soon as possible.

   Special instructions will be issued for utilization of materials.

   The previous field-gray (gray-green) Waffenröcke (Attila, Ulanka) will receive NCO braid instead of NCO lace bars and new-style shoulder straps once the existing ones are used up.

3. The following may be worn:

   a) dark blue* Waffenröcke etc. only in combination with mixed dark blue or gray trousers, but not with field gray ones.

   b) field-gray Waffenröcke etc., Feldröcke, the kleine Rock and blouses in combination with field-gray (gray-green) or gray trousers, but not with mixed dark blue ones.

   Any other combination of old and new clothing is acceptable.

4. **Re 3.** On the field-gray Waffenrock worn by NCOs as salaried personnel, the trim, piping, shoulder straps and buttons (yellow or white) are the same as on the dark-blue Waffenrock. The blouse receives the same shoulder straps and matching matte buttons.

   Junior paymasters, junior inspectors, junior medical officers, junior veterinary officers and one-year volunteer military pharmacists wear the former shoulder straps of the dark-blue uniform, of NCO braid, with the previous trim. Acting officers and enlisted men in senior official positions also wear trim on the shoulder straps of the blouse of NCO braid.

5. **Re 1 and 6.** The color of the basic material and trim in the field-gray (gray-green) peaked cap is the same as that of the field-gray (gray-green) field cap.

6. **As to 8.** The machine-gun battalions wear the uniform of the unit to which they are attached, with the badge of the next senior company etc. Special instructions will be issued concerning the use of their previous service dress.

   Landwehr officers attached to machine-gun battalions wear the Landwehr uniform of the arm of service to which the army corps machine-gun battalion is attached, with the Guards Corps the uniform of the Guards Machine-Gun Battalion No. 1.

   Headquarters orderlies wear the uniform of their unit.

7. a) **As to 9a.**

   Greatcoats, coats and capes of the previous style are to be fitted with collars of basic material; their shiny buttons, like those on the coat, are to be replaced with new-style ones.

   b) **As to 9b and e**

   The patches on the previous Feldröcken and Litewken are to be altered as soon as possible according to the directive for the blouse—including the cloth underlay—or for the kleine Rock, likewise the piping on the Litewken. The generals' Feldrock can be worn as is.

* The terms "dark blue" and "mixed dark blue" encompass all items of clothing except the field-gray (gray-green) field service dress.

8. **As to 10.** The kleine Rock is intended for officers only; it is not authorized for other classes (band leaders, junior paymasters).

9. **As to 11.** These badges are also not to be worn with the former field service dress.

10. **As to 13.** Manual laborers of the field artillery continue to wear long trousers and infantry boots.

11. **Re 14 and 23.** Officers may procure coats, tunics and breeches, as well as haversacks, canteens and drinking cups from unit stores, paying the cost price set annually by the Army Administration Department. The officers are responsible for any necessary alterations. As well, they may procure material for the above-mentioned items of clothing through their unit from the clothing offices. In addition to the enlisted men's cloth, the latter will also carry the lighter material for officers.

12. **Re 15.**

    a) The Tschapkas and covers worn by the troops in the field are to be replaced with the new style as soon as possible; old-style Tschapkas may, however, be worn in the homeland.

    b) The field badge on the shako (hussar cap, Tschapka) are not to be worn with the field uniform.

    c) Helmet spikes (balls, covers) are not to be worn in the field or on exercise.

13. **Re 17.** Directions on blackening will follow. Leather footwear and other items in unit stores will also continue to be stocked unblackened.

14. The necessary descriptions and patterns will be issued by the Army Administration Department.

    Manufacturers can purchase extra patterns of the materials from the Guards Corps clothing office—which will obtain the remaining pieces from the clothing department—in the district in which they reside. An announcement concerning the starting date of this procedure will be published in the Official Army Gazette.

15. Application:

    a) for the field-gray tunic material the pattern of 27 August 1914 – No. 796/8. 14. B. 3 —

    b) for the field-gray coat material the pattern of 29 June 1915 – No. 22/6. 15. B. 3 —

    c) for the gray neck band the pattern of 2 August 1914 – No. 1172/7. 14. B. 3 – and

    d) for the standard cavalry boot the pattern of 6 December 1914 – No. 611/12. 14. B 3 —

    Mention is also made of those items already introduced

    a) the gray basic material for the long trousers and breeches (pattern of 27 August 1914 – No. 796/8. 14. B 3 —

    b) the gray badges on helmet covers,

    c) the band to cover the trim stripe on field caps – decree of 29 March 1915 No. 649/3. 15. B 3 (Army Gazette, p. 141)

    } 15 August 1914 U.B.B1 G 315

16. **Re 26.** Wearing times will not be determined until after peace is concluded.

17. **Re 28.** Including, among others:

    a) Officers' field caps worn by NCOs and enlisted men.

b) Puttees, provided they are not prescribed for certain formations by the War Ministry, for officers and men.
c) Ankle boots with puttees for NCOs and enlisted men.

d) Brown gloves for NCOs and enlisted men, with the exception of bandmasters.

e) NCO badges in the form of chevrons or the like.

Such may still be worn by the field-gray troops as long as the new braid is not available.

Wild v. Hohenborn

Changes to the Uniforms of Army Administration Officials

(No. 736)

In response to the report given me, I decree that:

The uniform regulations contained in my order of 21 September 1915 also apply to the officials of the army administration.

As well, the uniforms worn by officials will incorporate the changes proposed to me.

The War Ministry is hereby directed to take the necessary steps.

Grand Headquarters, 21 September 1915

Wilhelm

To the War Ministry — Wild v. Hohenborn

War Ministry — Grand Headquarters, 27 September 1915
No. 2152/9. 15. B 3.

Implementing Regulations

The following brings to the attention of the army the preceding **Supreme Cabinet Order**:

1. Of the implementing regulations for the Supreme Cabinet Order of 21 September 1915 concerning changes in the uniforms of officers and enlisted men, subparagraphs 2, 3, 5, 7, 8, 11, 13, 14, 15, 16 and 17 also apply to officials.

2. Officials wear collar patches on the blouse collar as on the kleine Rock (see No. 4), but generally of cloth, as well as cornflower blue piping around the edges of the blouse, coat and cape collar. Officials with embroidery on the collar of the Waffenrock may wear a smaller version of this, but in matte finish, also on the collar patches of the blouse.

3. Junior officials, who until now have worn an Überrock instead of the Waffenrock, will be issued a field-gray Waffenrock. Collars, Swedish cuffs, piping and dished buttons in the color of the collar etc. on the previous Überrock.

4. **kleiner Rock for senior officials.**

   a) Cornflower-blue piping around the collar, down the front and around the cuffs.

   b) Lapel lining, only for officials with the rank of Rating 1st Class: same color as the piping on the collar patches.

   c) Collar Patches. Same color and fabric as Waffenrock collar; collar patch piping same as piping on the Waffenrock if this differs from the color of the patches.

5. **Civilian officials attached to Clothing Departments, Supply Offices, Field Magazines, Garrison Administrations, Homes for the Disabled and Hospital Administration** wear:

a) trim on the cap and the Waffenrock of cornflower-blue cloth;

b) piping on the cap and the Waffenrock of white material;

c) shoulder boards and swordknot of silver and blue silk, dished shiny buttons on the Waffenrock, helmet eagle with device band and gilt rosettes.

6. The changes under 5 also find use:

a) on the trim worn by paymasters;

b) on the Waffenrock buttons and the swordknot of military construction officials, heads of field workshops, materials administrators, airship hangar inspectors and superintendents of rolling stock in transport units;

c) on the same items, the trim and the shoulder boards of the field officials of the war chests;

d) on the helmet eagle of all classes of civilian official (including acting officials), provided they are not yet wearing the devices;

e) similarly on the uniforms of junior officials and junior inspectors of the various branches of service and on the uniforms of junior paymaster officials.

7. White silk replaces the yellow silk prescribed for the sword knot worn by junior official classes.

8. The field caps of officials who wear no uniform (Preliminary Note 7 of the summary of the uniforms and badges of officials) will be made of field-gray basic material with dark blue trim.

Wild v. Hohenborn

War Ministry
No. 2072/10. 15. B 3

Grand Headquarters, 1 November 1915

Wearing of Officers' Tanned and Dark Brown Footwear.

Drawing of Feldröcken and Coats from Unit Stores.

(No. 847)

Concerning Subparagraph 17 of the Supreme Cabinet Order of 21 September 1915 (Army Gazette p. 420), his majesty the Emperor and King has deigned to declare that officers are to be permitted to wear tanned or dark-brown footwear without blackening.

Further, it is pointed out that as long as the enlisted men are still wearing old pattern Feldröcke and coats, in order to promote complete harmony of dress with the enlisted men, officers requiring blouses or coats are authorized to draw items in the old pattern, meaning Feldröcke and gray coats, from unit stores (army clothing depots). General authorization for this has been given in Para. 11 of the War Ministry's Implementing Regulations for the Supreme Cabinet Order of 21 September 1915 (Army Gazette, p. 423).

Wild v. Hohenborn

Appendix 3.

Badges on the kleine Rock of Officers, Medical Officers and Veterinary Officers

A. Piping

Down the front and around the collar and cuffs generally poppy-red. With madder red, crimson, and pink collar patches or piping on these patches, the piping down the front and so on is crimson, madder red or pink.

B. Colored Lapel Linings

For generals and commanders of regiments etc. only, in the basic color of the collar patches, or—if these have piping—in the color of the piping, poppy-red for medical officers with the rank of general.

C. Colored Collar Patches

Of the color and material of the shoulder strap material with piping in the color of the border stripes, if such are present on the shoulder patches.

Generals:	poppy-red with smaller reproduction of the golden old-Prussian embroidery.
General-adjutants and aides-de-camp, aides-de-camp, generals à la suite of His Majesty the Emperor and King, and officers of the military cabinet:	silver with poppy-red piping.
Medical Officers:	dark blue with poppy-red piping.
Veterinary Officers:	black with crimson piping.

Appendix 2

Identification Markings on Officers' Shoulder Boards

Arm of Service etc.	Shoulder Boards	
	Base	Edge Stripe (on the base)
Infantry		
1st Foot Guards Regiment	white	silver braid
2nd Foot Guards Regiment	white	poppy red
3rd Foot Guards Regiment	white	lemon yellow
4th Foot Guards Regiment	white	pale blue
5th Foot Guards Regiment	white	—
Emperor Alexander Guards Grenadier Regiment No. 1	white	—
Emperor Franz Guards Grenadier Regiment No. 2	white	poppy red
Queen Elizabeth Guards Grenadier Regiment No. 3	white	lemon yellow
Queen Augusta Guards Grenadier Regiment No. 4	white	pale blue
Guards Grenadier Regiment No. 5	white	—
Guards Fusilier Regiment	white	lemon yellow
Grenadier Regiment King Wilhelm I (2nd West Prussian) No. 7	white	lemon yellow
Bodyguard Grenadier Regiment King Friedrich Wilhelm III (1st Brandenburg) No. 8	white	poppy red
Grenadier Regiment King Friedrich III (2nd Silesian) No. 11	white	lemon yellow
1st Baden Bodyguard Grenadier Regiment No. 109	white	silver braid
6th Baden Infantry Regiment Emperor Friedrich III No. 114	white	pale green
King's Infantry Regiment (6th Lothringen) No. 145	white	pale blue
The remaining grenadier, infantry and fusilier regiments	white	—
Light Infantry (Riflemen)		
Guards Light Infantry Battalion	pale green	—
Guards Rifle Battalion	pale green	black (velvet)
Line Light Infantry Battalions	pale green	—
Cuirassier		
Gardes du Corps	white trimmed with silver braid	same color as the piping on the enlisted men's shoulder straps, 1st Cuirassier Regiment velvet
The remaining cuirassier regiments	white	(same as above)

Arm of Service etc	Shoulder Boards	
	Base	Edge Stripe (on the base)
Dragoons	cornflower blue	same color as the piping on the enlisted men's shoulder straps, velvet for Dragoon Regiments 2, 6, 11, 12, 14 and 22, Dragoon Regiment 19 silver braid
Hussars	as before, but with prominent piping	—
Ulans	poppy red	same color as the piping on the enlisted men's shoulder straps
Mounted Rifles	pale green	same color as the piping on the enlisted men's shoulder straps
Guards and Provincial Home Defense Cavalry	cornflower blue	—
Field Artillery		
Guards Field Artillery Regiments	poppy red	1st Guards Field Artillery Regiment white 3rd " " " lemon yellow 4th " " " pale blue, otherwise no piping
Line field artillery regiments, field artillery gunnery school, provincial home defense field artillery	poppy red	—
Foot Artillery	gold yellow	—
Engineer and Pioneer Corps	black (velvet)	Poppy red
Transport Units	pale gray	Aviation Battalions: 1st Battalion white 2nd " poppy red 3rd " lemon yellow 4th " pale blue otherwise no piping
Train	potash blue	—
District Commands, Clothing Departments	white	—

Remarks

1. No changes in the shoulder boards of all officer classes not listed here.
2. The shoulder boards of staff officers, captains (Rittmeister) and lieutenants—except hussars—have an overall width of 5.5 cm; width of the protruding cloth base and edge stripe each 3 mm.
   Width of the shoulder board, including the 3-mm protruding cloth base, of hussar officers: staff officers 6.5 cm, Rittmeister etc 4.5 cm.
   The dimensions of the markings on the shoulder boards are generally the same as those for captains, etc.
3. Foot artillery officers wear two gilt crossed shells over the numbers; on shoulder boards with names they are combined with these.
4. The bases and edge stripes of field shoulder boards worn by staff officers, captains (Rittmeister) and lieutenants are similar to those of the normal shoulder board; average width 4.5 cm, without stiffener; cords and badges (pattern for captains, etc) matte.

Hesse

Extract from the Grand Ducal Hessian Regulations

Appendix 2

Identification Markings on Officers' Shoulder Boards

Arm of Service etc.	Shoulder Boards	
	Base	Edge Stripe (on the base)
Infantry		
Lifeguard Infantry Regiment No. 115	white	silver braid
Infantry Regiment "Kaiser Wilhelm" No. 116	white	—
Infantry Bodyguard Regiment "Grand Duchess" No. 117	white	potash blue
Infantry Regiment "Prince Karl" No. 118	white	lemon yellow
Infantry Regiment "Prince Karl" No. 168	white	poppy red
Cavalry		
Guards Dragoon Regiment No. 23	cornflower blue	poppy red (outer) and dark green
Bodyguard Dragoons Regiment No. 24	cornflower blue	white (outer) and dark green
Home Defense Cavalry	cornflower blue	—
Field Artillery		
Grand Ducal Artillery Corps, Field Artillery Regiment No. 25	poppy red	—
Field Artillery Regiment No. 61	poppy red	—
Home Defense Field Artillery	poppy red	—
Train	potash blue	—
District Commands	white	—

Remarks

1. No changes in the shoulder boards of all officer classes not listed here.
2. The width of the shoulder boards, of the protruding edge of the cloth base, and the width of the edge stripe are the same as those in the general army regulations; likewise the dimensions of the badges on the shoulder boards; the shoulder boards of dragoon officers, however, have a double edge stripe, with the identifying color (red or white) on the outside.
3. The bases and edge stripes of field shoulder boards worn by staff officers, captains (Rittmeister) and lieutenants are similar to those of the normal shoulder board; only on the field shoulder boards of the officers of Bodyguard Regiment No. 115 is the edge stripe poppy red.

Appendix 3

Badges on the kleine Rock Worn by Officers, Medical Officers and Veterinary Officers

The badges follow the guidelines set down in Army Gazette 1915, p. 452*. The collar patches of dragoon officers are of cornflower blue material and inside the red or white piping they have a dark green edge stripe 4 mm wide.

Changes to the Uniforms Worn by Officials of the Army Administration

The uniforms of officials of the Army Administration follow the guidelines set down in Army Gazette 1915, p. 453 with the proviso that the helmet adornment remain unchanged.

Mecklenburg-Schwerin

Extract from the Grand Ducal Mecklenburg-Schweriner Regulations of 18 May 1916.

Changes to the Uniforms of the Officers and Enlisted Men

The imperial decree of 21 September 1915 concerning changes to the uniforms of the officers and enlisted men, including implementing regulations by the Imperial War Ministry and Appendices 1 to 3, is also generally applicable to the Grand-Ducal contingent; Appendices A to E*, which include a number of deviations ordered by the Grand Duke, are authoritative with respect to the identifying symbols of the arms of service and units.

The bases of officers' shoulder boards are: for generals and all other officers not specially designated, etc, unchanged; for adjutant-generals and aides-de-camp poppy-red with silver edge stripes, for Grenadier-Regiment 89 white with silver edge stripe, for Fusilier Regiment 90 Kaiser Wilhelm and district commands white, for Light Infantry Battalion 14 pale green, for Field Artillery Regiment 60 poppy-red, for Dragoon Regiments 17 and 18 cornflower-blue with poppy-red and black edge stripes respectively.

The embroidery or Litzen embroidery on the tunic collar patches of generals and officers are the same as those worn on the Feldrock.

A supreme decision is still pending with respect to the piping on the seams of the gray trousers worn by Dragoon Regiment 18 and Field Artillery Regiment 60.

The former summer tunics of white linen or denim can continue to be worn in closed areas as well as for bicycle riding and horseback riding while off duty.

---

* Appendices A to E expressed by the "Schematic Representation of the Enlisted Man's Uniform" (Plates I to V).

According to a note to Appendix A the Bodyguard Company of Grenadier Regiment No. 89 wore helmet chin scales during parades and similar occasions.

Mecklenburg-Schwerin

Extract from the Grand Ducal Mecklenburg-Schweriner Regulations of 31 May 1916.

Changes to the Uniforms of the Officers and Enlisted Men

1) in II/89.*
Waffenrock: sleeve patches field-gray with Litzen as before.
Piping: poppy-red.
Shoulder straps: poppy-red piping.
Tunic: double Litze [decorative bar] on the collar, poppy-red stripe in center of Litze, stripes yellow.
Shoulder strap piping: poppy-red.

Contrary to §139 of A. 4 and 5, of Appendix II of the Clothing Order, Part II, Feldwebel (sergeants) will also wear Auszeichnungsknöpfe [a button in the state colors worn by NCOs on each side of the collar to indicate rank].

2) 3rd Battery, Field Artillery Regiment No. 24.*
The poppy-red piping remains, even on the bottom edge of the collar on the Waffenrock.

3) **General:**
The NCO braid will receive stripes in the national colors.
In future the Auszeichnungsknöpfe for Feldwebel (Waffenmeister), Vizefeldwebel (Vizewachtmeister), Sergeanten, Gefreite and as per § 166 of 1 of Appendix II of the Clothing Order, Part II will receive the Mecklenburg coat of arms with crown instead of the royal crown.

4) **Officers:**
Shoulder boards in II/89 white base with poppy-red piping.
Collar patches on the kleine Rock white with poppy-red piping.
The buttons on the Waffenrock and kleine Rock remain yellow gilded in II/89 and 3/24.
In II/89, curved sleeve patches on the Waffenrock (see appendix to the Officers Clothing Regulation, No. 6, Subparagraph 68).
Collar Litzen on the tunic for II/89 in yellow or gold.

---

* See the schematic representations

Munich, 1 April 1916

Supreme Cabinet Order of the King of Bavaria

No. 33730

In the supreme decision of 31/3/1916, His Majesty the King graciously deigned to issue the following regulations concerning the reuniforming of the Bavarian Army:

I.

Changes in the Uniforms of the Officers and Enlisted Men.

I decree that:

1. In future the basic material of the Waffenrock, trousers and peaked cap will be field-gray.

   Henceforth the cape will also be field-gray; it will receive a collar of the basic material and have a slit in back.

2. The trim material of the Heavy Horse will in future be lemon-yellow, that of the 1st and 2nd Light Horse Regiments orange-red, the train potash-blue.

3. The former colors of the shoulder straps and shoulder board bases are replaced by those illustrated in the appendices.

4. Instead of cuffs with patches, in future the Waffenrock will generally have simple cuffs (so-called "Swedish"). The Ulans will retain their existing pointed cuffs (so-called "Polish"), and the Heavy Horse will receive the same cuffs.

   The entire cavalry will receive the Cheveauleger (light horse) tunic with two rows of buttons, the Ulans retain their existing piping in the sleeve and back seams.

In future the braid on trumpeters' swallow's nests will be sewn vertically, instead of slanted as at present.

5. In future the Auszeichnungsknöpfe will be marked with a crowned lion holding the Bavarian shield.

6. The Bavarian Army will receive a special emblem, consisting of a narrow white-blue (officers silver-blue) braid (for items of field uniform in gray—officers matt silver—basic color, to be attached to the collars of all items of clothing of the new style, specifically at the top and front on standing collars, and around the outer edge of stand-and-fall collars.

7. For all arms, the long field-gray service trousers are to be given piping in the color of the piping on the Waffenrock.
   The broad stripes on the long trousers of the cavalry and field artillery are thus deleted. Generals, adjutant-generals and aides-de-camp, officers of the War Ministry and the General Staff, as well as medical officers holding general's rank will retain the existing stripes, specifically on their boot trousers.
   The riding breeches and boot trousers worn by officers and enlisted men of all arms will have no piping.

8. Lance-corporals (Gefreite) and the ranks of all arms will henceforth wear a peak on their own caps.

9. The cockades on the peaked and field caps of officers and enlisted men will in future be manufactured according to a new pattern.

10. The special uniforms worn by machine-gun battalions and headquarters orderlies are discontinued.

11. I approve the following designs submitted to me:

   a) A field-gray greatcoat of standard cut for unmounted and mounted troops with collars of basic material for all arms in place of the existing coats for officers and enlisted men, for generals with poppy-red lapel lining and identical piping. Special Bavarian identity markings gray or matt silver.
   In future officers will wear the saber (single-edge sword) outside the field-gray greatcoat; to this end a slit approximately 8 cm long will be added to allow the carrying strap to pass through, either a horizontal one high in the rear part of the left coat pocket or a vertical one behind the pocket, depending on body shape.

   b) A field-gray blouse in place of the existing field-gray Waffenrock, of the same cut for all arms of service with collar of basic material (with two breast pockets and poppy-red piping on the collar and around the cuffs for generals) as well as the embroidery, Litzen and NCO braid instead of lace. Special Bavarian emblems as on the greatcoat collar.

   c) The buttons for Waffenrock, greatcoat and blouse. With the exception of number buttons, all Waffenrock buttons are dull—also for the Infantry Bodyguard Regiment--, the buttons on the greatcoat and blouse will bear the Royal Crown as a special marking.

   d) New embroidery for the collars and cuffs of the generals.

   e) A field-gray "kleine Rock" for officers together with the badges illustrated in Appendix 3. Bavarian emblems bright silver.

   f) Shoulder straps with a width of 4.5 cm. Shoulder straps replace epaulettes for Ulan enlisted men.

   g) A common belt for the enlisted men of all arms of service with a common belt buckle instead of the existing Leibriemen, outside belt and sword belt with buckle or clasp, plus a dark brown leather field belt in place of the discontinued Feldbinde for officers.
   Instead of the Leibbinde, bandmasters will wear the enlisted men's belt with the matt buckle of the Leibbinde.

   h) A gray neck stock (cloth) in place of the neckerchief and the black and field-gray neck stocks. Officers are permitted to wear a collar visible to a height of 3 mm under the neck stock with the kleine Rock and blouse (except in the field).

i) A new cavalry boot.

k) The black ankle boots and puttees for officers.

l) A field cap for officers and a field-gray peak for all peaked caps.

m) Shoulder boards for temporarily- and permanently-retired officers.

n) A simplified monogram for the 3rd Infantry Regiment.

12. The previously-authorized overcoat (Überrock) and the current officer's Litewka disappear from the inventory; the kleine Rock takes the place of the former for officers. For temporarily- and permanently-retired officers and for officers commissioned for the duration, this is only an authorized item.

13. Not to be worn with the blouse:

a) badges of flag and standard bearers, rifleman badges, marksmanship awards, King's badge and Kaiser shooting prizes, the badges for artillery gunners, fencers, Prussian Infantry Instruction Battalion and Military Riding Institute, shooting schools, NCO schools and pre-schools, and signalers;

b) flag and standard bearer's gorgets;

c) fur garters and swallow's nests.

14. Officers' boot trousers will henceforth be identical to the enlisted men's riding trousers in width and seat.

15. Unmounted members of the foot artillery will wear cavalry boots and boot trousers, those of the machine-gun battalions infantry boots and long service trousers.

16. Tricot may also be used in the Waffenröcke and the officers' kleine Rock, corduroy may also be used in boot trousers, on the other hand field caps, coats and blouses must be of cloth whose appearance is fully compatible with the approved pattern for enlisted men.

17. The enlisted men of the field artillery and of the train will receive the Helmet 96, the helmets of the officers and men of the field and foot artillery, likewise of the ordnance officers and NCOs, will receive a ball instead of the spike.

All helmets and Tschapkas will receive removable spikes (balls) or covers. Chin straps will generally be worn (also by officers) with covered helmets (shako, Tschapka). For helmets etc without cover, scale chains for the metal helmet are approved only for officers.

The helmets of all officers remain otherwise unchanged. The plumes of generals etc and the white plumes of aides-de-camp, officers of the War Ministry and of the general staff as well as of the cavalry are being retained, the red plumes of the field artillery and the black ones of the train are being discarded.

18. Bandolier and cartridge pouch are leaving the equipment of NCOs and enlisted men. Officers are exempted from this order.

19. Leather articles (bark-tanned for all arms of service), footwear, as well as binocular cases, pistol holsters and map cases, are to be worn blackened. The color of riding equipment has not changed. Cavalry enlisted men will wear with the parade Rabatte [colored cloth cover] a white leather belt with the same dimensions and buckle as the standard belt.

20. Officers of all arms of service may on any occasion wear black ankle boots with puttees instead of high boots.

21. Officers will always wear heel-fixing spurs with ankle boots and puttees.

22. The adjutant's sash will only be worn with the peacetime uniform; adjutants will wear the field belt with the field uniform like all other officers.

In future the court sash will also be worn by officers of the Heavy Horse.

23. The existing ribbon bar will be replaced by
    a large ribbon bar (with medals) and
    a small ribbon bar (without medals).

24. Epaulettes and epaulette holders are discontinued. In the field officer's shoulder boards of a design approved by me must be worn with the blouse.

25. To the field equipment of non-mounted officers with the foot troops will be added the haversack, canteen and drinking cup of the type for enlisted men.

26. The clothing and equipment of the Leibgarde der Hartschiere (Bavarian Palace Guards) remains unchanged.

27. Adjutant-generals and aides-de-camp will wear collars, cuffs, cap bands and shoulder board bases of poppy-red material.

28. Old-style pieces must no longer be procured. Continued production of gray trousers during the war is unaffected by this.

    No attempt will be made to enforce uniformity in officers' dress within units during the wearing time.

29. The War Ministry is to take the necessary steps.

    Regulations concerning the wearing of previous items I reserve to myself until after peace is concluded.

30. Now that the army's clothing and equipment have been revised to incorporate the lessons learned in the war, I expect all special orders, permits and concessions issued by various headquarters to be rescinded. Deviations from the regulations and the introduction of special badges, even during the war, require my express authorization.

II.

Changes in the Uniforms of Officials of the Army Administration

1. The uniform regulations issued for officers are also applicable to the officials of the Army Administration. In addition, the following changes are being made in the uniforms worn by the officials.

2. Officials will wear on their tunic collars collar patches in the same colors as on the kleine Rock, however generally of cloth, as well as cornflower-blue piping around the edge of the blouse, greatcoat and cape collar. Officials who have embroidery on the Waffenrock collar may continue to wear a smaller, matte version of this, even on the blouse collar patches.

3. Junior officials, who until now have had an overcoat instead of the Waffenrock, will receive a field-gray Waffenrock. Collars, simple (Swedish) cuffs, piping and dished buttons in the color of the collar etc on the previous overcoat.

4. Kleine Rock for senior officials:

   a) Piping around the collar, down the front and around the cuffs cornflower-blue.

   b) Lapel linings, only for officials of Class I of senior officials; same color as the piping on the collar patches.

   c) Collar Patches. Same color and material as the Waffenrock collar; collar patch piping the same as piping on the Waffenrock if this is different than the color of the patches.

5. Officials attached to the clothing department, rations department, field magazines and garrison or hospital administrations, the officials of the military training and military prison installations, and the remount inspectorate, depot and institute will wear:

   a) Trim on the cap and Waffenrock of cornflower-blue cloth;

   b) Piping on the cap and Waffenrock of white cloth.

6. The changes under 5 are also applicable to:

   a) the trim worn by paymasters, cashiers of the peacetime assets, paymaster officials of the general staff and the field officials of the war chests;

   b) likewise on the uniforms of junior officials and junior inspectors of the various branches of service and on the uniform of the junior paymaster.

7. The shoulder boards and sword knots of all officials will in future be of silver and blue silk, all rosettes gilded, the buttons the same as those of the officers.

   White silk replaces the yellow prescribed for sword knots of the junior official class.

8. The service caps of officials wearing no uniform (Preliminary Note 6 of the Summary of Uniforms and Badges of the Officials) will be of field-gray material with trim of dark-blue material.

9. Concerning the Bavarian emblem, the same applies to the officials as to the officers; for junior officials the enlisted men's pattern applies.

Concerning this the War Ministry decrees:

Implementing Regulations

I.

The following brings the preceding Supreme Cabinet Order to the attention of the army:

1. The changes ordered for the uniforms of officers or the regulations listed below are also generally applicable to medical and veterinary officers. Medical officers will retain the Feldbinde for occasions when officers wear the sash. Veterinary officers are not to wear the new leather field belt.

2. The existing items of clothing and equipment are to continue to be worn unchanged (exception see Subpara. 7a, however not to be worn are: Feldbinden without wrapping, adjutant's sashes with the field uniform, bandoliers and cartridge pouches by NCOs and enlisted men, epaulettes and epaulette holders. Old style shoulder boards are to be replaced by the new type as soon as possible.

   Special instructions will issued for the utilization of materials

   The previous field-gray Waffenröcke will receive NCO braid and, once the existing shoulder straps are used up, ones of the new pattern.

3. Any combination of old and new clothing is authorized until further notice.

4. **Re 3.** On the field-gray Waffenrock worn by NCOs as salaried personnel, the trim, piping, shoulder straps and buttons (yellow or white) are the same as on the blue* Waffenrock. The blouse receives the same shoulder straps and matching matte buttons.

   Junior paymasters, junior inspectors, junior medical officers, junior veterinary officers and one-year volunteer military pharmacists wear the former shoulder straps of the dark-blue uniform, of NCO braid, with the previous trim. Acting officers and enlisted men in senior official positions also wear trim on the blouse shoulder straps of NCO braid.

5. **Re 1 and 8.** The colors of the basic material and trim in the field gray peaked cap are the same as those of the field-gray field cap. For the piping on the long service trousers of medical orderlies Appendix 1 applies.

6. **Re 10.** The machine-gun battalion wears the uniform of the unit to which it is attached, with the badge of the next senior company etc. Special instructions will be issued concerning the use of their previous service dress.

   Landwehr officers attached to machine-gun battalions wear the Landwehr uniform of the arm of service to which the army corps machine-gun battalion is attached.

   Headquarters orderlies wear the uniform of their unit.

7. a) **Re 11a.** Greatcoats, coats and capes of the previous style are to be fitted with collars of basic material; their shiny buttons, like those on the new-style coat, are to be replaced with new-style ones.

   Old-style enlisted men's coats are to retain the previous buttons.

   The regulation for the wearing of the officer's sword outside the field-gray coat also applies to former NCOs with permission to wear the uniform.

   b) **Re 11 b and c.** The patches on the previous Feldröcke—including the cloth backing--are to be modified as soon as possible as per the regulation.

   The general's Feldrock can continue to be worn as is.

---

*The term "blue" refers to all items of clothing except the field-gray field service dress.

c) **Re 11g.** The introduction of the standard belt is limited to new procurements. Stocks of old-style Leibriemen, outside belts and sword belts are therefore to be used up without alteration.

d) **Re 11l.** On service caps (§ 6 Clothing Order II) with matte field-gray peak, the outer side of the chin strap and the pull buckle must also be matte field-gray, the metal buttons to attach the strap to the cap shiny field-gray.

8. **Re 12.** The kleine Rock is reserved for officers only (excluding Feldwebel-Leutnante); it is not authorized for other classes (bandmasters, junior paymasters, etc).

9. **Re 13.** This badge is no longer to be worn, even with the earlier field service dress.

10. **Re 15.** Manual laborers of the field artillery will continue to wear long trousers and infantry boots.

11. **Re 16 and 25.** All officers, medical officers and veterinary officers may procure coats, tunics and breeches, as well as haversacks, canteens and drinking cups from unit stores or clothing depots, paying the cost price set annually by the Army Administration Department. They are personally responsible for any necessary alterations. As well, they may procure material for the above-mentioned items of clothing through their unit from the clothing depots. In addition to the enlisted men's cloth, these will also carry the lighter material for officers. § 53 of the Clothing Order I and Para. 2 of the decree of 5/8/15 No. 72669—Army Gazette p. 724—is amended accordingly.

    As long as the enlisted men are still wearing old pattern Feldröcke and coats, in order to promote complete harmony of dress with the enlisted men, officers requiring blouses or coats are authorized to purchase items in the old pattern, meaning Feldröcke and gray coats, from unit stores (army clothing depots) at the cost prices set down in the gazette.

12. **Re 17.**

    a. The previous-style helmets are to be worn. The Tschapkas with covers of the troops in the field are to be replaced by the new pattern as soon as possible; however, the old-style Tschapkas are to be worn in the homeland.

    b. The field badge on the shako (Tschapka) is not to be worn with the field uniform.

    c. Helmet spikes (balls, covers) will not be worn in the field or on exercise.

13. Re 19. Directions on blackening will follow. Leather footwear and other items in unit stores will also continue to be stocked unblackened.

14. The necessary descriptions and patterns will be issued by the War Ministry. Manufacturers can purchase extra patterns of the materials from the Guards Corps clothing office—which will obtain the remaining pieces from the I Army Corps clothing depot—in the district in which they reside. An announcement concerning the starting date of this procedure will be published in the Army Gazette.

15. Application:

    a. for the field-gray tunic material the pattern of 6/9/14 No. 31267

    b. for the field-gray greatcoat material the pattern of 4/9/15 No. 79478

    c. for the gray neck stock, the description issued by the decree of 21/9/14 No. 32975

    d. for the new cavalry boot the design prescribed by decree on 9/5/14 with stiffening.

    e. the pattern for the field-gray trouser material will not be issued until after disarmament.

16. **Re. 28.** Officers etc are authorized to wear the tanned or dark-brown boots and shoes without blackening.

17. **Re 30.** Included among these are:

    a. Officer's field caps worn by NCOs and enlisted men,

    b. Puttees, provided they are not prescribed by the War Ministry for particular formations, for officers and enlisted men,

    c. Ankle boots and puttees for all NCOs and enlisted men, however approval is given for those non-commissioned officers who were formerly authorized to wear puttees by the decree of 13/3/12 No. 4995—Army Gazette p. 253—to wear the puttees currently in their possession. The decree of 4/10/15 No. 90308 therefore does not apply,

    d. brown gloves for NCOs and enlisted men, excepting bandmasters,

    e. NCO insignia in the form of chevrons or the like; among the fighting troops these may be continue to be worn as long as the new braid is not available.

II.

Of the Implementing Regulations Part I, subparagraphs 2, 3, 5, 7, 8, 11, 13, 14, 15, 16 and 17 also apply to civilian officials; the regulation on the wearing of the officer's sword outside the field-gray greatcoat may also be applied to junior officials equipped with a short bayonet.

Freiherr v. Kreß

Appendix 2

Identifying Badges on Officers' Shoulder Boards

Arm of Service etc	Shoulder Boards	
	Base	Piping (on the base)
Aides-de-camp	poppy-red	—
Infantry	white	—
Jäger	pale green	—
Cavalry		
1st and 2nd Heavy Horse Regiments	lemon-yellow	Steel-green (only on field shoulder boards)
1st and 2nd Lancer Regiments	crimson	" " " " " " "
1st and 2nd Light Horse Regiments	orange-red	" " " " " " "
3rd and 6th " " "	peach-red	" " " " " " "
4th and 5th " " "	poppy-red	" " " " " " "
7th and 8th " " "	white	" " " " " " "
Field Artillery	poppy-red	—
Foot Artillery	gold-yellow	—
Engineer Corps and Pioneers	black velvet	Poppy red
Transport Units	pale gray	—
Train	potash-blue	—
District Commands, Clothing Departments	white	—

Remarks

1. No changes in the shoulder boards of all officer classes not listed here.
2. The shoulder boards of staff officers, captains, etc have an overall width of 5.5 cm; width of the protruding cloth base and edge stripe each 3 mm; the dimensions of the markings on the shoulder boards are generally the same as those for captains, etc.
3. The bases and piping of field shoulder boards worn by staff officers, captains (Rittmeister) and lieutenants are similar to those of the normal shoulder board; average width 4.5 cm, without stiffener; cords and badges (pattern for captains, etc) matte.

Appendix 3

Badges on the kleine Rock of Officers, Medical Officers and Veterinary Officers

A. Piping

Down the front and around the collar and cuffs the same color as the piping on the Waffenrock.

B. Colored Lapel Linings

For generals and commanders of regiments etc only, in the basic color of the collar patches, or—if these have colored piping—in the color of the piping, poppy-red for medical officers with the rank of general.

C. Colored Collar Patches

In general the same color and material as the shoulder board base; cavalry officers will normally wear steel-green collar patches with piping in the color of the regiment in question, therefore, for example, heavy horse with lemon-yellow, 7th and 8th Light Horse Regiments with white piping; the officers of the engineer corps and the pioneers wear black velvet collar patches with poppy-red piping.

Generals:	poppy-red with smaller reproduction of the silver general's embroidery.
Adjutant-Generals: / **Aides-de-camp:**	poppy-red with miniaturized embroidery
Medical Officers:	dark blue with poppy-red piping
Veterinary Officers:	black with crimson piping

Dresden, 9 November 1915

Supreme Cabinet Order of the King of Saxony

Changes in the Uniforms of Officers and Enlisted Men (No. 265)

Concerning the proposals submitted to me, I decree:

1. Henceforth the basic material of the Waffenrock (Attila, Ulanka) and the peaked cap shall be field gray, for light infantry and riflemen gray-green, specifically the darker gray-green authorized by me. There is no change in the basic material of the peaked caps worn by the hussars. The Guards Horse and carabineer regiments will receive peaked caps of white basic material with colored trim bands and piping.

   Henceforth the cape is also field gray; it will have a collar of coat trim material and a slit in the rear and will be issued only to authorized units.

2. The trim material of the light infantry is pale green, the train potash blue, and for the ordnance and fortress construction personnel black (officers velvet).

3. The previous colors of shoulder straps and shoulder board bases are replaced by those illustrated in the appendices.

4. The hussars will carry their regimental number on their shoulder cords, provided they do not have a title.

5. The 1st Lancer Regiment No. 17 "Emperor Franz Joseph of Austria, King of Hungary" and the 2nd Lancer Regiment No. 18 will receive buttons and Tschapka fittings of nickel-silver.

6. Lance-corporals (Gefreite) and the ranks of all arms will henceforth wear a peak on their own caps.

7. The special uniforms worn by machine-gun battalions and headquarters orderlies are discontinued.

8. I approve the following designs submitted to me:

a) A single-breasted field-gray greatcoat, of identical cut for mounted and unmounted personnel and with identical trim material on the collar for all arms instead of the previous greatcoat and instead of the officer's greatcoat; for generals with poppy-red lapel lining and piping;

b) A field-gray (gray-green) blouse in place of the existing field-gray (gray-green) Waffenrock, of the same cut and with the same field-gray trim material on the collar for all arms of service, for light infantry and riflemen with gray-green trim material, as well as the embroidery, Litzen and NCO braid instead of lace on this blouse;

c) a Waffenrock for the Heavy Horse to replace the existing Waffenrock;

d) an Attila for the Hussars to replace the existing Attila;

e) a field-gray officer's Litewka, henceforth called the "kleine Rock", instead of the existing gray, together with the badges illustrated in Appendix 3;

f) the shoulder straps and cords with a width of 4.5 cm, for the foot artillery with two crossed shells. Shoulder straps replace epaulettes for Ulan enlisted men;

g) A standard belt for the enlisted men of all arms of service instead of the existing Leibriemen and sword belt, plus a dark brown leather field belt in place of the discontinued Feldbinde for officers.

The Lancer's Leibbinde is discontinued.

Instead of a buckle, the Hussars will wear a closing ring when the belt is worn under the coat.

Instead of the Leibbinde, bandmasters will wear the enlisted men's belt with the matt buckle of the Leibbinde.

h) A gray neck stock in place of the neckerchief and both the black and field-gray neck stocks. Officers are permitted to wear a collar visible to a height of 3 mm under the neck stock with the kleine Rock and blouse (except in the field).

i) a standard cavalry boot instead of the existing boot for the Heavy Horse, the cavalry boot and the hussar boot;

k) the black ankle boot and puttees for officers;

l) a field cap for officers and a field-gray peak for all peaked caps;

m) shoulder boards for temporarily- and permanently-retired officers.

9. The overcoat (Überrock) and interim Attila disappear from the inventory; the kleine Rock takes their place for officers. For temporarily and permanently retired officers and for officers commissioned for the duration, this is only a permitted item.

10. Not to be worn with the blouse:

a) badges of flag bearers, rifleman badges, marksmanship awards, King's badge and Kaiser shooting prizes, the badges for artillery gunners, fencers, Infantry Instruction Battalion, Military Riding Institute, gunnery schools, NCO schools and pre-schools, and signalers;

b) flag and standard bearer's gorgets;

c) fur garters and swallow's nests.

11. Officers' boot trousers will henceforth be identical to the enlisted men's riding trousers in width and seat.

12. Unmounted members of the foot artillery will wear cavalry boots and boot trousers, those of the machine-gun battalions infantry boots and long service trousers.

13. Tricot may be used in Waffenröcke (Attila, Ulanka) and the officers' kleine Rock, and corduroy may be used in boot trousers, on the other hand field caps, coats and blouses must be of cloth whose appearance is fully compatible with the valid pattern for enlisted men.

14. All helmets and Tschapkas will receive removable spikes (balls) or covers. Chin straps will generally be worn with covered helmets (Shako, hussar cap, Tschapka). For helmets etc without cover, scale chains are reserved for the metal helmet only, for both grenadier regiments and for officers.

15. Bandolier and cartridge pouches are leaving the equipment of NCOs and enlisted men. Officers are exempted from this order.

16. Leather articles (bark-tanned for all arms of service), footwear, as well as binocular cases, pistol holsters and map cases, are to be worn blackened. The color of riding equipment has not changed.

    Officers are authorized to wear tanned or dark-brown footwear without blackening.

17. Officers of all arms of service may on any occasion wear black ankle boots with putties instead of high boots.

18. Officers shall generally wear strap-on spurs of the type approved by me instead of heel-fixing spurs with high boots as well as with ankle boots and puttees.

19. The adjutant's sash will only still be worn with the peacetime uniform.; like all other officers, adjutants will wear the field belt with the field uniform.

20. The existing ribbon bar will be replaced by
    a large ribbon bar (with medals) and
    a small ribbon bar (without medals).

21. Epaulettes and epaulette holders are discontinued. In the field, officer's shoulder boards of a design approved by me must be worn with the blouse.

22. To the field equipment of non-mounted officers with the foot troops will be added the haversack, canteen and drinking cup of the type for enlisted men.

23. My Guards Horse Regiment will wear the cornflower-blue Waffenrock, Kirsenhose and the previous riding boots with the parade and gala uniforms. The rest of this regiment's gala uniform also remains unchanged. As well, the gala trousers specified for the officers of various units are discontinued.

24. The pelisse [over jacket trimmed with fur] of the commanders and generals à la suite of hussar regiments, as well as of temporarily- and permanently-retired generals who have been authorized to wear the uniform of a hussar regiment, will still be worn only with the parade, gala and court ball uniforms.

25. Old-style pieces must no longer be procured. No attempt will be made to enforce uniformity in officers' dress within units during the wearing time.

26. The War Ministry is to take the necessary steps, especially in establishing rules and regulations for the wearing of earlier pieces in keeping with my directions.

27. Now that the army's clothing and equipment have been revised to incorporate the lessons learned in the war, I expect all special orders, permits and concessions issued by various headquarters to be rescinded.

    Deviations from the regulations and the introduction of special badges, even during the war, require my express authorization.

Dresden, 9 November 1915

Friedrich August

To the War Ministry

v. Wilsdorf

War Ministry Dresden, 9/11/15
No. 5505 II C.

Implementing Regulations

The following brings the preceding Supreme Cabinet Order to the attention of the army:

1. The changes ordered for the uniforms of officers or the regulations listed below are also generally applicable to medical and veterinary officers. Medical officers will retain the Feldbinde for occasions when officers wear the sash. Veterinary officers are not to wear the new leather field belt.

2. The existing items of clothing and equipment are to continue to be worn unchanged, however the following are no longer to be worn: Feldbinden without wrapping, adjutant's sashes with field uniform, bandolier and cartridge pouches by NCOs and enlisted men, epaulettes and epaulette holders. Old-style shoulder boards are to be replaced by new-style ones as soon as possible.

   Special instructions will be issued for utilization of materials.

   The previous field-gray (gray-green) Waffenröcke (Attila, Ulanka) will receive NCO braid instead of NCO lace and new-style shoulder straps once the existing ones are used up.

3.The following may be worn:

   a) dark blue* Waffenröcke etc only in combination with mixed dark-blue or gray trousers, but not with field-gray ones;

   b) field-gray Waffenröcke etc, Feldröcke, blouses and the kleine Rock in combination with field-gray (gray-green) or gray trousers, but not with mixed dark-blue ones. Any other combination of old and new clothing is acceptable.

   The Supreme Decision of 9/4/1915 No. 1933 II C – Army Gazette 1915, Page 127 – remains in effect until the end of the war, however.

4. **Re 2 and 3**. On the field-gray Waffenrock worn by lower-ranking ordnance and fortress construction personnel, the piping and buttons (yellow or white) are the same as on the dark green Waffenrock, however the shoulder straps are of black velvet or cloth with poppy-red piping. The blouse receives the same shoulder straps and matching matte buttons.

   Junior paymasters, junior inspectors, junior medical officers, junior veterinary officers and one-year volunteer military pharmacists wear the former shoulder straps of the dark-blue uniform with the previous trim; on blouses the trim is of NCO braid. Acting officers and enlisted men in senior official positions also wear trim on the blouse shoulder straps of NCO braid.

5. **Re 1 and 6.** The color of the basic material and trim of the field-gray (gray-green) peaked caps is the same as that of the field-gray (gray-green) field cap.

6. **Re 7.** The machine-gun battalion wears the uniform of the unit it is attached to, with the badge of the next senior company etc. Special instructions will be issued concerning the use of their previous service dress.

   Landwehr officers attached to machine-gun battalions wear the Landwehr uniform of the arm of service to which the army corps machine-gun battalion is attached.

   Headquarters orderlies wear the uniform of their unit.

7. a) **Re 8a.**

   Greatcoats and capes of the previous style are to be fitted with collars of basic material; their shiny buttons are to be replaced with new-style ones like those on the new-style coat.

   b) **Re 8b and e.**

   The patches on the existing Feldröcke and Litewkas are to be modified as soon as possible in keeping with regulations for the blouse--and the cloth backing--or the kleine Rock; likewise the piping on the Litewkas.

   The general's Feldrock can continue to be worn as is.

---

* The terms "dark blue" and "mixed dark blue" encompass all items of clothing except the field-gray (gray-green) field service dress.

8. **Re 9.** The kleine Rock is reserved for officers only; it is not authorized for other classes (bandmasters, junior paymasters, etc).

9. **Re 10.** This badge is also no longer to be worn with the earlier field dress.

10. **Re 12.** Manual laborers of the field artillery will continue to wear long trousers and infantry boots.

11. **Re 13 and 22.** Officers may procure coats, tunics and breeches, as well as haversacks, canteens and drinking cups from unit stores or clothing depots, paying the cost price set annually by the Army Administration Department. They are personally responsible for any necessary alterations. As well, they may procure material for the above-mentioned items of clothing through their unit from the clothing depots. In addition to the enlisted men's cloth, these will also carry the lighter material for officers.

    In no case may the material used in officer's dress differ in color from that of the enlisted men's cloth.

12. **Re 14.**

    a) The Tschapkas with covers of the troops in the field are to be replaced by the new pattern as soon as possible; the old-style Tschapkas are to be worn in the homeland, however.

    b) The field badge on the shako (hussar cap, Tschapka) is not to be worn with the field uniform.

    c) Spikes (balls, covers) are not to be worn with the helmet etc in the field or during exercises in field uniform.

13. **Re 16.** Directions on blackening will follow. Leather footwear and other items in unit stores will also continue to be stocked unblackened.

14. The necessary descriptions and patterns are being issued by the Army Administration Department.

    Manufacturers can purchase extra patterns of the materials from the Guards Corps clothing office—which will obtain the remaining pieces from the XII (1.K.S.) Army Corps clothing depot—in the district in which they reside. An announcement concerning the starting date of this procedure will be published in the Military Gazette.

15. Application:

    a) for the field-gray tunic fabric the pattern of 3 September 1914 – No. 2373 II C/14 --,

    b) for the field-gray greatcoat fabric the pattern of 27 August 1915 – No. 3583 II C/15 --,

    c) for the gray neck stock the pattern of 20 August 1914 – No. 2012 II C/14 – and

    d) for the standard cavalry boot the pattern of 9 March 1915 – No. 1221 II C/15.

    Reference is made to the following, which have already been introduced:

    a) the gray basic fabric for the long trousers, riding trousers and boot trousers (pattern of 3 September 1914 – No. 2373 II C/14),

    b) the green badges on the helmet covers – directive of 29 August 1914 No. 172 (Military Gazette p. 189) --,

    c) the band to cover the trim stripe on the field cap – directive of 22 April 1915 No. 101 (Military Gazette p. 145).

16. **Re 25.** Wearing times will not be determined until peace has been concluded.

17. **Re 27.** Included among these are:

    a) Officer's field caps worn by NCOs and enlisted men,

b) puttees for officers and enlisted men,

c) ankle boots with puttees for NCOs and enlisted men,

d) brown gloves for NCOs and enlisted men, excepting bandmasters.

e) NCO insignia in the form of chevrons or the like. These may continue to be worn by the fighting troops as long as the new braid is not available.

v. Wilsdorf

No. 266

Changes in the Uniforms of the Officials of the Army Administration

Concerning the proposals submitted to me, I decree:

The uniform regulations contained in my order of 21 September 1915 also apply to the officials of the army administration.

As well, the uniforms worn by officials will incorporate the changes proposed to me.

The War Ministry is hereby directed to take the necessary steps.

Friedrich August

v. Wilsdorf

War Ministry
No. 5505 II C.

Dresden,
9/11/15

Implementing Regulations

The following brings to the attention of the army the preceding Supreme Cabinet Order:

1. Of the implementing regulations for the Supreme Cabinet Order of 9 November 1915 concerning changes in the uniforms of officers and enlisted men, subparagraphs 2, 3, 5, 7, 8, 11, 13, 14, 15, 16 and 17 also apply to civilian officials.

2. Officials wear collar patches on the blouse collar as on the kleine Rock (see No. 4), but generally of cloth, as well as cornflower blue piping around the edges of the blouse, coat and cape collar. Officials with embroidery on the collar of the Waffenrock may wear a smaller version of this, but in matte finish, also on the collar patches of the blouse.

3. Junior officials, who until now have worn an Überrock instead of the Waffenrock, will be issued a field-gray Waffenrock. Collars, Swedish cuffs, piping and dished buttons in the color of the collar etc. on the previous Überrock.

4. kleiner Rock for senior officials.

   a) cornflower-blue piping around the collar, down the front and around the cuffs.

   b) Collar Patches. Same color and fabric as Waffenrock collar; collar patch piping same as piping on the Waffenrock if this differs from the color of the patches.

c) Lapel lining, only for officials who have been personally awarded the rank of Class II Group 11 of the court rank order: same color as the piping on the collar patches.

5. Civilian officials attached to Clothing Departments, Supply Offices, Field Magazines, Garrison Administrations and Hospital Administration wear:

   a) trim on the cap and the Waffenrock of cornflower-blue cloth;

   b) the piping on the cap and the Waffenrock of white material;

   c) shoulder straps and swordknot of silver and blue silk, dished shiny buttons on the Waffenrock, helmet eagle with device band and gilt rosettes.

6. The changes under 5 also find use:

   a) on the trim worn by paymasters;

   b) on the Waffenrock buttons and swordknot of military construction officials, heads of field workshops, materials administrators, airship hangar inspectors and superintendents of rolling stock in transport units;

   c) on the same items, the trim and the shoulder straps of the field officials of the war chests;

   d) similarly on the uniforms of junior officials and junior inspectors of the various branches of service and on the uniforms of junior paymaster officials.

7. White silk replaces the yellow silk prescribed for the sword knot worn by junior official classes.

8. The field caps of officials who wear no uniform (Preliminary Note 14 of the summary of the uniforms and badges of officials) will be made of field-gray basic material with dark blue trim.

v. Wilsdorf

Appendix 2

Identifying Badges on Officers' Shoulder Boards

Arm of Service etc	Shoulder Boards	
	Base	Piping (on the base)
Infantry		
1st (Bodyguard) Grenadier Rgt. No 100	white	silver braid
2nd Grenadier Regiment No. 101	the same	—
The remaining infantry regiments	the same	—
Light Infantry (Riflemen)		
Light Infantry Battalions	pale green	—
Rifle (Fusilier) Rgt. No. 108	the same	black (velvet)
Heavy Horse		
Guards Horse Regiment	cornflower-blue	silver braid
Carbineer Regiment	the same	black (velvet)
Hussars	as before, but prominent like piping	—
Lancers	poppy-red	same color as the piping on the enlisted men's shoulder straps
Landwehr Cavalry	cornflower-blue	—
Field Artillery	poppy-red	1st Field Artillery Regiment No. 12 white 3rd " " 32 the same the remaining field artillery regiments –
Foot Artillery	gold-yellow	—
Engineer and Pioneer Corps	black (velvet)	Poppy red
Transport Troops	pale gray	3rd (Royal Saxon) Company of the Royal Prussian Aviation Battalion No. 1:
Train	potash-blue	—
District Commands, Clothing Departments	white	—
Ordnance and Fortress Construction Officers	black (velvet)	—

Remarks

1. No changes in the shoulder boards of all officer classes not listed here.
2. The shoulder boards of staff officers, captains (Rittmeister) and lieutenants have an overall width of 5.5 cm; width of the protruding cloth base and piping each 3 mm. Width of the shoulder boards, including the 3 mm projecting cloth base, of hussar officers: staff officers 6.5 cm, Rittmeister etc 4.5 cm.
3. Foot artillery officers wear two crossed shells over the numbers.
4. The bases and piping of field shoulder boards worn by staff officers, captains (Rittmeister) and lieutenants are similar to those of the normal shoulder board; average width 4.5 cm, without stiffener; cords and badges (pattern for captains, etc) matte.

Badges on the kleine Rock of Officers, Medical Officers and Veterinary Officers

A. Piping

Down the front and around the collar and cuffs generally poppy-red; with crimson-red and purple-red collar patches the piping down the front is crimson-red or purple-red, respectively.

B. Colored Collar Patches

General:
the same color and material as the shoulder board base. If the shoulder boards have edge stripes, the collar patches will also be given piping in the same color as the edge stripes.

In particular:

Generals: poppy-red with gold embroidery.

Adjutant-Generals and aides-de-camp, generals à la suite of His Majesty the King: poppy-red with silver embroidery.

Personal adjutants of the Royal Princes: silver with dark blue piping

Medical Officers: dark blue with poppy-red piping

Veterinary Officers: black with crimson piping

C. Colored Lapel Linings

Only for generals and commanders of regiments etc, in the base color of the collar patches. However, if the collar patches have piping, the lapel lining will be the same color as the piping on these collar patches. The lapel lining is poppy-red for medical officers with the rank of general.

Stuttgart, 10 October 1915

Supreme Cabinet Order of the King of Württemberg

Changes in the Uniforms of Officers and Enlisted Men as well as Officials (No. 761)

His Majesty the King, in agreement with a decree issued by His Majesty the Kaiser for the Royal Prussian Army, has graciously deigned to decree:

1. Henceforth the basic material of the Waffenrock (Ulanka) and the peaked cap shall be field gray. There is no change, however, in the basic material of the peaked caps worn by the dragoons.

   Henceforth the cape is also field gray; it will have a collar of coat trim material and a slit in the rear and will be issued only to authorized units.

2. Gold-yellow trim material replaced the lemon-yellow; the train's trim material is potash-blue.

3. The previous colors of shoulder straps and sleeve patches as well as the bases of shoulder boards are replaced by those illustrated in the appendices.

4. The hussars will generally receive nickel buttons.

5. Lance-corporals (Gefreite) and the ranks of all arms will henceforth wear a peak on their own caps.

6. The special uniforms worn by machine-gun battalions and headquarters orderlies are discontinued.

7. New designs are being introduced:

   a) For a field-gray greatcoat, of identical cut for mounted and unmounted personnel and with identical trim material on the collar for all arms instead of the previous greatcoat and instead of the officer's greatcoat and overcoat, for generals with poppy-red lapel lining and piping;

b) For a field-gray blouse in place of the existing field-gray Waffenrock (Ulanka), of the same cut and with identical trim material on the collar for all arms of service, as well as for the embroidery, Litzen and NCO braid instead of lace on this blouse;

c) a field-gray officer's Litewka, henceforth called the "kleine Rock", instead of the existing gray, together with the badges illustrated in Appendix 3;

d) For shoulder straps with a width of 4.5 cm, with two crossed shells for the foot artillery. Shoulder straps replace epaulettes for Ulan enlisted men;

e) For a standard belt and buckle for the enlisted men of all arms of service instead of the existing Leibriemen, outside belt, and sword belt, plus a dark brown leather field belt in place of the discontinued Feldbinde for officers.

The Lancer's Leibbinde is discontinued.

Instead of the Leibbinde, bandmasters will wear the enlisted men's belt with the matt buckle of the Leibbinde.

f) For a gray-green neck stock in place of the neckerchief and both the black and field-gray neck stocks. Officers are permitted to wear a collar visible to a height of 3 mm under the neck stock with the kleine Rock and blouse (except in the field).

g) For a standard cavalry boot.

h) For black ankle boots and puttees for officers;

i) For a field cap for officers and a field-gray peak for all peaked caps;

k) For shoulder boards for temporarily- and permanently-retired officers.

8. The overcoat (Überrock) disappears from the inventory; the kleine Rock takes its place for officers. For temporarily and permanently retired officers and for officers commissioned for the duration, this is only a permitted item.

9. Not to be worn with the blouse:

a) badges of flag bearers, rifleman badges, marksmanship awards, King's badge and Kaiser shooting prizes, the badges for artillery gunners, fencers, Infantry Instruction Battalion, Military Riding Institute, gunnery schools, NCO schools and pre-schools, and signalers;

b) flag and standard bearer's gorgets;

c) swallow's nests.

10. Officers' boot trousers will henceforth be identical in width and seat to the enlisted men's riding trousers, and will only have piping in the side seams if accompanied by trim stripes.

11. Unmounted members of the foot artillery will wear cavalry boots and boot trousers, those of the machine-gun battalions infantry boots and long service trousers.

12. Tricot may be used in Waffenröcke (Ulanka) and the officers' kleine Rock, and corduroy may be used in boot trousers, on the other hand field caps, coats and blouses must be of cloth whose appearance is fully compatible with the valid pattern for enlisted men.

13. All helmets and Tschapkas will receive removable spikes (balls) or covers. Chin straps will generally be worn with covered helmets (Shako, hussar cap, Tschapka). For helmets etc without cover, scale chains continue to be reserved for officers only.

14. Bandolier and cartridge pouches are leaving the equipment of NCOs and enlisted men. Officers are exempted from this order.

15. Leather articles (bark-tanned for all arms of service), footwear, as well as binocular cases, pistol holsters and map cases, are to be worn blackened. The color of riding equipment has not changed.

16. Officers of all arms of service may on any occasion wear black ankle boots with putties instead of high boots.

17. Officers shall generally wear new-style strap-on spurs instead of heel-fixing spurs with high boots as well as with ankle boots and puttees.

18. The adjutant's sash will only still be worn with the peacetime uniform.; like all other officers, adjutants will wear the field belt with the field uniform.

19. The existing ribbon bar will be replaced by
    a large ribbon bar (with medals) and
    a small ribbon bar (without medals).

20. Epaulettes and epaulette holders are discontinued. A newly-introduced style of officer's shoulder board will be worn with the blouse.

21. To the field equipment of non-mounted officers with the foot troops will be added the haversack, canteen and drinking cup of the type used by enlisted men.

22. The basic color of the gala trousers for all officers is gray.

23. The clothing and equipment of the Palace Guard Company remains unchanged.

24. Old-style pieces may no longer be procured. No attempt will be made to enforce uniformity in officers' dress within units during the wearing period.

25. The War Ministry is to take the necessary steps and issue rules and regulations for the wearing of earlier pieces.

26. Now that the army's clothing and equipment have been revised to incorporate the lessons learned in the war, I expect all special orders, permits and concessions issued by various headquarters to be rescinded.

    Deviations from the regulations and the introduction of special badges require my express authorization, even during the war.

The following

Implementing Regulations

bring to attention:

1. The changes ordered for the uniforms of officers or the regulations listed below are also generally applicable to medical and veterinary officers. Medical officers will retain the Feldbinde for occasions when officers wear the sash.

2. The existing items of clothing and equipment are to be worn unchanged, however the following are no longer to be worn: Feldbinden without wrapping, adjutant's sashes with field uniform, bandoliers and cartouches by NCOs and enlisted men, epaulettes and epaulette holders. Old-style shoulder boards are to be replaced by new-style ones as soon as possible.

   Special instructions will be issued for utilization of materials.

   The previous field-gray (gray-green) Waffenröcke (Ulanka) will receive NCO braid instead of NCO lace and new-style shoulder straps once the existing ones are used up.

3. The following may be worn:

   a) dark blue* Waffenröcke etc only in combination with mixed dark-blue or gray trousers, but not with field-gray ones;

* The terms "dark blue" and "mixed dark blue" encompass all items of clothing except the field-gray (gray-green) field service dress.

b) field-gray Waffenröcke etc, Feldröcke, the kleine Rock and blouses in combination with field-gray (gray-green) or gray trousers, but not with mixed dark-blue ones. Any other combination of old and new clothing is acceptable.

4. **Re 3.** On the field-gray Waffenrock worn by non-commissioned officers as members of the salaried class, the trim, piping shoulder straps and buttons (yellow or white) are the same as on the dark blue Waffenrock. The blouse receives the same shoulder straps and matching matte buttons.

Junior paymasters, junior inspectors, junior medical officers, junior veterinary officers, junior pharmacists and one-year volunteer military pharmacists wear the former shoulder straps of the dark-blue uniform with the previous trim; on blouses the trim is of NCO braid. Acting officers and enlisted men in senior official positions also wear trim of NCO braid on the blouse shoulder straps.

5. **Re 1 and 5.** The color of the basic material and trim of the field-gray (gray-green) peaked caps is the same as that of the field-gray (gray-green) field cap.

6. **Re 6.** The machine-gun battalions wear the uniform of the unit they are attached to, with the badge of the next senior company etc. Special instructions will be issued concerning the use of their previous service dress.

Landwehr officers attached to machine-gun battalions wear the Landwehr officer uniform of the arm of service to which the army corps machine-gun battalion is attached.

Headquarters orderlies wear the uniform of their unit.

7. a) **Re 7a.**

Overcoats, greatcoats and capes of the previous style are to be fitted with collars of basic material; their shiny buttons are to be replaced by new-style ones like those on the new-style coat.

b) Re 7b and c.

The patches on the previous Feldröcke and Litewkas are to be modified as soon as possible in keeping with regulations for the blouse—including the cloth backing--or the kleine Rock; likewise the piping on the Litewka.

The general's Feldrock can continue to be worn as is.

8. **Re 8.** The kleine Rock is reserved for officers only; it is not authorized for other classes (bandmasters, junior paymasters, etc).

9. **Re 9.** This badge is also no longer to be worn with the earlier field dress.

10. **Re 11.** Manual laborers of the field artillery will continue to wear long service trousers and infantry boots.

11. **Re 12 and 21.** Officers may procure coats, tunics and breeches, as well as haversacks, canteens and drinking cups from unit stores or clothing depots, paying the cost price set annually by the War Ministry. They are personally responsible for any necessary alterations. As well, they may procure material for the above-mentioned items of clothing through their unit from the clothing depot. In addition to the enlisted men's cloth, these will also carry the lighter material for officers.

12. **Re 13.**

a) The Tschapkas with covers worn by the troops in the field are to be replaced by the new pattern as soon as possible; the old-style Tschapkas are to be worn in the homeland, however.

b) the field badge on the Shako (Tschapka) is not to be worn with the field uniform;

c) Spikes (balls, covers) are not to be worn with the helmet etc in the field or during exercises in field uniform.

13. **Re 15.** Directions on blackening will follow. Leather footwear and other items in unit stores will also continue to be stocked unblackened.

14. The necessary descriptions and patterns are being issued by the War Ministry.

Manufacturers can purchase extra patterns from the Guards Corps clothing office. An announcement concerning the starting date of this procedure will be published in the Military Gazette.

15. Application:

a) for the field-gray tunic fabric the pattern of 13 September 1914 – No. 833. K.B.4 --;

b) for the field-gray greatcoat fabric the pattern of 14 July 1915 – No. 11995. K.B. 5 --,

c) for the gray neck stock the pattern of 11 August 1914 – No. 2347 II. B. – and

d) for the standard cavalry boot the pattern of 31 January 1915 – No. 5209 K.B.2.

Reference is made to the following, which have already been introduced:

a) the gray basic fabric for the long service trousers, riding trousers and boot trousers (pattern of 13 September 1914 – No. 833. K.B.4.);

b) the green badges on the helmet covers;

} August 1914 No. 582 K.B.

c) the band to cover the trim stripe on the field cap – directive of 13 April 1915 No. 7922. K.B. (Military Gazette p. 181).

16. **Re 24.** Wearing times will not be determined until peace has been concluded.

17. **Re 26.** Included among these are:

a) Officer's field caps worn by NCOs and enlisted men,

b) Provided they are not prescribed for individual formations by the War Ministry, puttees for officers and enlisted men,

c) ankle boots with puttees for NCOs and enlisted men,

d) brown gloves for NCOs and enlisted men, excluding bandmasters.

e) NCO insignia in the form of chevrons or the like. These may continue to be worn by the fighting troops as long as the new braid is not available.

18. **Re 27. Uniform of Officials**

a) Subparagraphs 2, 3, 5, 7, 8, 11, 13, 14, 15, 16 and 17 of the preceding Implementing Regulations also apply to officials.

b) Officials wear patches on the blouse collar as on the kleine Rock (see d), but generally of cloth, as well as cornflower blue piping around the edges of the blouse, coat and cape collar. Officials with embroidery on the collar of the Waffenrock may wear a smaller version of this, but in matte finish, also on the collar patches of the blouse.

c) Junior officials, who until now have worn an Überrock instead of the Waffenrock, will be issued a field-gray Waffenrock. Collars, Swedish cuffs, piping and dished buttons in the color of the collar etc on the previous Überrock.

d) **kleiner Rock for senior officials.**

a) cornflower-blue piping around the collar, down the front and around the cuffs.

b) Lapel lining, only for officials at the 3rd stage of rank order: same color as the piping on the collar patches.

c) Collar Patches. Same color and fabric as the Waffenrock collar; collar patch piping same as piping on the Waffenrock if this has different color patches.

e) **Officials attached to Clothing Departments, Supply Offices, Field Magazines, Garrison Administrations and Hospital Administrations** wear:

a) trim on the cap and the Waffenrock of cornflower-blue material;

b) the piping on the cap and the Waffenrock of white material;

c) shoulder straps and sword knot of silver and blue silk, dished shiny buttons on the Waffenrock, and gilt rosettes.

f) **The changes under e also find use:**

a) on the trim worn by paymasters;

b) on the Waffenrock buttons and sword knot of military construction officials and airship hangar inspectors;

c) on the same items, the trim and the shoulder straps of the field officials of the war chests;

d) similarly on the uniforms of junior officials and junior inspectors of the various branches of service and on the uniforms of junior paymaster officials.

g) White silk replaces the yellow silk prescribed for the sword knot worn by junior official classes.

h) The field caps of officials who wear no uniform (Preliminary Note 7 of the summary of the uniforms and badges of officials) will be made of field-gray basic material with dark blue trim.

v. Marchtaler

Appendix 2

Identifying Badges on Officers' Shoulder Boards

Arm of Service etc	Shoulder Boards	
	Base	Piping (on the base)
Infantry	white	—
Dragoons	cornflower-blue	Same color as the piping on the enlisted men's shoulder straps
Lancers	poppy-red	Same color as the piping on the enlisted men's shoulder straps
Landwehr Cavalry	cornflower-blue	—
Field Artillery	poppy-red	—
Foot Artillery	gold-yellow	—
Engineer and Pioneer Corps	black (velvet)	poppy-red
Transport Troops	pale gray	—
Train	potash blue	—
District Commands, Clothing Departments	white	—

Remarks

1. No changes in the shoulder boards of all officer classes not listed here.
2. The shoulder boards of staff officers, captains (Rittmeister) and lieutenants have an overall width of 5.5 cm; width of the protruding cloth base and piping each 3 mm.
   The badges on shoulder boards are generally similar in size to the badges for captains etc.
3. Foot artillery officers wear two crossed shells over the numbers.
4. The bases and piping of field shoulder boards worn by staff officers, captains (Rittmeister) and lieutenants are similar to those of the normal shoulder board; average width 4.5 cm without stiffener; cords and badges (pattern for captains) matte.

Appendix 3

Badges on the kleine Rock of Officers, Medical Officers and Veterinary Officers

A. Piping

Down the front and around the collar and cuffs generally poppy-red; if the collar patches or piping on the patches is crimson-red, the piping down the front is also crimson-red.

B. Colored Lapel Linings

Only for generals and commanders of regiments etc, in the base color of the collar patches or—if these have piping—in the color of the piping, for medical officers with the rank of general poppy-red.

C. Colored Collar Patches

Color and material same as the shoulder board base, with piping the same color as the edge stripes, if such are present on the shoulder boards.

Generals: poppy-red with smaller reproduction of the golden embroidery on the previous Feldrock.

Adjutant-Generals:
Aides-de-camp:
generals à la suite: } silver with poppy-red piping.

Medical Officers: dark blue with poppy-red piping

Veterinary Officers: black with crimson piping

Darstellungen der vorschriftsmäßigen Uniformen

Vorderansicht

Der Mantel

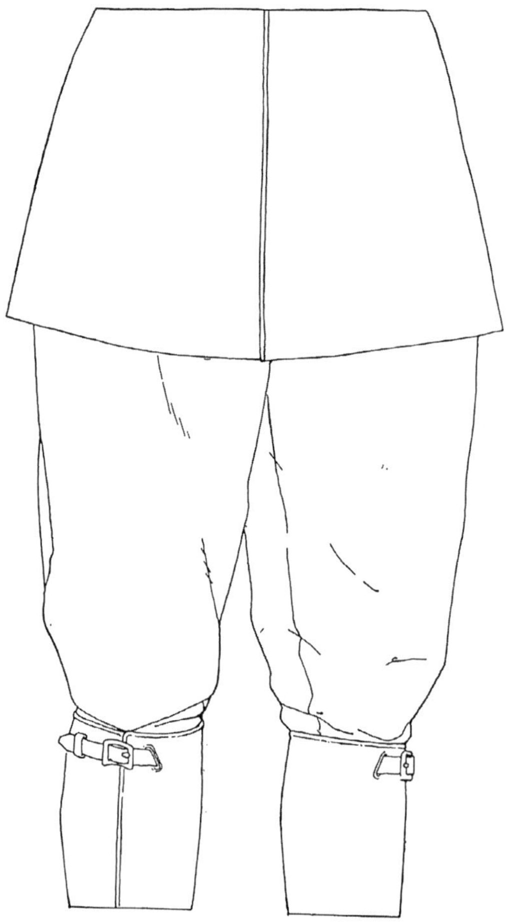

Die vorschriftsmäßige Stiefelhose

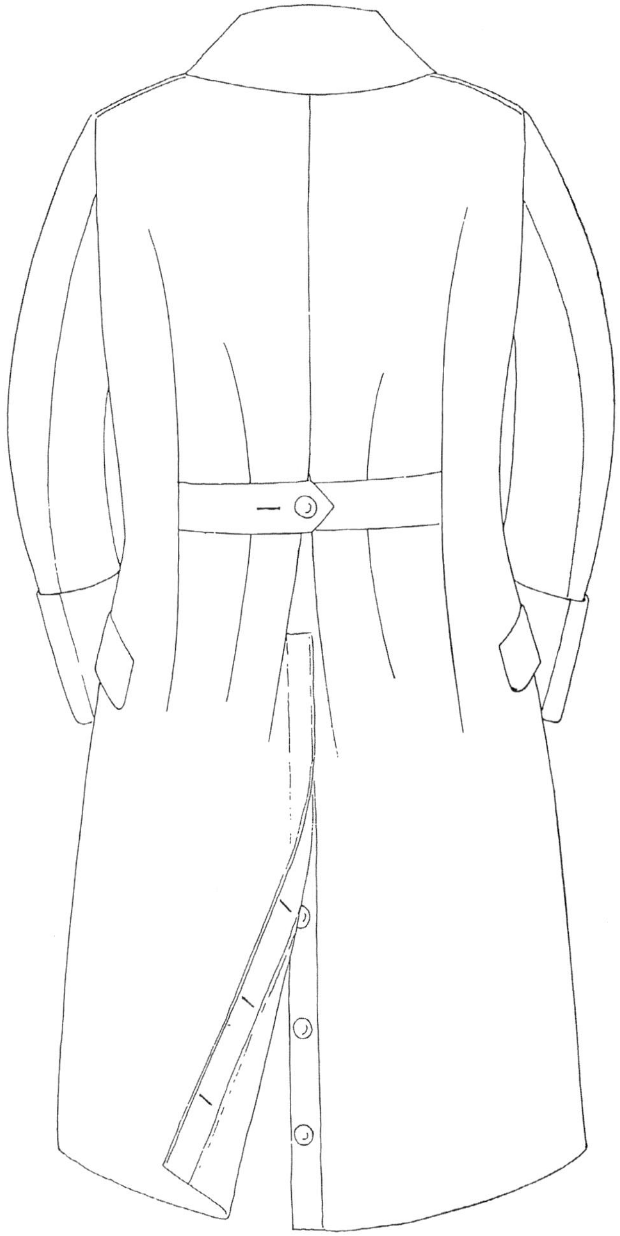

Rückansicht

Der Mantel

Vorderansicht Rückansicht

Der Attila für die Offiziere der Preußischen Husaren-Regimenter (ausschließlich Leib-Garde-Husaren-R.)

Vorderansicht Rückansicht

Der kleine Rock für Offiziere und obere Beamte
(Für die Offiziere und oberen Beamten der Bayerischen Armee mit blau-silberner Hoheitsborde um den Kragen)

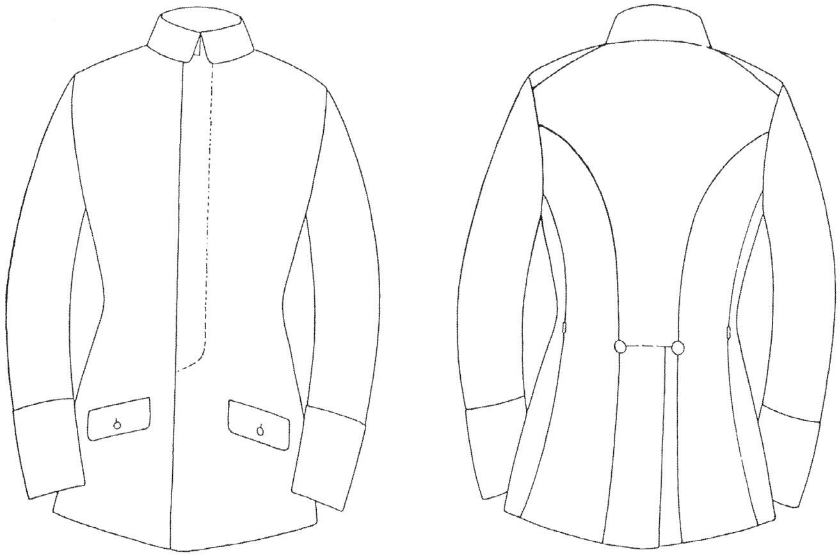

Vorderansicht Rückansicht

Die Bluse
Einheitliches Bekleidungsstück für den Felddienst für Offiziere und Mannschaften der Armee
(Für die Bayerischen Truppen blau-silber bezw. blau-weiße Hoheitsborde um den Kragen)

Vorderansicht Rückansicht

Der Waffenrock der Garde-Infanterie (für Linien-Infanterie Kragen ohne Litze, vorn abgerundet)
Desgl. der Garde-Dragoner, Garde-Jäger, Garde-Schützen, Garde-Pioniere, Garde-Verkehrstruppen, Garde-Train, Garde-Artillerie und Krankenwärter des Gardekorps

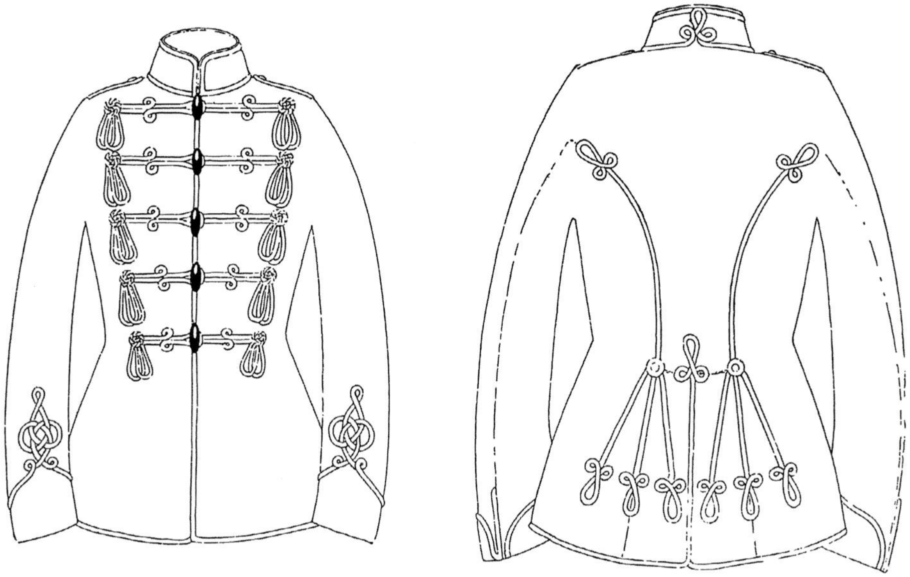

Vorderansicht Rückansicht

Der Attila für Mannschaften der **Preußischen** Husaren-Regimenter

Vorderansicht Rückansicht

Der Waffenrock der Kürassier-Regimenter

Vorderansicht Rückansicht

Die Ulanka (hier Garde), Linien-Regimenter Kragen ohne Litzen, vorn abgerundet

Vorderansicht Rückansicht

Der Waffenrock der Regimenter Jäger zu Pferde

Vorderansicht — Rückansicht

Der allgemeine Waffenrock der Bayerischen Armee

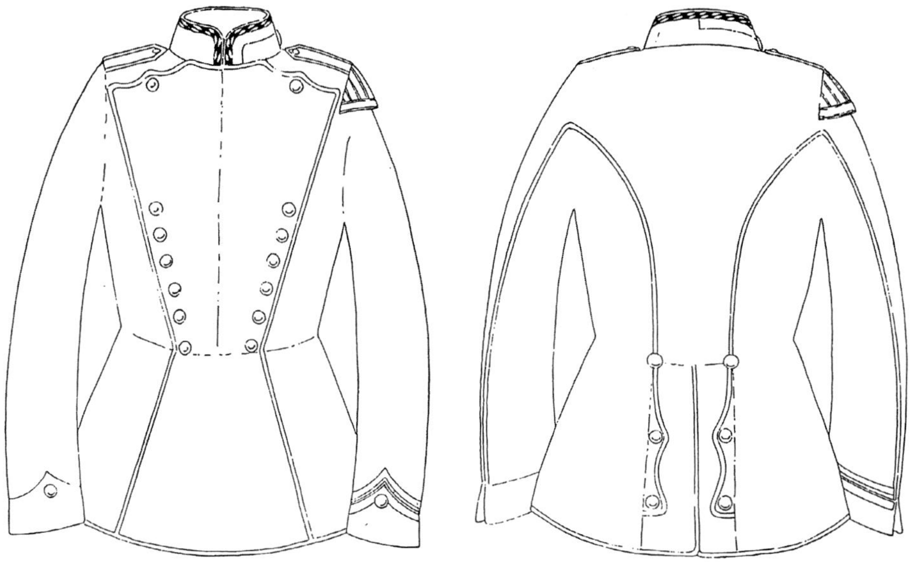

Vorderansicht — Rückansicht

Die Ulanka der Bayerischen Ulanen-Regimenter

Vorderansicht

Der Waffenrock der Chevaulegers-Regimenter

Rückansicht wie bei der Ulanka ohne Vorstoß in den Ärmel- u. Rückennähten

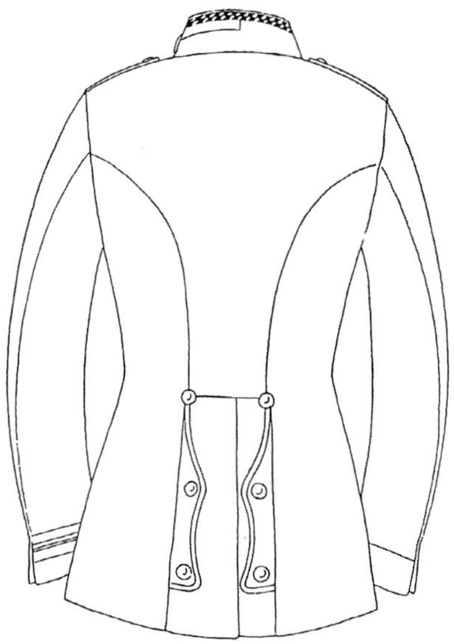

Rückansicht

Der Waffenrock der Schweren Reiter-Regimenter

Vorderansicht wie beim Waffenrock der Chevaulegers-Regimenter jedoch ohne Vorstoß unten um die Schöße des Waffenrocks

Vorderansicht — Rückansicht

Der allgemeine Waffenrock der Sächsischen Armee

Vortragender General-Adjutant
(Generaloberst)
im Waffenrock

General der Infanterie
in der Bluse
(Bei d. fechtenden Truppe ohne
Besatzstreifen a. d. Stiefelhose)

Flügel-Adjutant Sr. M. des Kaisers
in der Bluse

Gr. Generalstab
Major in der Bluse

Kriegsministerium
Major im Waffenrock

Militär-Kabinett
Major in der Bluse

Persönlicher Adjutant
der Prinzen des Königl. Hauses
Major im Waffenrock

1. Garde-R. z. F.
Oberst im Waffenrock

2. Garde-R. z. F.
Oberstleutnant in der Bluse

4. Garde-R. z. F.
Major im Waffenrock
Parade

Kaiser Alexander
Garde-Gren.-R. Nr. 1
Hauptmann im Waffenrock
Parade

Kaiser Franz
Garde-Gren.-R. Nr. 2
Oberleutnant im Kleinen Rock

Königin Elisabeth
Garde-Gren.-R. Nr. 3
Leutnant in der Bluse

Königin Augusta Garde-Gren.-R. Nr. 4
Oberleutnant im Waffenrock
(als Adjutant)
Parade

Garde-Gren.-R. Nr. 5
Oberleutnant im Waffenrock
Parade

Leib-Grenadier-R.
König Friedrich Wilhelm III. Nr. 8
Oberst im Waffenrock
Parade

Grenadier-R.
König Friedrich I Nr. 5
Oberstleutnant im Waffenrock
Parade

Grenadier-R.
König Friedrich der Große Nr. 4
Major im Waffenrock
Parade

Grenadier-R. Kronprinz Nr. 1
Hauptmann in der Bluse

Füsilier-R. Nr. 80
Oberleutnant in der Bluse

Infanterie-R. Nr. 17
Leutnant im Waffenrock
(als Adjutant)

Eisenbahn-R. Nr. 1
Hauptmann im Waffenrock
Parade

Flieger-Bat. Nr. 2
Leutnant in der Bluse

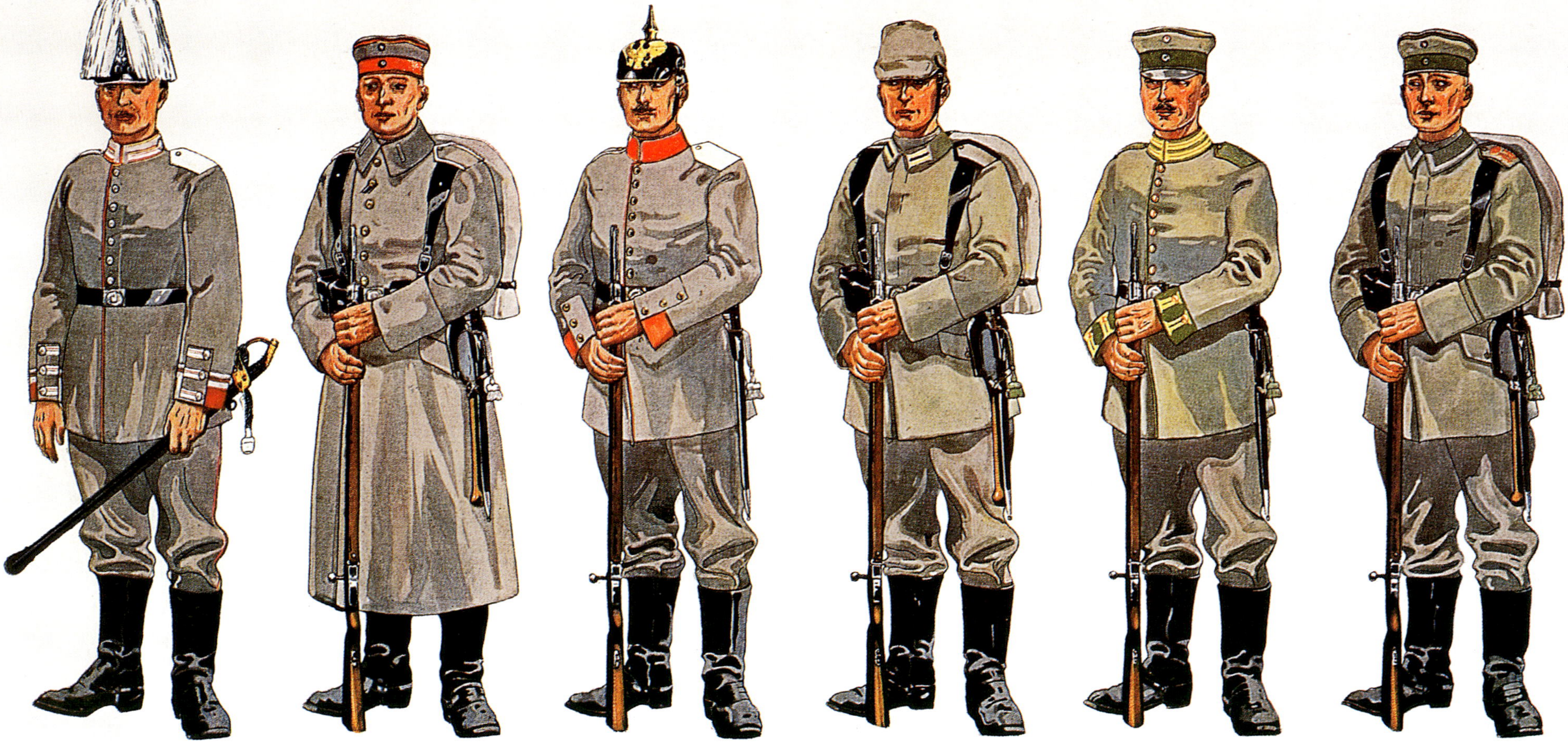

5. Garde-R.	Garde-Gren.-R. Nr. 5	Unteroffizierschule in Potsdam	Garde-Schützen-Bat.	Garde-Jäger-Bat.	Jäger-Bat. Nr. 11
Feldwebel im Waffenrock	Unteroffizier im Mantel	(Im Waffenrock)	(In der Bluse)	(Im Waffenrock)	Unteroffizier in der Bluse

Grenadier-R. Nr. 1
Unteroffizier in der Bluse

Grenadier-R. Nr. 4
(Im Waffenrock)

Infanterie-R. Nr. 92
(In der Bluse)

1. Bad. Leib-Grenadier-R. Nr. 109
(Im Waffenrock)

2. Bad. Grenadier-R. Nr. 110
(In der Bluse)

6. Bad. Infanterie-R. Nr. 114
(Im Waffenrock)

Grenadier-R. Nr. 5
(In der Bluse)

Grenadier-R. Nr. 7
(Im Waffenrock)

Grenadier-R. Nr. 11
(In der Bluse)

Füsilier-R. Nr. 80
(Im Waffenrock)

Königs-Inf.-R. Nr. 145
(In der Bluse)

Infanterie-R. Nr. 17
(Im Waffenrock)

Garde-Pionier-Bat. (In der Bluse) | Pionier-Versuchs-Kompagnie (Im Waffenrock) | Pionier-Bat. Nr. 1 (In der Bluse) | Telegraphen-Bat. Nr. 1 (In der Bluse) | Kraftfahr-Bat. (In der Bluse) | Eisenbahn-R. Nr. 1 (Im Waffenrock) | Luftschiffer-Bat. Nr. 1 (In der Bluse)

Garde-Pionier-Bat. (In der Bluse)	Pionier-Versuchs-Kompagnie (Im Waffenrock)	Pionier-Bat. Nr. 1 (In der Bluse)	Telegraphen-Bat. Nr. 1 (In der Bluse)	Kraftfahr-Bat. (In der Bluse)	Eisenbahn-R. Nr. 1 (Im Waffenrock)	Luftschiffer-Bat. Nr. 1 (In der Bluse)

Infanterie-Leib-R. (Im Waffenrock) — 2. Infanterie-R. (In der Bluse) — 4. Infanterie-R. (Im Waffenrock) — 1. Schweres Reiter-R. (Im Waffenrock mit Paraderabatte) — 1. Ulanen-R. (In der Ulanka mit Paraderabatte) — 4. Chevaulegers-R. König (Im Waffenrock)

Bayern

Garde-Reiter-R. (Im Waffenrock) — Karabinier-R. (Im Waffenrock) — Ulanen-R. Nr. 17 Unteroffizier in der Bluse — Feldartillerie-R. Nr. 48 (Im Waffenrock) — Schützen-(Füsilier-)R. Nr. 108 (Im Waffenrock) — (Leib-)Grenadier-R. Nr. 100 (In der Bluse) — Infanterie-R. Nr. 102 Unteroffizier im Waffenrock — Jäger-Bat. Nr. 12 (Im Waffenrock)

Sachsen

„Deutschlands Armee in feldgrauer Kriegs- und Friedens-Uniform“ Ta

Infanterie-R. Nr. 125
(7. Württembergisches)
Unteroffizier im Waffenrock

Dragoner-R. Nr. 25
(1. Württembergisches)
(Im Waffenrock)

Ulanen-R. Nr. 20
(In der Ulanka)

Württemberg

Leibgarde-Infanterie-R. Nr. 115
(1. Großherz. Hessisches)
Unteroffizier im Waffenrock

Garde-Dragoner-R. Nr. 23
(1. Großherz. Hessisches)
Vize-Wachtmeister im Waffenrock

Hessen

Großherz. Mecklenburg.
Grenadier-R. Nr. 89, I. u. III. Bat.
(In der Bluse)

Großherz. Mecklenburg.
Grenadier-R. Nr. 89, II. Bat.
Gefreiter im Waffenrock

Mecklenburg

Garde-Schützen-Bat.
Oberstleutnant im Waffenrock

1. Jäger-Bat. König
Hauptmann in der Bluse
Bayern

Garde-Jäger-Bat.
Hauptmann im Waffenrock

1. Garde-Feldartillerie-R.
Oberleutnant im Waffenrock
(als Adjutant)

Fußartillerie-R. Nr. 9
Major im Waffenrock

2. Garde-Train-Abt.
Oberleutnant im Kleinen Rock

1. Train-Bat.
Leutnant im Waffenrock (Parade)
Bayern

1. Garde-Train-Abt.
Wachtmeister im Waffenrock

Infanterie-Leib-R.
Hauptmann im Waffenrock

Bayern

Dragoner-R. Nr. 25
(1. Württembergisches)
Oberleutnant im Waffenrock
Parade

Württemberg

5. Chevaulegers-R.
Oberleutnant im Waffenrock
Parade

Bayern

Leib-Dragoner-R. Nr.24
(2. Großherz. Hessisches)
Rittmeister i. Waffenrock
Parade

Hessen

2. Ulanen-R. König
Major im Waffenrock

Bayern

Grenadier-R. Nr. 119
(1. Württembergisches)
Leutnant im Waffenrock

Württemberg

Dragoner-R. Nr. 18
(2. Großherz. Mecklenburgisches)
Rittmeister im Waffenrock

Mecklenburg

Schützen-(Füsilier-R.) Nr. 108
Hauptmann im Waffenrock

Sächs. Pionier-Bat. Nr. 12
Oberleutnant im Waffenrock.

Zugleich Festungsbauoffizier
mit Beamten-Achselstück

Sachsen

Regiment der Gardes du Corps
Major im Waffenrock

Leib-Kürassier-R. Großer Kurfürst (Schlesisches) Nr. 1
Leutnant im Waffenrock

1. Garde=Dragoner=R.
Oberleutnant im Waffenrock

2. Garde=Dragoner=R.
Leutnant im Waffenrock (Adjutant)

Grenadier-R. z. Pferde Freiherr von Derfflinger (Neumärkisches) Nr. 3
Leutnant im Waffenrock

Dragoner-R. von Bredow (1. Schlesisches) Nr. 4
Rittmeister in der Bluse (Feldordensschnalle)

3. Badisches Dragoner=R. Prinz Karl Nr. 22

Rittmeister im Waffenrock

Leib=Garde=Husaren=R.

Rittmeister in der Bluse

1. Leib-Husaren-R. Nr. 1
Leutnant in der Attila

Husaren-R. König Wilhelm I. (1. Rheinisches) Nr. 7
Leutnant in der Attila

1. Garde=Ulanen=R.
Leutnant in der Ulanka

3. Garde=Ulanen=R.
Leutnant in der Ulanka

2. Pommersches Ulanen=R. Nr. 9
Leutnant in der Ulanka

Ulanen=R. Kaiser Alexander II. von Rußland (1. Brandenburgisches) Nr. 3
Leutnant in der Ulanka

Regiment Königs-Jäger zu Pferde Nr. 1

Leutnant in der Bluse

Jäger-R. zu Pferde Nr. 12

Major im Waffenrock

Kürassier-R. Nr. 6
(Im Waffenrock)

Dragoner-R. Nr. 8
(Im Waffenrock)

Leib-Garde-Husaren-R.
(In der Bluse)

Regiment der Gardes du Corps
(In der Bluse)

1. Garde-Feldartillerie-R., reit. Abt.
Wachtmeister im Waffenrock

Kavallerist in der Bluse
mit umgeschnalltem Karabiner

Königl. Sächs. Garde-Reiter-R.
(1. schweres Regiment)
Sachsen

1. Schweres Reiter-R.
Prinz Karl von Bayern
Bayern

Generalarzt
m. d. Range als Gen.-Major
im Waffenrock

Oberstabsarzt
m. d. Range als Major
in der Bluse

Korpsstabsveterinär
im Waffenrock

Kriegsgerichtsrat
im Waffenrock

Korpsstabsapotheker
in der Bluse

Armee-Musikinspizient
in der Bluse

Zahlmeister
m. d. Range als Rechnungsrat
in der Bluse

Proviantamts-Offizier
im Waffenrock

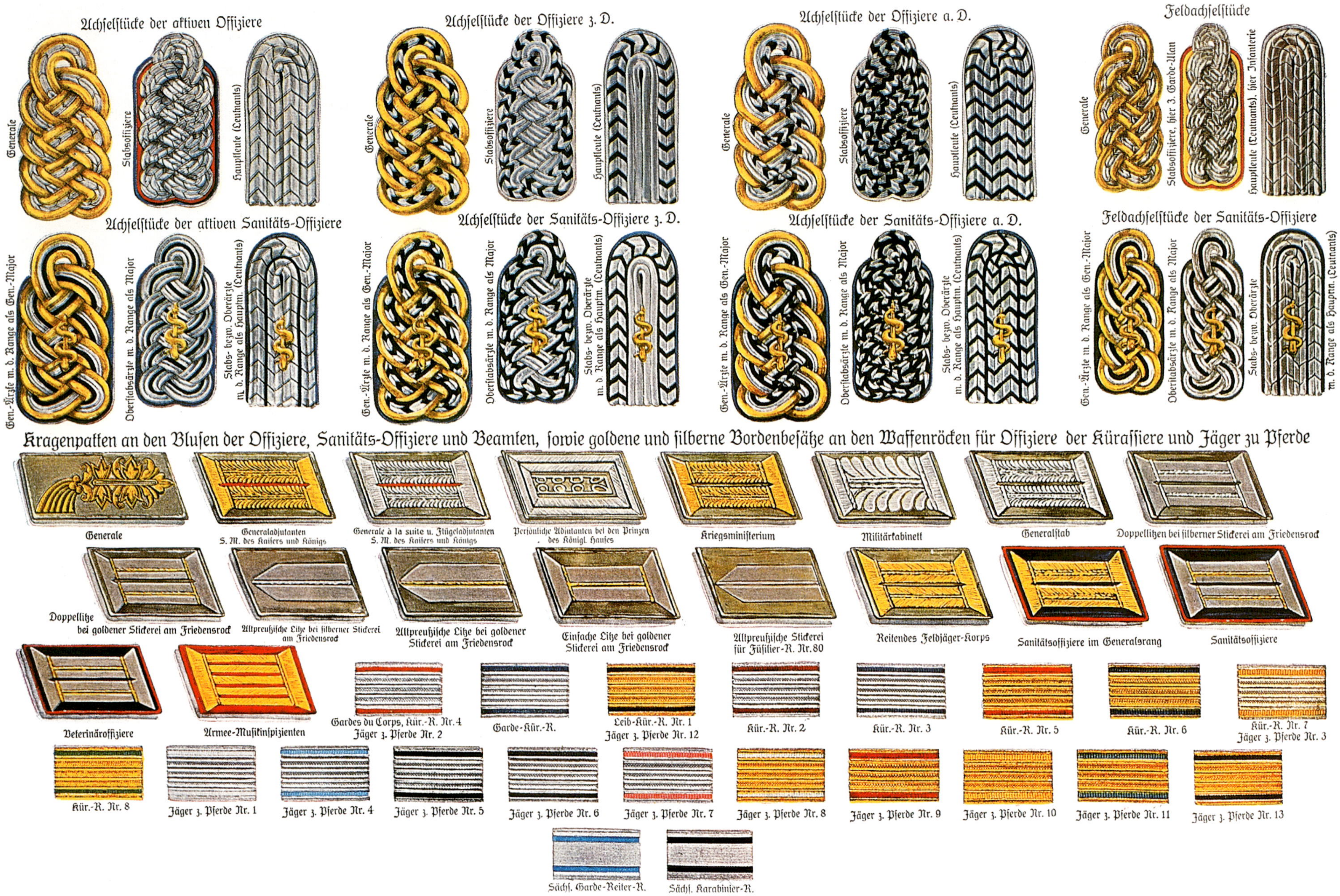

Achselstücke der aktiven Offiziere
Generale
Stabsoffiziere
Hauptleute (Leutnants)
Achselstücke der Offiziere z. D.
Generale
Stabsoffiziere
Hauptleute (Leutnants)
Achselstücke der Offiziere a. D.
Generale
Stabsoffiziere
Hauptleute (Leutnants)
Feldachselstücke
Generale
Stabsoffiziere, hier 3. Garde-Ulan
Hauptleute (Leutnants), hier Infanterie
Achselstücke der aktiven Sanitäts-Offiziere
Gen.-Ärzte m. d. Range als Gen.-Major
Oberstabsärzte m. d. Range als Major
Stabs- bezw. Oberärzte m. d. Range als Hauptm. (Leutnants)
Achselstücke der Sanitäts-Offiziere z. D.
Gen.-Ärzte m. d. Range als Gen.-Major
Oberstabsärzte m. d. Range als Major
Stabs- bezw. Oberärzte m. d. Range als Hauptm. (Leutnants)
Achselstücke der Sanitäts-Offiziere a. D.
Gen.-Ärzte m. d. Range als Gen.-Major
Oberstabsärzte m. d. Range als Major
Stabs- bezw. Oberärzte m. d. Range als Hauptm. (Leutnants)
Feldachselstücke der Sanitäts-Offiziere
Gen.-Ärzte m. d. Range als Gen.-Major
Oberstabsärzte m. d. Range als Major
Stabs- bezw. Oberärzte m. d. Range als Hauptm. (Leutnants)
Kragenpatten an den Blusen der Offiziere, Sanitäts-Offiziere und Beamten, sowie goldene und silberne Bordenbesätze an den Waffenröcken für Offiziere der Kürassiere und Jäger zu Pferde
Generale
Generaladjutanten S. M. des Kaisers und Königs
Generale à la suite u. Flügeladjutanten S. M. des Kaisers und Königs
Persönliche Adjutanten bei den Prinzen des Königl. Hauses
Kriegsministerium
Militärkabinett
Generalstab
Doppellitzen bei silberner Stickerei am Friedensrock
Doppellitze bei goldener Stickerei am Friedensrock
Altpreußische Litze bei silberner Stickerei am Friedensrock
Altpreußische Litze bei goldener Stickerei am Friedensrock
Einfache Litze bei goldener Stickerei am Friedensrock
Altpreußische Stickerei für Füsilier-R. Nr. 80
Reitendes Feldjäger-Korps
Sanitätsoffiziere im Generalsrang
Sanitätsoffiziere
Veterinäroffiziere
Armee-Musikinspizienten
Gardes du Corps, Kür.-R. Nr. 4 Jäger z. Pferde Nr. 2
Garde-Kür.-R.
Leib-Kür.-R. Nr. 1 Jäger z. Pferde Nr. 12
Kür.-R. Nr. 2
Kür.-R. Nr. 3
Kür.-R. Nr. 5
Kür.-R. Nr. 6
Kür.-R. Nr. 7 Jäger z. Pferde Nr. 3
Kür.-R. Nr. 8
Jäger z. Pferde Nr. 1
Jäger z. Pferde Nr. 4
Jäger z. Pferde Nr. 5
Jäger z. Pferde Nr. 6
Jäger z. Pferde Nr. 7
Jäger z. Pferde Nr. 8
Jäger z. Pferde Nr. 9
Jäger z. Pferde Nr. 10
Jäger z. Pferde Nr. 11
Jäger z. Pferde Nr. 13
Sächs. Garde-Reiter-R.
Sächs. Karabinier-R.

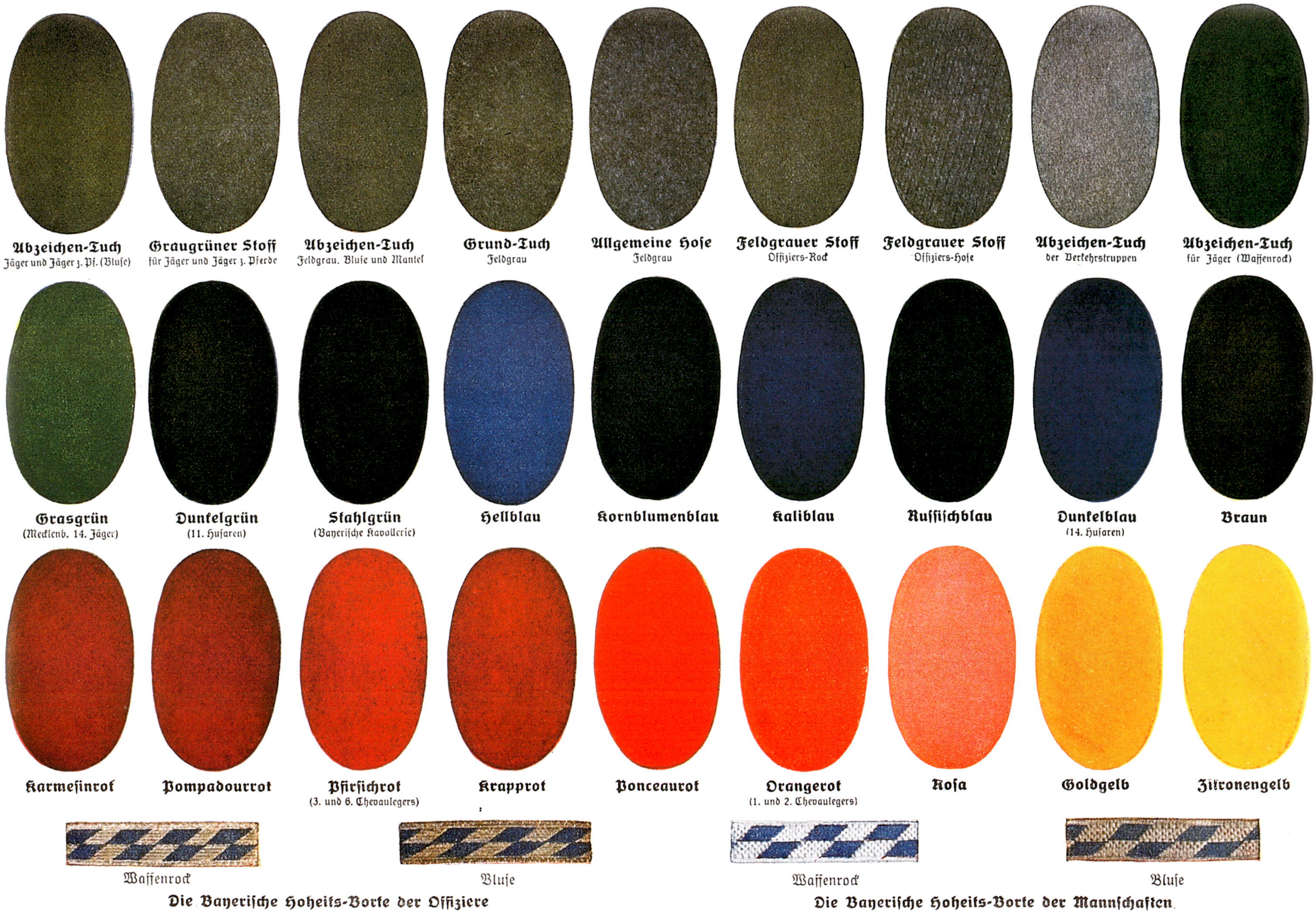
Abzeichen-Tuch
Jäger und Jäger z. Pf. (Bluse)
Graugrüner Stoff
für Jäger und Jäger z. Pferde
Abzeichen-Tuch
Feldgrau, Bluse und Mantel
Grund-Tuch
Feldgrau
Allgemeine Hose
Feldgrau
Feldgrauer Stoff
Offiziers-Rock
Feldgrauer Stoff
Offiziers-Hose
Abzeichen-Tuch
der Verkehrstruppen
Abzeichen-Tuch
für Jäger (Waffenrock)
Grasgrün
(Mecklenb. 14. Jäger)
Dunkelgrün
(11. Husaren)
Stahlgrün
(Bayerische Kavallerie)
Hellblau
Kornblumenblau
Kaliblau
Russischblau
Dunkelblau
(14. Husaren)
Braun
Karmesinrot
Pompadourrot
Pfirsichrot
(3. und 6. Chevaulegers)
Krapprot
Ponceaurot
Orangerot
(1. und 2. Chevaulegers)
Rosa
Goldgelb
Zitronengelb
Waffenrock
Bluse
Die Bayerische Hoheits-Borte der Offiziere
Waffenrock
Bluse
Die Bayerische Hoheits-Borte der Mannschaften.

Schematische Darstellung

aller Mannschafts-Uniformen der Deutschen Armee.

Tafel I bis V Preußen

einschließlich

der **Badischen, Hessischen** und **Mecklenburgischen** Kontingente.

Bildliche Darstellung der **Anlage 1** der Allerhöchsten Kabinetts-Ordre Sr. Maj. des Kaisers und Königs.

Die hier nicht dargestellten Grenadier-, Füsilier- und Infanterie-Regimenter unterscheiden sich von den Infanterie-Regimentern Nr. 17, 21, 25, 52 und 76, abgesehen von kleinen Auszeichnungen (hellblauen Gedenk-Bändern um die rechte Ärmelpatte des Waffenrockes bei Infanterie-Regiment Nr. 73 u. 79 und Jäger-Bataillon Nr. 10), nur durch ihre Regiments-Nummer. Es dienen als Muster:

Das Infanterie-Regiment Nr. 17 für die nicht dargestellten Regimenter des XXI. Armeekorps.

Das Infanterie-Regiment Nr. 21 für die nicht dargestellten Regimenter des V., VI., XVI., XVII. Armeekorps.

Das Infanterie-Regiment Nr. 25 für die nicht dargestellten Regimenter des VII., VIII., XVIII., XX. Armeekorps.

Das Infanterie-Regiment Nr. 52 für die nicht dargestellten Regimenter des III., IV., XI., XIV., XV. Armeekorps.

Das Infanterie-Regiment Nr. 76 für die nicht dargestellten Regimenter des I., II., IX., X. Armeekorps.

Tafel VI Bayern.

Bildliche Darstellung der **Anlage 1** der Allerhöchsten Kabinetts-Ordre Sr. Maj. des Königs von Bayern.

Tafel VII Sachsen.

Bildliche Darstellung der **Anlage 1** der Allerhöchsten Kabinetts-Ordre Sr. Maj. des Königs von Sachsen.

Tafel VIII Württemberg.

Bildliche Darstellung der **Anlage 1** der Allerhöchsten Kabinetts-Ordre Sr. Maj. des Königs von Württemberg.

Gold- und Silber-Stickereien

an den Waffenröcken der Offiziere*)

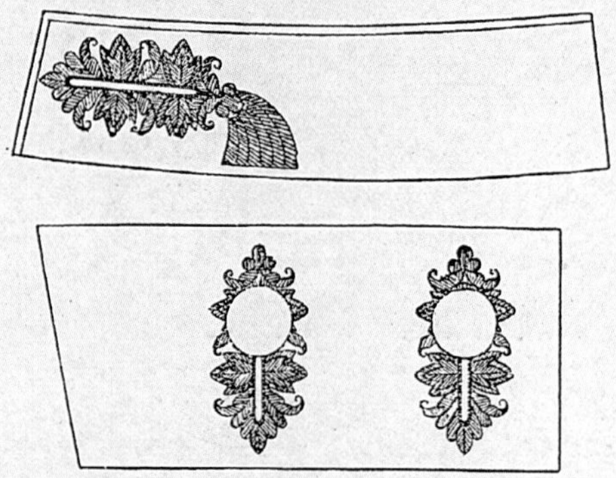

Preußische Generale. Gold-Stickerei.
Bayerische Generale. Silber-Stickerei.
Laut M. V. Bl. v. 1. IV. 16.

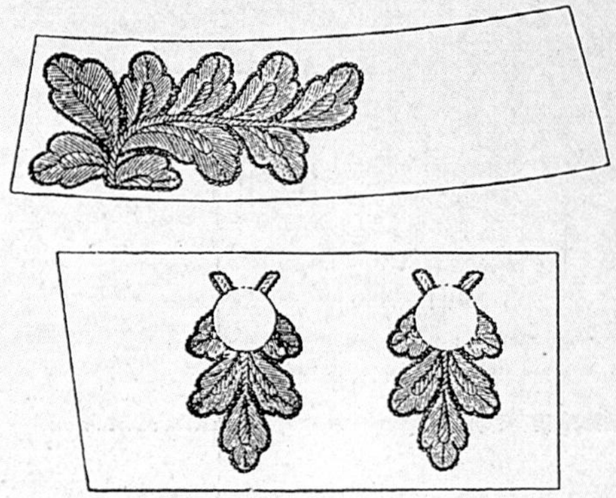

Generale des Großh. Mecklenburgischen Kontingents. Silber-Stickerei.

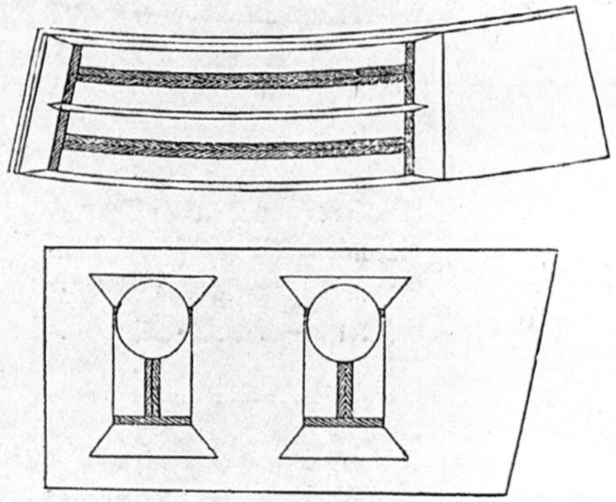

Silberne Stickerei

für Offiziere des 1. Garde-Regiments z. F., Garde-Füsilier-Regiments, der Grenadier-Regimenter 100, 109, 119 u. 123, des 1. Garde-Landwehr- und Garde-Füsilier-Landwehr-Regiments, des Bayerischen Infanterie-Leib-Regiments, des Mecklenburgischen Jäger-Bataillons 14, des 2. Garde-Dragoner-Regiments und der Dragoner-Regimenter 18, 23 u. 25, der Schutztruppen, für Militär-Gerichts- und Intendantur-Beamte, sowie Beamte der technischen Institute.

Goldene Stickerei

für Offiziere des 2., 3. u. 4. Garde-Regiments z. F., der Garde-Jäger, des Garde-Trains, der Gendarmerie, des Reitenden Feldjägerkorps, des 2., 3. u. 4. Garde-Landwehr-Regiments, des Garde-Landwehr-Trains und der Garde-Landwehr-Jäger, des Grenadier-Regiments 101, des 1. Garde-Dragoner-Regiments, des Dragoner-Regiments 17, des Sanitäts- und Veterinärkorps und des Sanitäts- und Veterinärkorps der Schutztruppen.

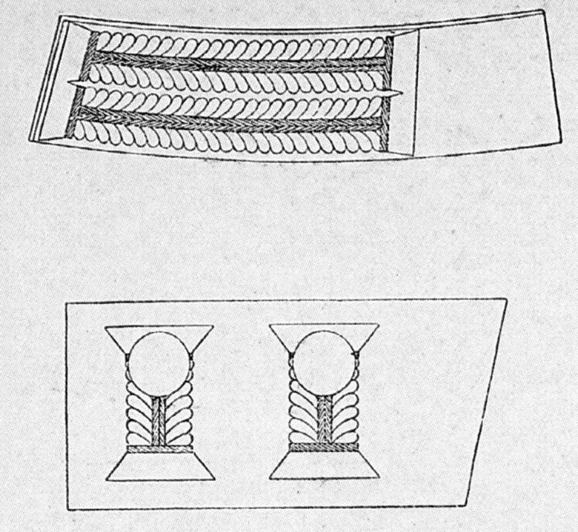

Offiziere d. Kriegsministeriums u. Gen.-Adj. Goldene Kolben-Stickerei.

Offiziere des Generalstabes und Flügel-Adjutanten, des Ingenieur- u. Pionierkorps, der Eisenbahn-R., der Luftschiffer- u. Flieger-Bat., d. Kraftfahr-Bat., d. Telegraphen-Truppen. Silberne Kolben-Stickerei.

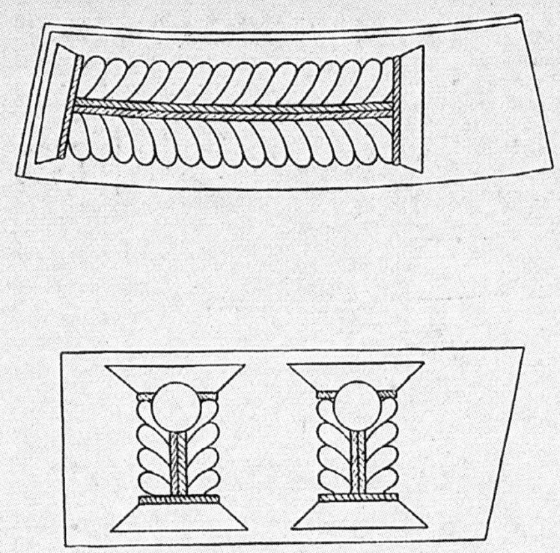

Militär-Kabinett. Silber-Stickerei.

Prinzliche Adjutanten. Silber-Stickerei.

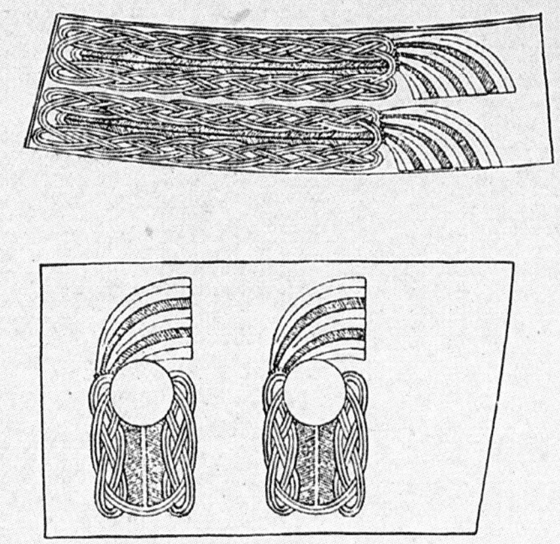

Offiziere des Kadettenkorps. Gold-Stickerei.

Offiziere d. 5. Garde-R. z. F.
Silber-Stickerei.
Offiziere d. Garde-Gren.-R. 5.
Gold-Stickerei.

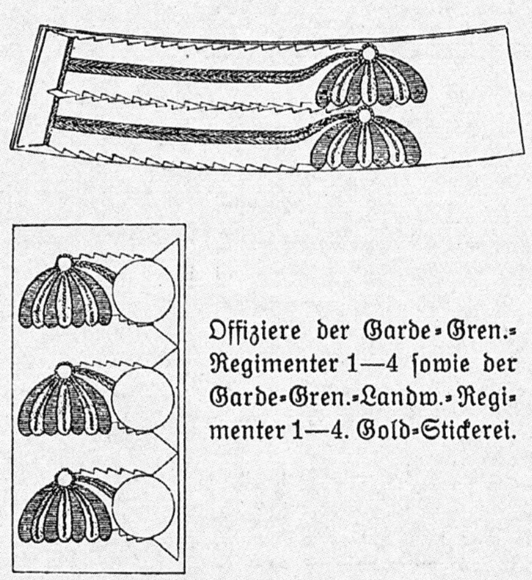

Offiziere der Garde-Gren.-Regimenter 1—4 sowie der Garde-Gren.-Landw.-Regimenter 1—4. Gold-Stickerei.

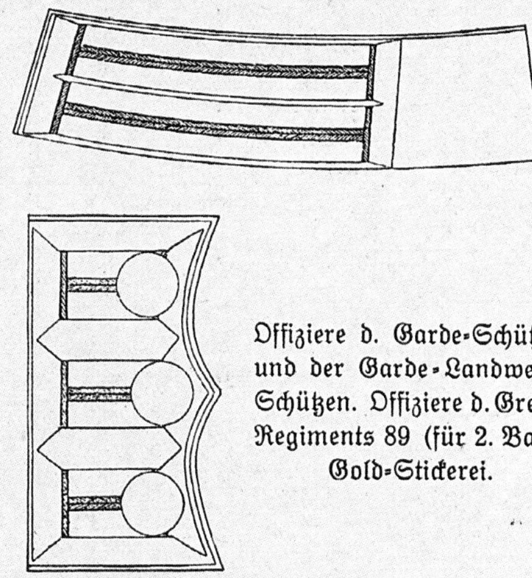

Offiziere d. Garde-Schützen und der Garde-Landwehr-Schützen. Offiziere d. Gren.-Regiments 89 (für 2. Bat.).
Gold-Stickerei.

Offiziere d. Grenadier-R. 1.
Gold-Stickerei.

Offiziere d. Grenadier-R. 2.
Gold-Stickerei.

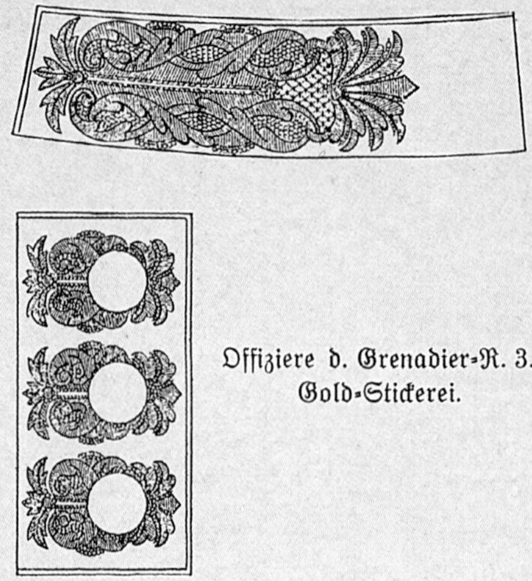

Offiziere d. Grenadier-R. 3.
Gold-Stickerei.

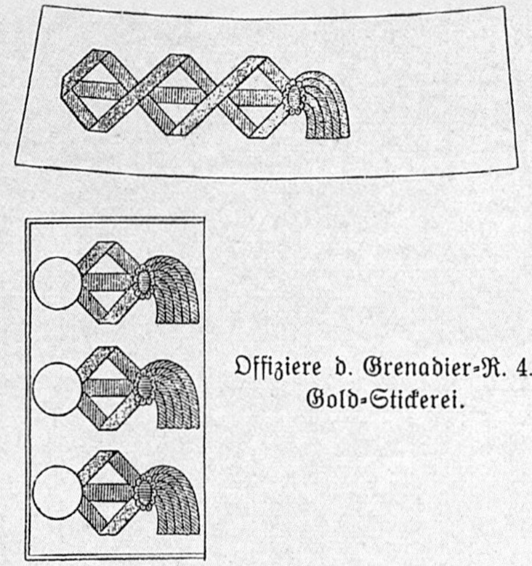

Offiziere d. Grenadier-R. 4.
Gold-Stickerei.

Offiziere d. Grenadier-R. 5.
Gold-Stickerei.

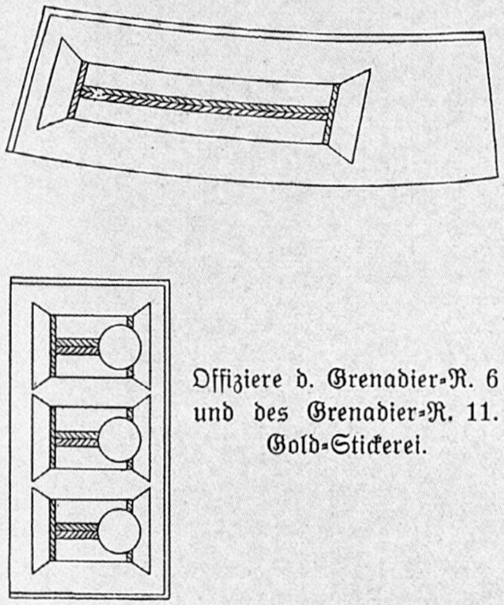

Offiziere d. Grenadier-R. 6
und des Grenadier-R. 11.
Gold-Stickerei.

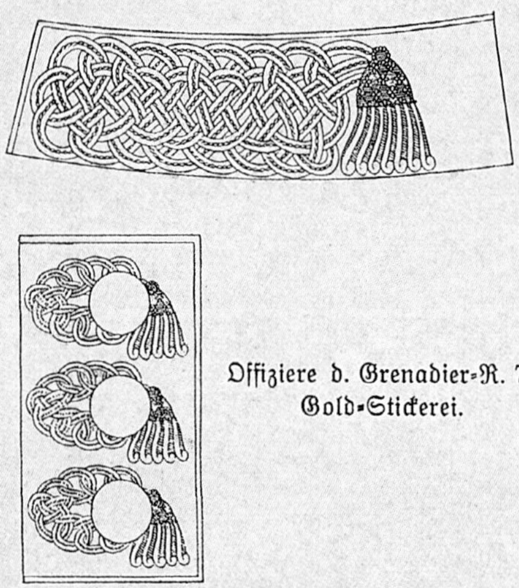

Offiziere d. Grenadier-R. 7.
Gold-Stickerei.

Offiziere d. Grenadier-R. 8.
Gold-Stickerei.

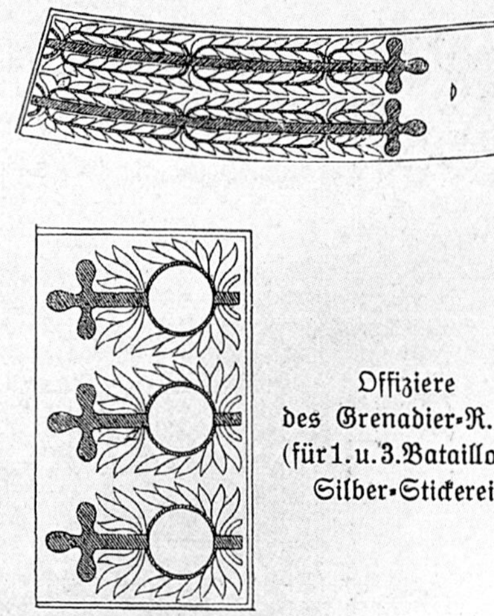

Offiziere
des Grenadier-R. 89
(für 1. u. 3. Bataillon).
Silber-Stickerei.

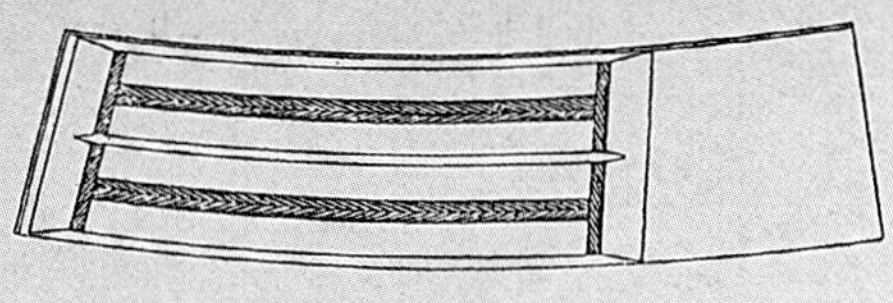

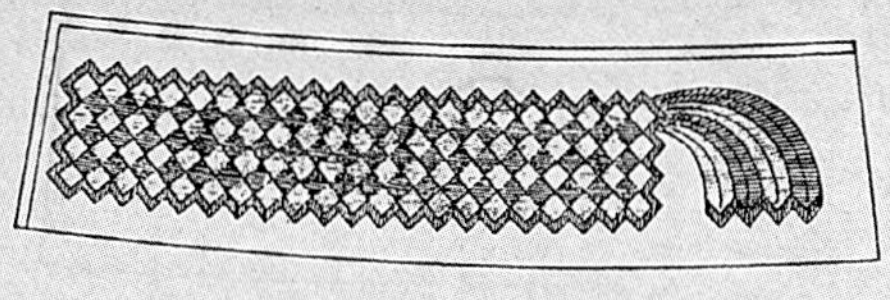

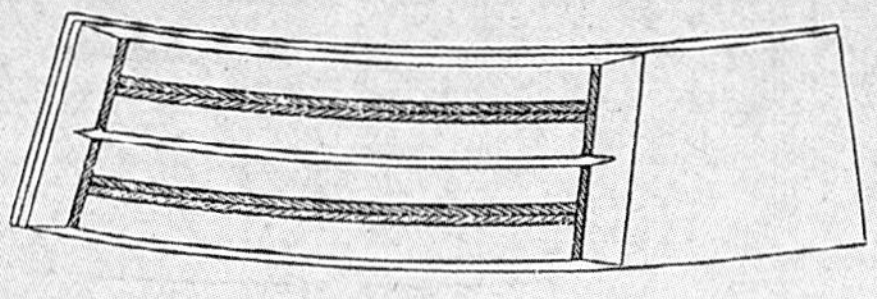

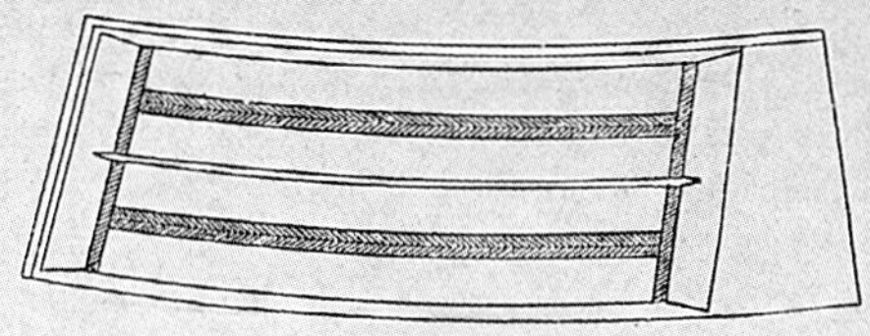

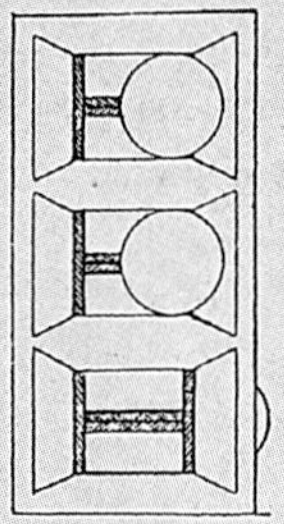

Offiziere d. Infanterie-R. 115 u. Meckl.-Strel. Flügel-Adjutanten. Silber-Stickerei.

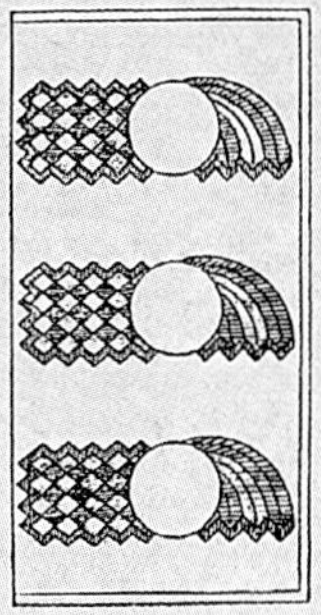

Offiziere des Füsilier-R. 80. Gold-Stickerei.

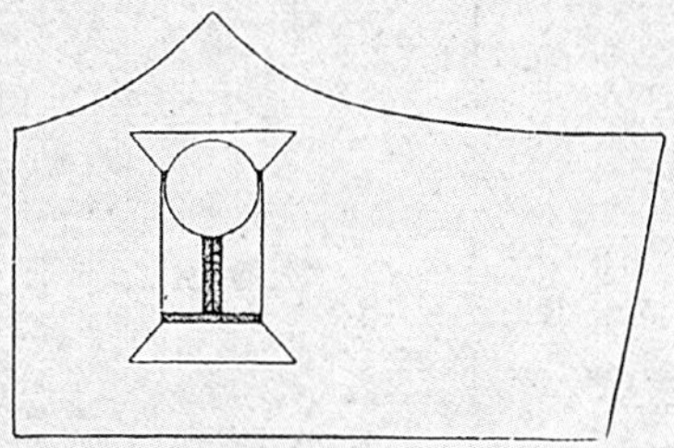

Offiziere des Garde-Ulanen-R. 2 und des Ulanen-R. 18. Gold-Stickerei.

Offiziere der Garde-Ulanen-R. 1 u. 3 und der Ulanen-Regimenter 17, 19 u. 21. Silber-Stickerei.

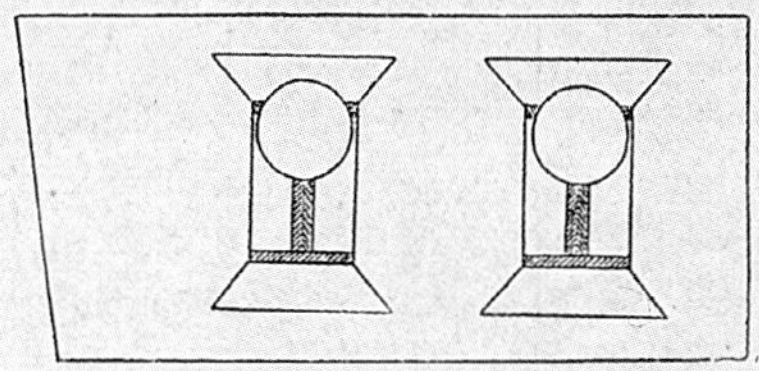

Offiziere der Garde-Artillerie und des 1. Großh. Hess. Feld-Artillerie-R. 25. Gold-Stickerei.

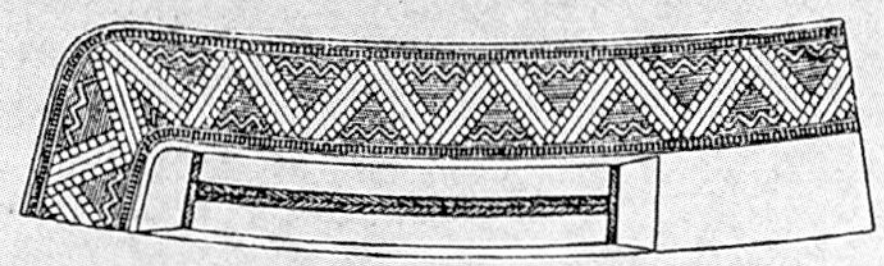

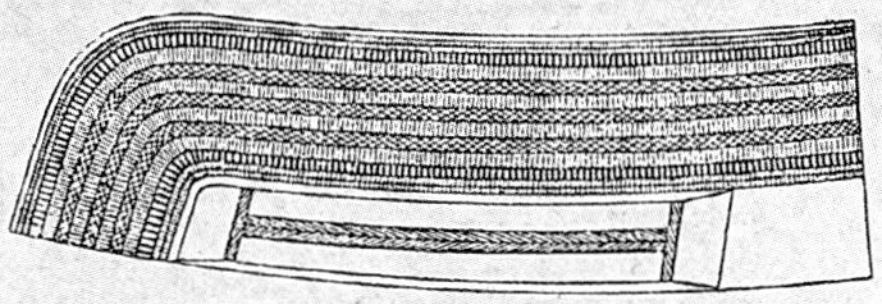

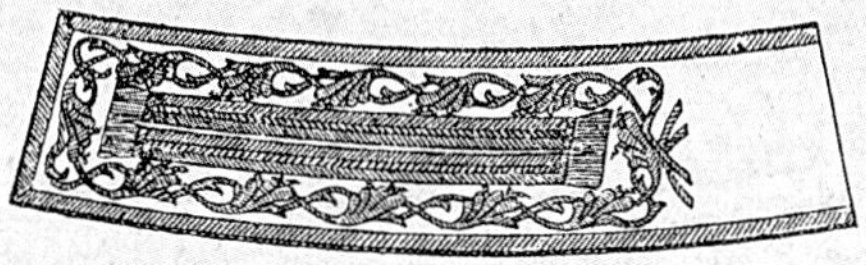

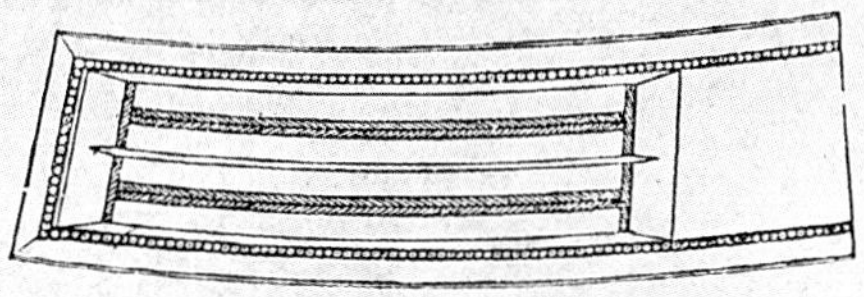

Offiziere der Garde-Landwehr-Kavallerie. Gold-Stickerei.

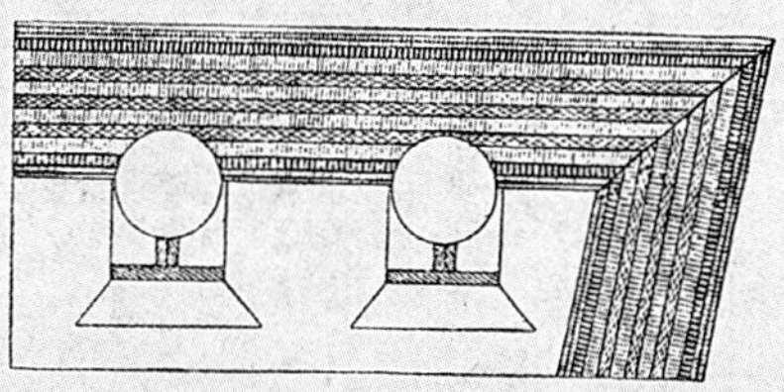

Offiziere der Gardes du Corps und der Garde-Kürassiere. Silber-Stickerei.

Senats-Präsidenten des Reichsmilitär-Gerichts. Silber-Stickerei.

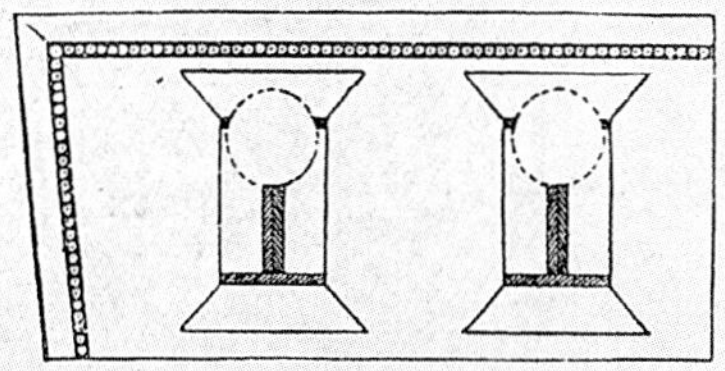

Ober-Militäranwälte d. Reichsmilitär-Gerichts m. d. Range d. Räte II. Klasse. Silber-Stickerei.

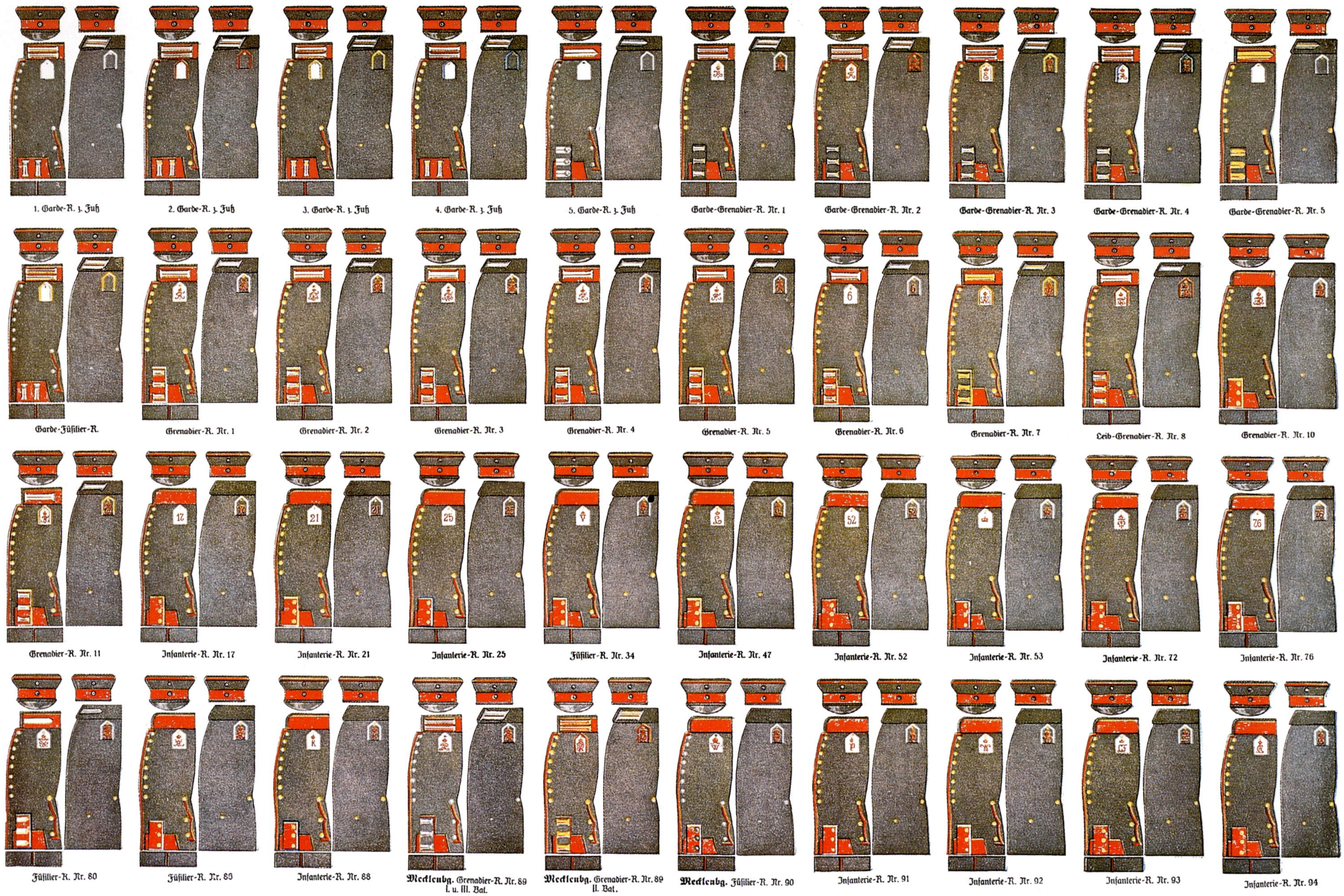

Die hier nicht dargestellten Grenadier-, Füsilier- und Infanterie-Regimenter wie die Infanterie-Regimenter Nr. 17, 21, 25, 52 und 76 mit ihrer Regiments-Nummer und den Vorstößen um die Ärmelpatte in der Farbe ihres Armeekorps.

An den Ärmelpatten haben Vorstöße in der Farbe der Schulterklappen am bisherigen dunkelblauen Waffenrock die Infanterie-Regimenter beim I., II., IX. und X. A.-K.: weiß, siehe Infanterie-Regiment Nr. 76 — V., VI., XVI. und XVII. A.-K.: zitronengelb, siehe Infanterie-Regiment Nr. 21 — VII., VIII, XVIII und XX A.-K.: hellblau, siehe Infanterie-Regiment Nr. 25 — XXI A.-K.: hellgrün, siehe Infanterie-Regiment Nr. 17. — Ohne Vorstöße an den Ärmelpatten. III., IV., XI, XIV., XV. Armeekorps wie Infanterie-Regiment Nr. 52.

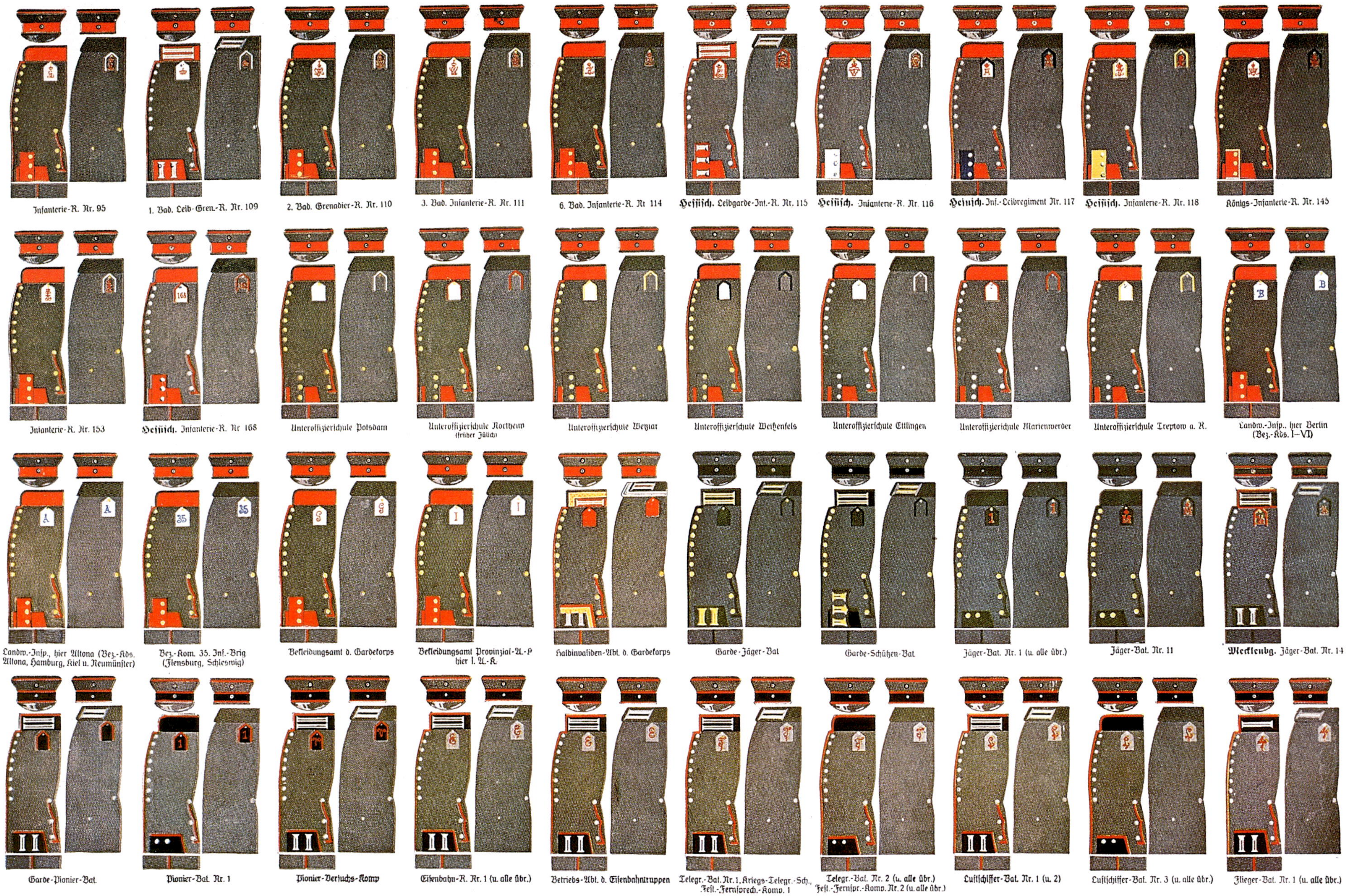

Die hier nicht dargestellten Grenadier-, Jiifilier- u. Infanterie-Regimenter wie die Inf.-Regimenter Nr. 17, 21, 25, 52 u. 76 mit ihrer Regiments-Nr. und den Vorstößen um die Ärmelpatte in der Farbe ihres Armeekorps. — Die Abkürzung: (u. alle übr.) = und alle übrigen mit ihrer Regiments- bezw. Bataillons-Nr. An den Ärmelpatten haben Vorstöße in der Farbe der Schulterklappen am bisherigen dunkelblauen Waffenrock die Infanterie-Regimenter beim I., II., IX. und X. A.-K.: weiß, siehe Infanterie-Regiment Nr. 76 — V., VI., XVI. und XVII. A.-K.: zitronengelb, siehe Infanterie-Regiment Nr. 21 — VII., VIII., XVIII und XX. A.-K.: hellblau, siehe Infanterie-Regiment Nr. 25 — XXI. A.-K.: hellgrün, siehe Infanterie-Regiment Nr. 17. — Ohne Vorstöße an den Ärmelpatten. III., IV., XI., XIV., XV. Armeekorps wie Infanterie-Regiment Nr. 52.

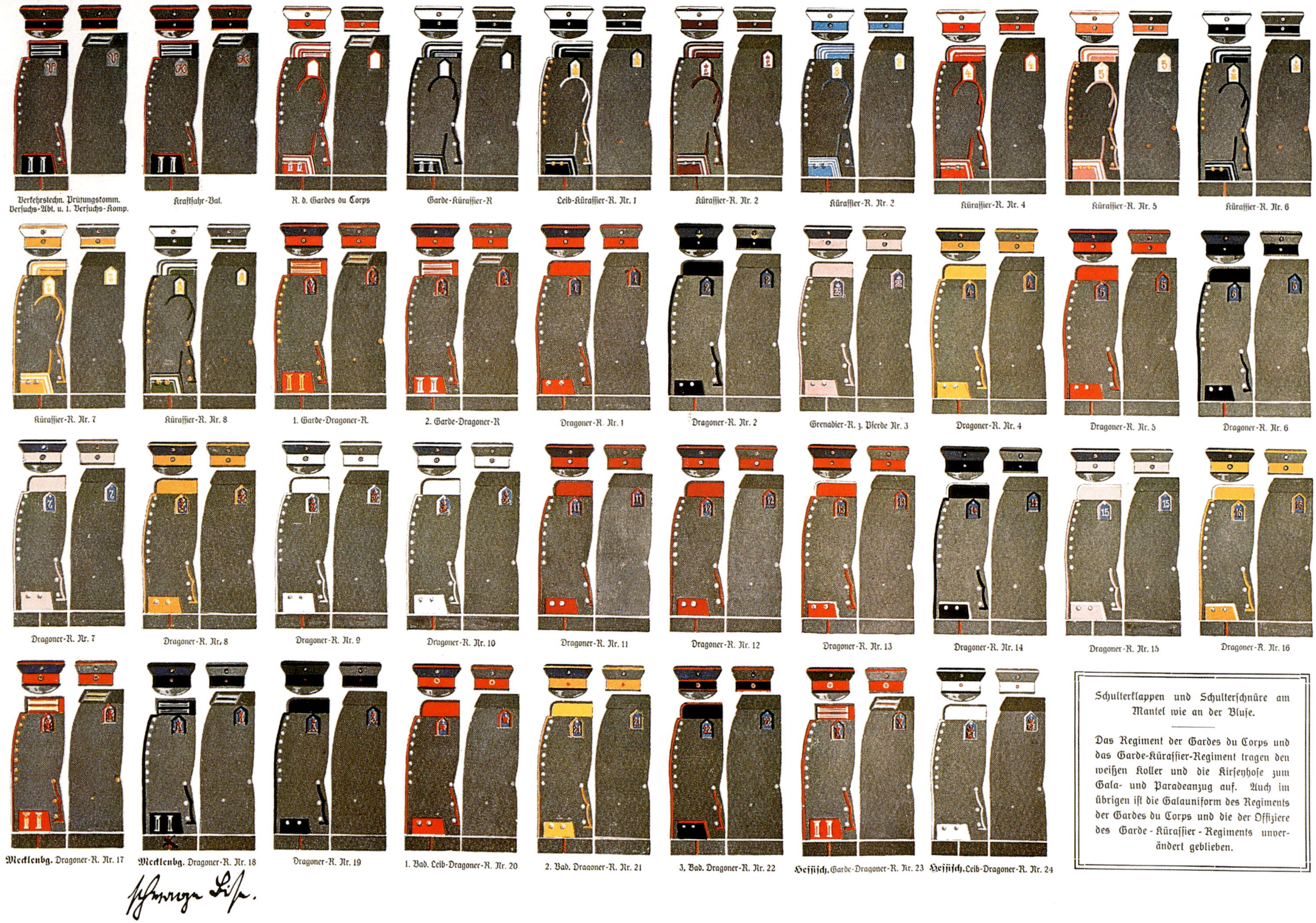

Schulterklappen und Schulterschnüre am Mantel wie an der Bluse.

Das Regiment der Gardes du Corps und das Garde-Kürassier-Regiment tragen den weißen Koller und die Kirseyhose zum Gala- und Paradeanzug auf. Auch im übrigen ist die Galauniform des Regiments der Gardes du Corps und die der Offiziere des Garde-Kürassier-Regiments unverändert geblieben.

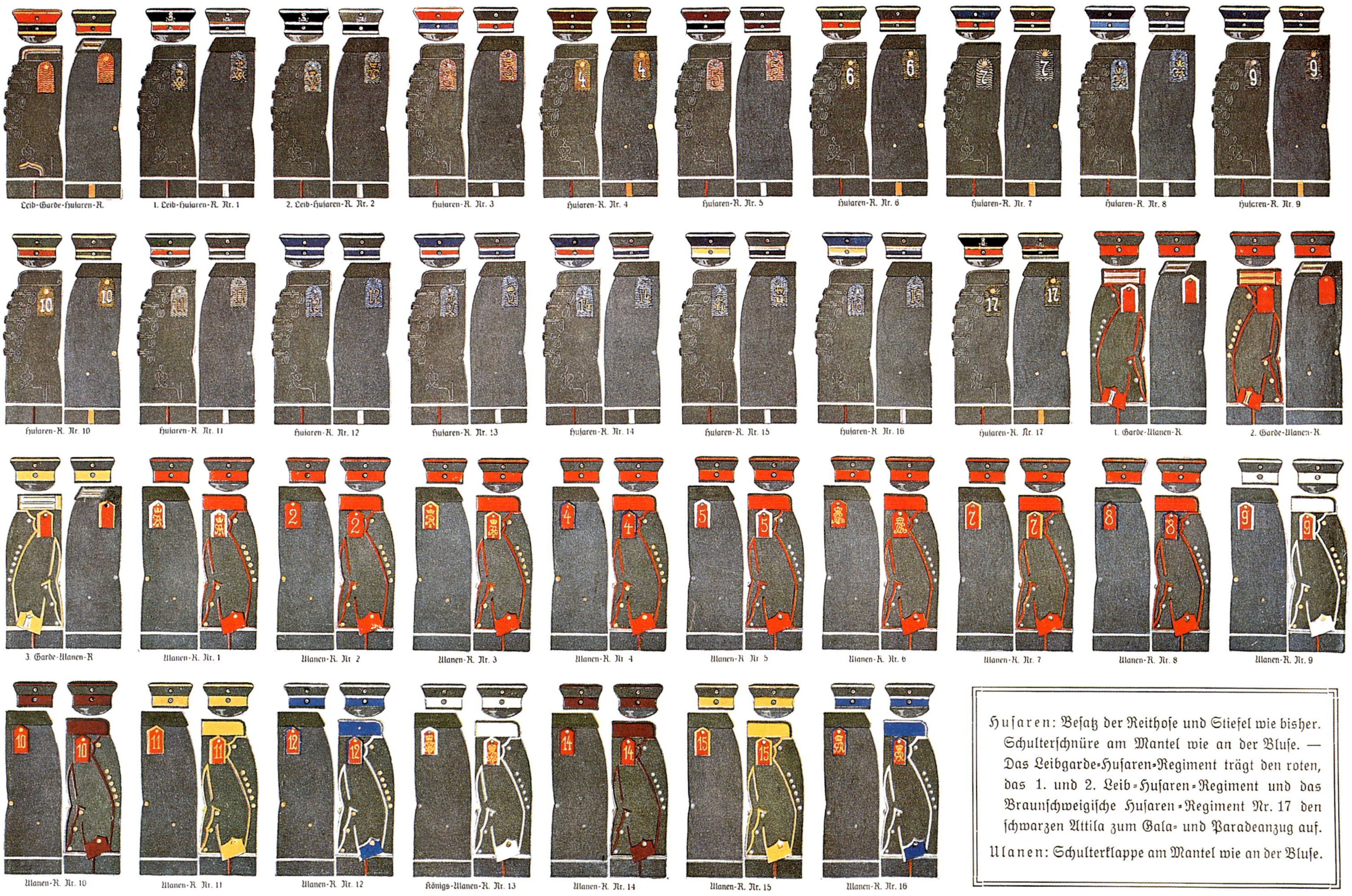

Husaren: Besatz der Reithose und Stiefel wie bisher. Schulterschnüre am Mantel wie an der Bluse. — Das Leibgarde-Husaren-Regiment trägt den roten, das 1. und 2. Leib-Husaren-Regiment und das Braunschweigische Husaren-Regiment Nr. 17 den schwarzen Attila zum Gala- und Paradeanzug auf.

Ulanen: Schulterklappe am Mantel wie an der Bluse.

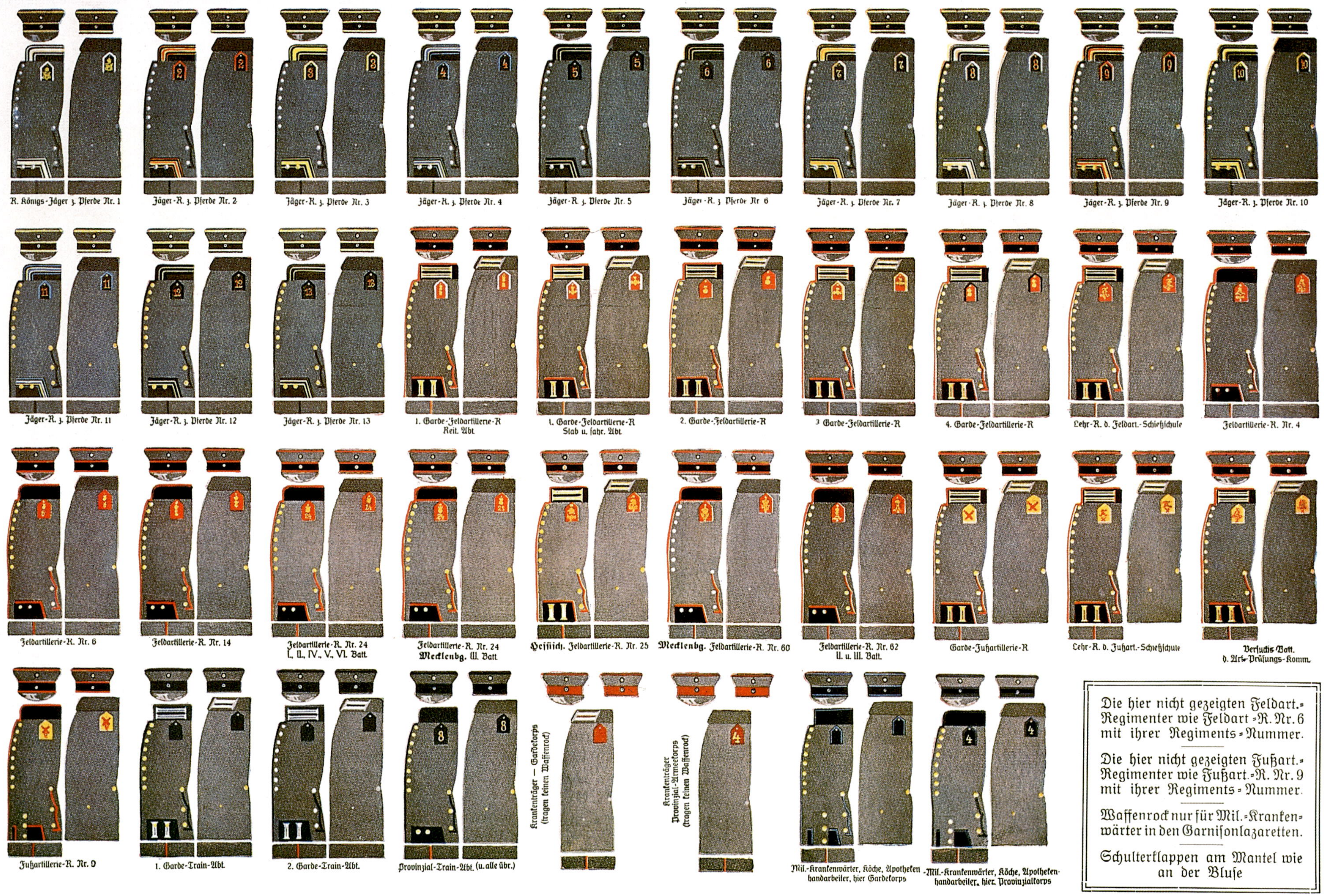

K. Königs-Jäger z. Pferde Nr. 1
Jäger-R. z. Pferde Nr. 2
Jäger-R. z. Pferde Nr. 3
Jäger-R. z. Pferde Nr. 4
Jäger-R. z. Pferde Nr. 5
Jäger-R. z. Pferde Nr. 6
Jäger-R. z. Pferde Nr. 7
Jäger-R. z. Pferde Nr. 8
Jäger-R. z. Pferde Nr. 9
Jäger-R. z. Pferde Nr. 10
Jäger-R. z. Pferde Nr. 11
Jäger-R. z. Pferde Nr. 12
Jäger-R. z. Pferde Nr. 13
1. Garde-Feldartillerie-R. Reit. Abt.
1. Garde-Feldartillerie-R. Stab u. fahr. Abt.
2. Garde-Feldartillerie-R.
3. Garde-Feldartillerie-R.
4. Garde-Feldartillerie-R.
Lehr-R. d. Feldart.-Schießschule
Feldartillerie-R. Nr. 4
Feldartillerie-R. Nr. 6
Feldartillerie-R. Nr. 14
Feldartillerie-R. Nr. 24 I., II., IV., V., VI. Batt.
Feldartillerie-R. Nr. 24 Mecklenbg. III. Batt.
Hessisch. Feldartillerie-R. Nr. 25
Mecklenbg. Feldartillerie-R. Nr. 60
Feldartillerie-R. Nr. 62 II. u. III. Batt.
Garde-Fußartillerie-R.
Lehr-R. d. Fußart.-Schießschule
Versuchs-Batt. d. Art.-Prüfungs-Komm.
Fußartillerie-R. Nr. 9
1. Garde-Train-Abt.
2. Garde-Train-Abt.
Provinzial-Train-Abt. (u. alle übr.)
Krankenträger — Gardekorps (tragen keinen Waffenrock)
Krankenträger Provinzial-Armeekorps (tragen keinen Waffenrock)
Mil.-Krankenwärter, Köche, Apotheken-handarbeiter, hier Gardekorps
Mil.-Krankenwärter, Köche, Apotheken-handarbeiter, hier Provinzialkorps
Die hier nicht gezeigten Feldart.-Regimenter wie Feldart.-R. Nr. 6 mit ihrer Regiments-Nummer.
Die hier nicht gezeigten Fußart.-Regimenter wie Fußart.-R. Nr. 9 mit ihrer Regiments-Nummer.
Waffenrock nur für Mil.-Krankenwärter in den Garnisonlazaretten.
Schulterklappen am Mantel wie an der Bluse

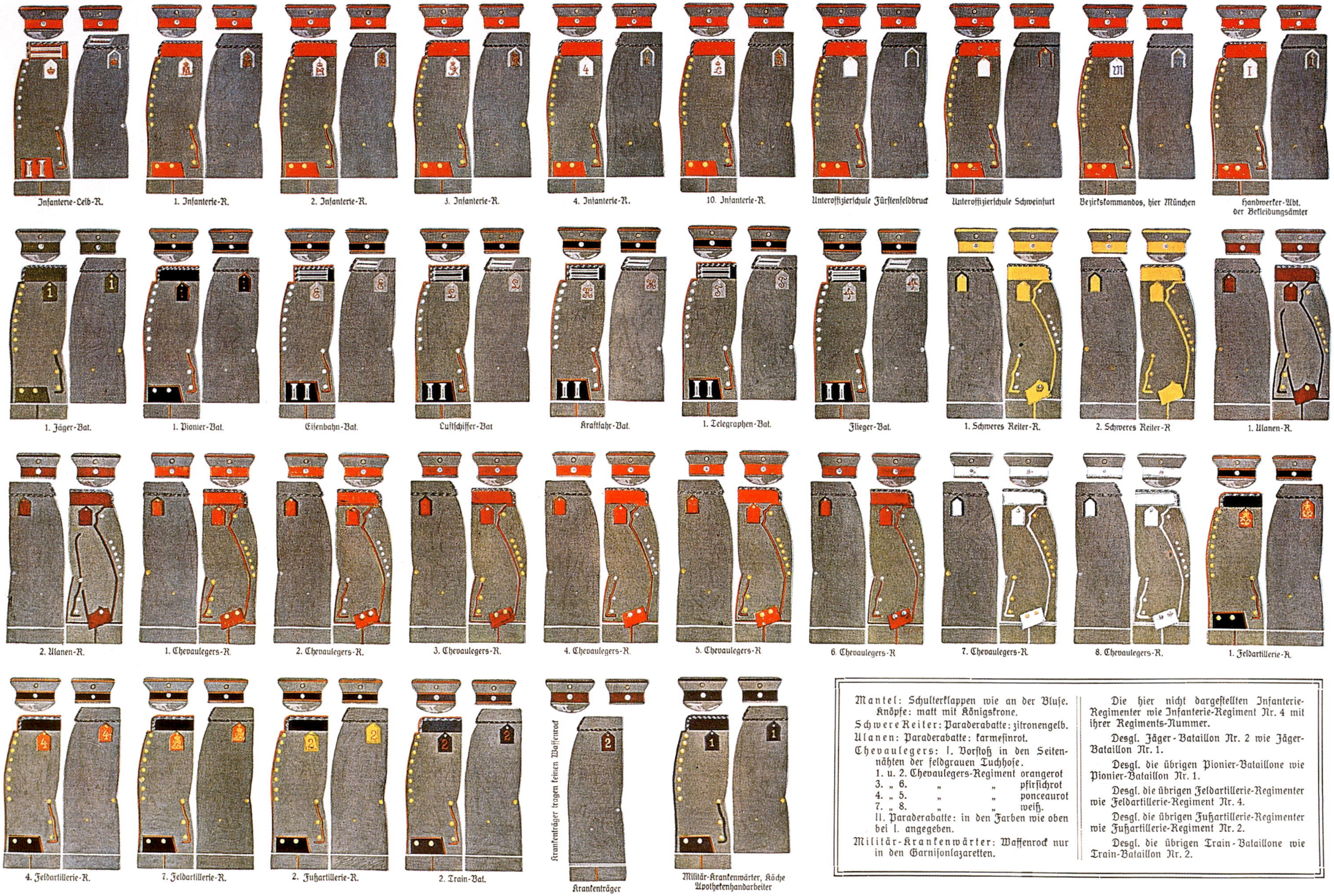

Mantel: Schulterklappen wie an der Bluse. Knöpfe: matt mit Königskrone.

Schwere Reiter: Paraderabatte: zitronengelb.

Ulanen: Paraderabatte: karmesinrot.

Chevaulegers: I. Vorstoß in den Seitennähten der feldgrauen Tuchhose.

1. u. 2. Chevaulegers-Regiment orangerot
3. „ 6. „ „ pfirsichrot
4. „ 5. „ „ ponceaurot
7. „ 8. „ „ weiß.

II. Paraderabatte: in den Farben wie oben bei I. angegeben.

Militär-Krankenwärter: Waffenrock nur in den Garnisonlazaretten.

Die hier nicht dargestellten Infanterie-Regimenter wie Infanterie-Regiment Nr. 4 mit ihrer Regiments-Nummer.

Desgl. Jäger-Bataillon Nr. 2 wie Jäger-Bataillon Nr. 1.

Desgl. die übrigen Pionier-Bataillone wie Pionier-Bataillon Nr. 1.

Desgl. die übrigen Feldartillerie-Regimenter wie Feldartillerie-Regiment Nr. 4.

Desgl. die übrigen Fußartillerie-Regimenter wie Fußartillerie-Regiment Nr. 2.

Desgl. die übrigen Train-Bataillone wie Train-Bataillon Nr. 2.

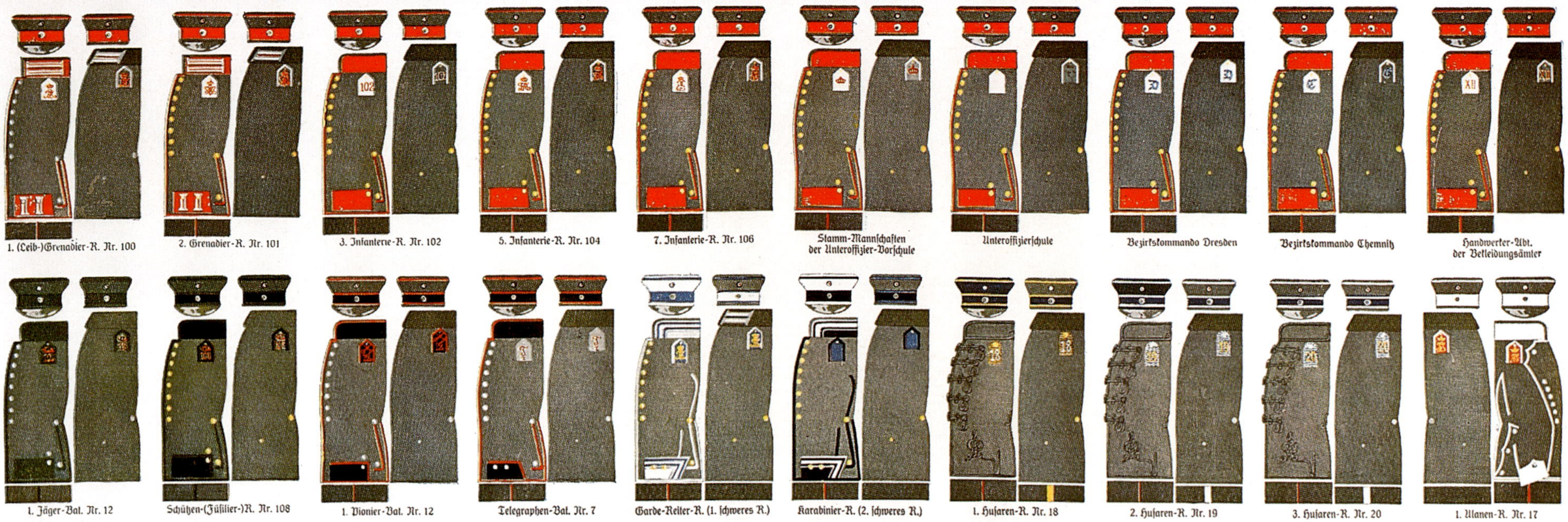

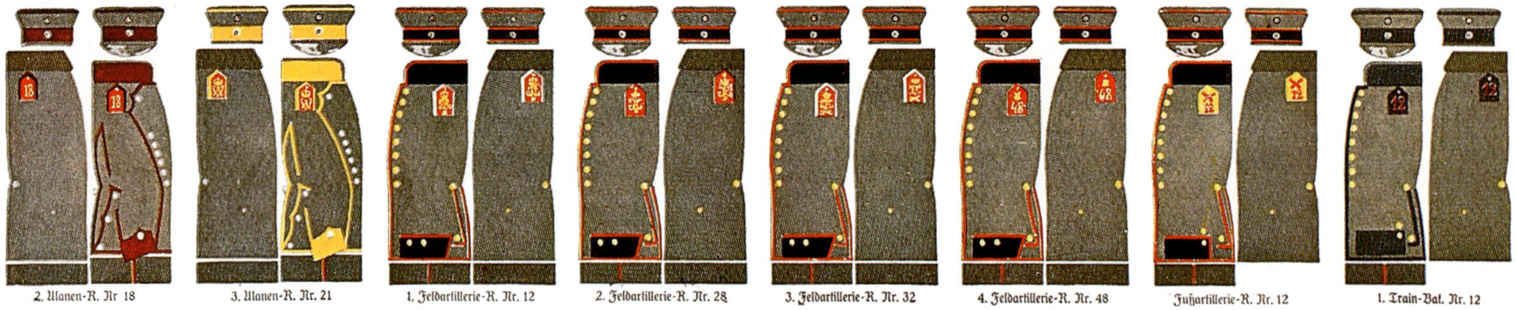

Schulterklappen am Mantel wie an der Bluse.

Unteroffiziertresse der Schweren Reiter nur 1,6 cm breit, wie die besondere Tresse für die Wachtmeister.

Paraderabatte bei den Ulanen von der Farbe des Stehkragens und der Ärmel-Aufschläge.

Die hier fehlenden Infanterie-Regimenter wie Inf.-R. Nr. 102 mit ihrer Regiments-Nummer. Jäger-Bataillon Nr. 13 wie Jäger-Bataillon Nr. 12 mit seiner Bataillons-Nummer. Pionier-Bataillon Nr. 22 wie Pionier-Bataillon Nr. 12 mit seiner Bataillons-Nummer. Fußartillerie-Regiment Nr. 19 wie Fußartillerie-R. Nr. 12 mit seiner Regiments-Nummer. Train-Bataillon Nr. 19 wie Train-Bataillon Nr. 12 mit seiner Bataillons-Nummer. Krankenträger sowie Krankenwärter, Köche, Apothekenhandarbeiter in den Farben **wie die preußischen auf Tafel V (Preußen)** mit sächsischem Rockschnitt, Hoheits-Abzeichen und roter 12.

Sächs. (II.) Bataillon beim Königl. Preuß. Eisenbahn-Regiment Nr. 1 — Sächs. Detachement für die Betriebs-Abteilung der Königl. Preuß. Eisenbahntruppen — Sächs. (3.) Kompagnie des Königl. Preuß. Luftschiffer-Bataillons Nr. 2 — Sächs. Detachement der 2. Kompagnie des Königl. Preuß. Kraftfahr-Bataillons — Sächs. Detachement bei der Königl. Preuß. Verkehrstechnischen Prüfungskommission nebst Versuchs-Abteilung — Sächs. (3.) Kompagnie des Königl. Preuß. Flieger-Bataillons Nr. 1 — **wie die preußischen auf Tafel II (Preußen)** mit ihren sächsischen Hoheits-Abzeichen.

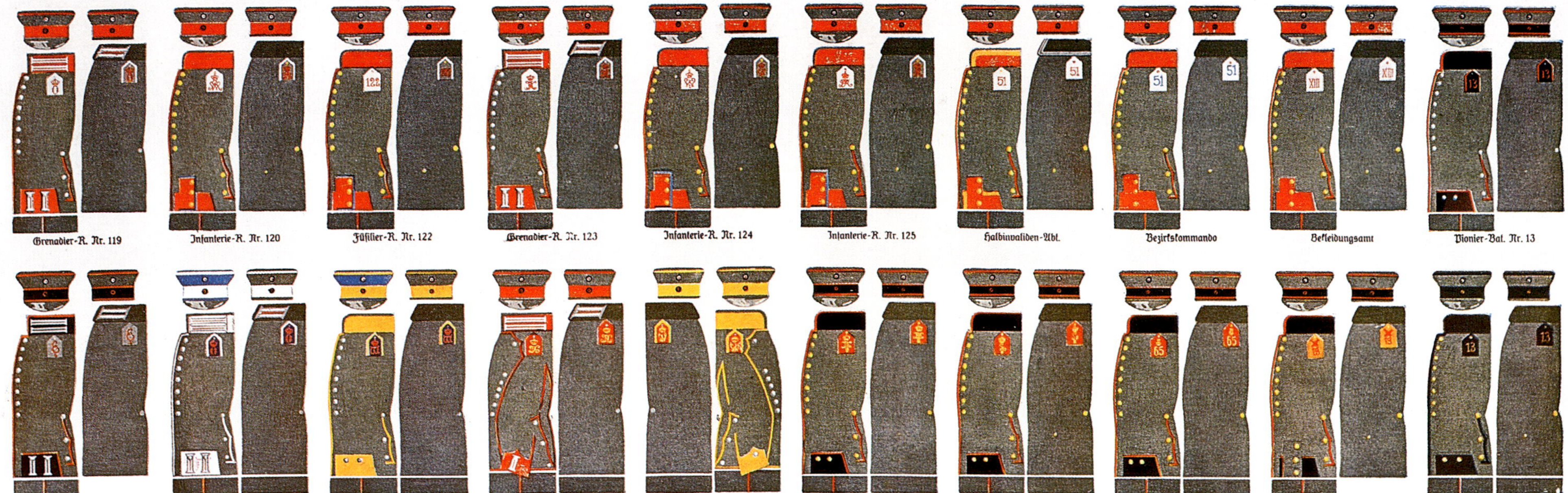

Grenadier-R. Nr. 119 — Infanterie-R. Nr. 120 — Füsilier-R. Nr. 122 — Grenadier-R. Nr. 123 — Infanterie-R. Nr. 124 — Infanterie-R. Nr. 125 — Halbinvaliden-Abt. — Bezirkskommando — Bekleidungsamt — Pionier-Bat. Nr. 13

Komp. beim Preuß. Eisenb.-Bat. Nr. 4 — Dragoner-R. Nr. 25 — Dragoner-R. Nr. 26 — Ulanen-R. Nr. 19 — Ulanen-R. Nr. 20 — Feldartillerie-R. Nr. 13 — Feldartillerie-R. Nr. 29 — Feldartillerie-R. Nr. 65 — Fußartillerie-R. Nr. 13 — Train-Bat. Nr. 13

Schulterklappen am Mantel wie an der Bluse.

Die hier nicht dargestellten Infanterie-Regimenter wie Füsilier-Regiment Nr. 122 mit ihrer Regiments-Nummer.

Ulanen: Paraderabatte wie bisher, beim Ulanen-Regiment Nr. 20 aber goldgelb.

Krankenträger, sowie Militär-Krankenwärter, Köche, Apothekenhandarbeiter: **wie auf Tafel V (Preußen)** mit ihren württembergischen Hoheits-Abzeichen und auf den Schulterklappen mit gelber 13.

Detachement bei der Kgl. Preuß. Betriebsabteilung der Eisenbahntruppen — Detachement beim Kgl. Preuß. Kraftfahr-Bataillon — Detachement bei der Kgl. Preuß. Versuchsabteilung nebst Versuchskompagnie — Kompagnie beim Kgl. Preuß. Telegraphen-Bataillon Nr. 4 mit Detachement bei der Kgl. Preuß. Festungs-Fernsprech-Kompagnie Nr. 4 — Kompagnie beim Kgl. Preuß. Luftschiffer-Bataillon Nr. 4 — **wie die preußischen auf Tafel II (Preußen)** mit ihren württembergischen Hoheits-Abzeichen.

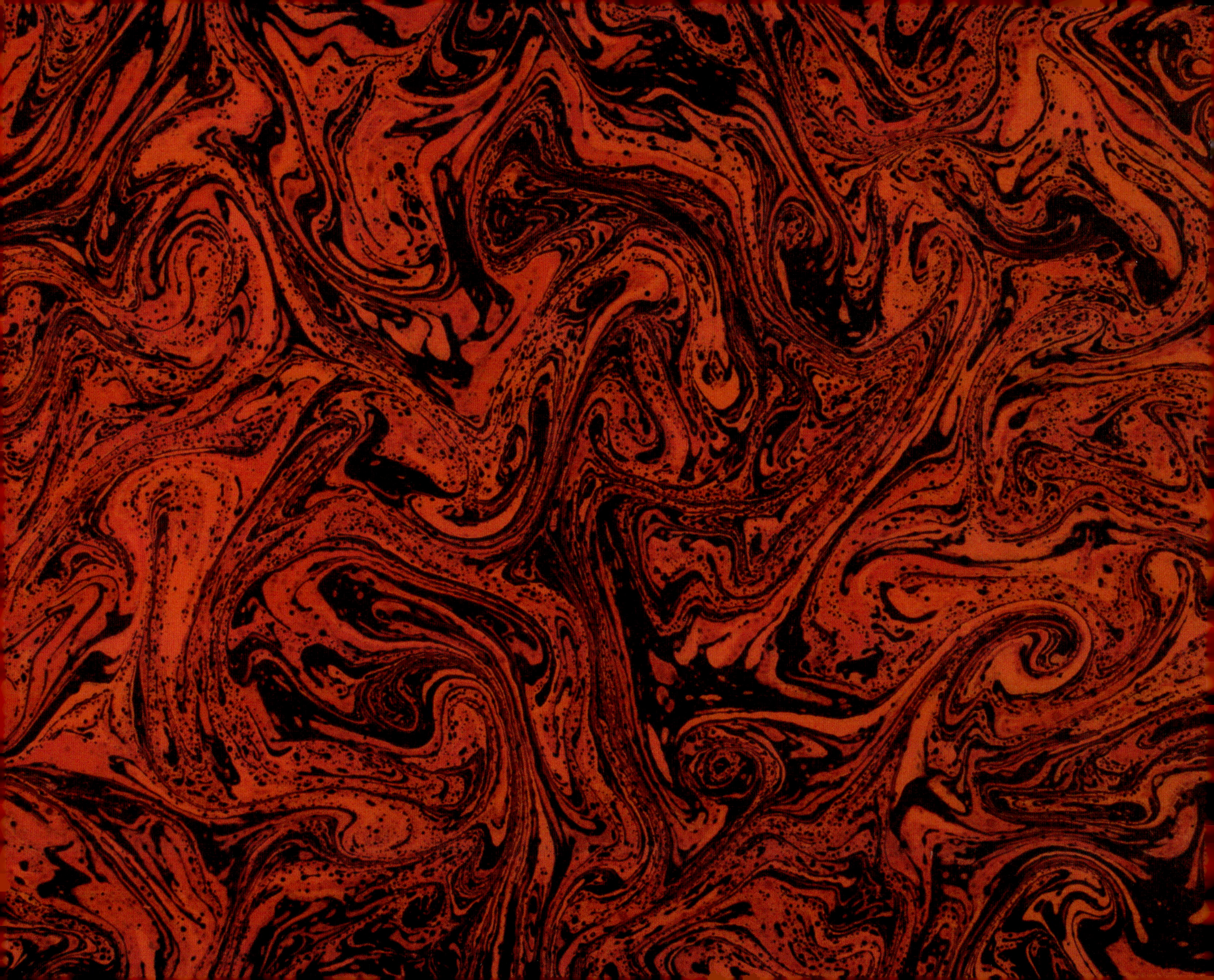

Feldgrau in Krieg u. Frieden

I. Teil

Mannschaften

2. Auflage.

Uniformtafeln

nach der Allerhöchsten Kabinettsordre vom 21. September 1915 mit Genehmigung des Königl. Preuß. Kriegsministeriums herausgegeben von
Otto Weiß

Berlin 1916 · Druck u. Verlag von H. S. Hermann · Preis 2 Mark

Feldgrau in Krieg und Frieden

Uniformtafeln sämtlicher Truppenteile

der Kgl. Preußischen Armee / ausschl. des Mecklenburgischen und Hessischen Kontingents / nach der Allerhöchsten Kabinettsordre vom 21. September 1915

Mit Genehmigung des Kgl. Preuß. Kriegsministeriums herausgegeben von

Otto Weiß

Ob. Mil. Intendantursekretär kdt. zur Bekleidungs-Abteilung des Kgl. Preuß. Kriegsministeriums

Druck und Verlag von H. S. Hermann in Berlin SW 19, Beuthstr. 8

Inhaltsverzeichnis

Linien-Infanterie:

Inhaltsverzeichnis

Abbildungen der neuen Uniformen.

Mantel
für alle Waffengattungen.
Vorderansicht.

Waffenrock.

Infanterie.
(1. Garde-R. z. F.)

Kürassiere.
(R. der Gardes du Corps.)

Jäger zu Pferde.
(R. Königs-J. z. Pf. 1.)

Abbildungen der neuen Uniformen.

Attila.

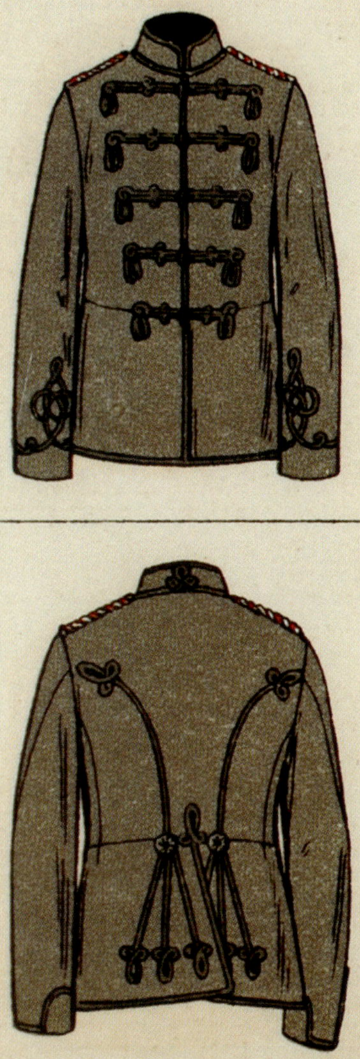

Ulanka.
(1. Garde-Ul. R.)

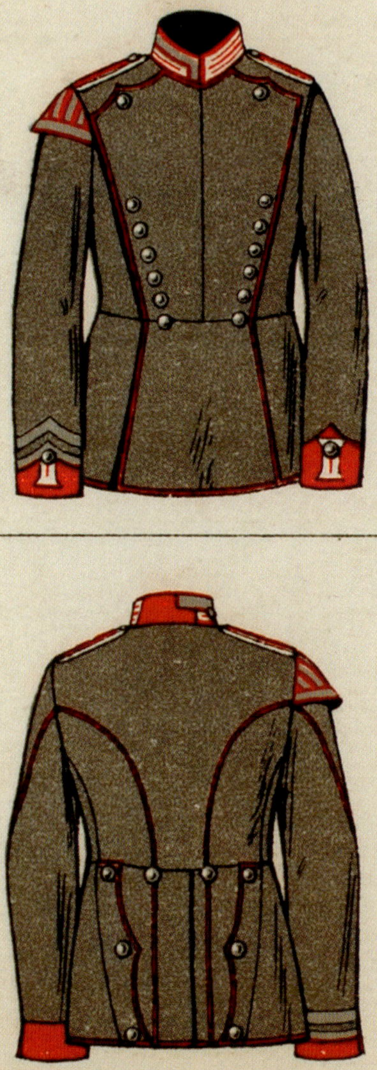

Bluse
für alle Waffengattungen.

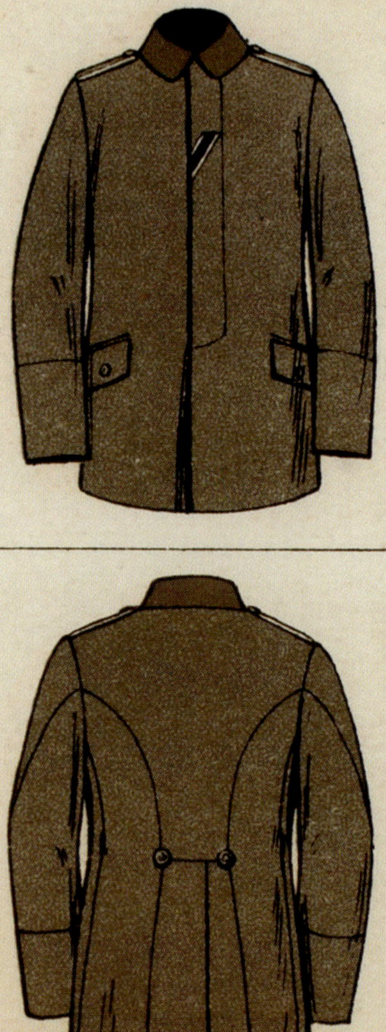

Mantel
für alle Waffengattungen.
Rückansicht.

Infanterie.

Infanterie-Regimenter.

Gardekorps.

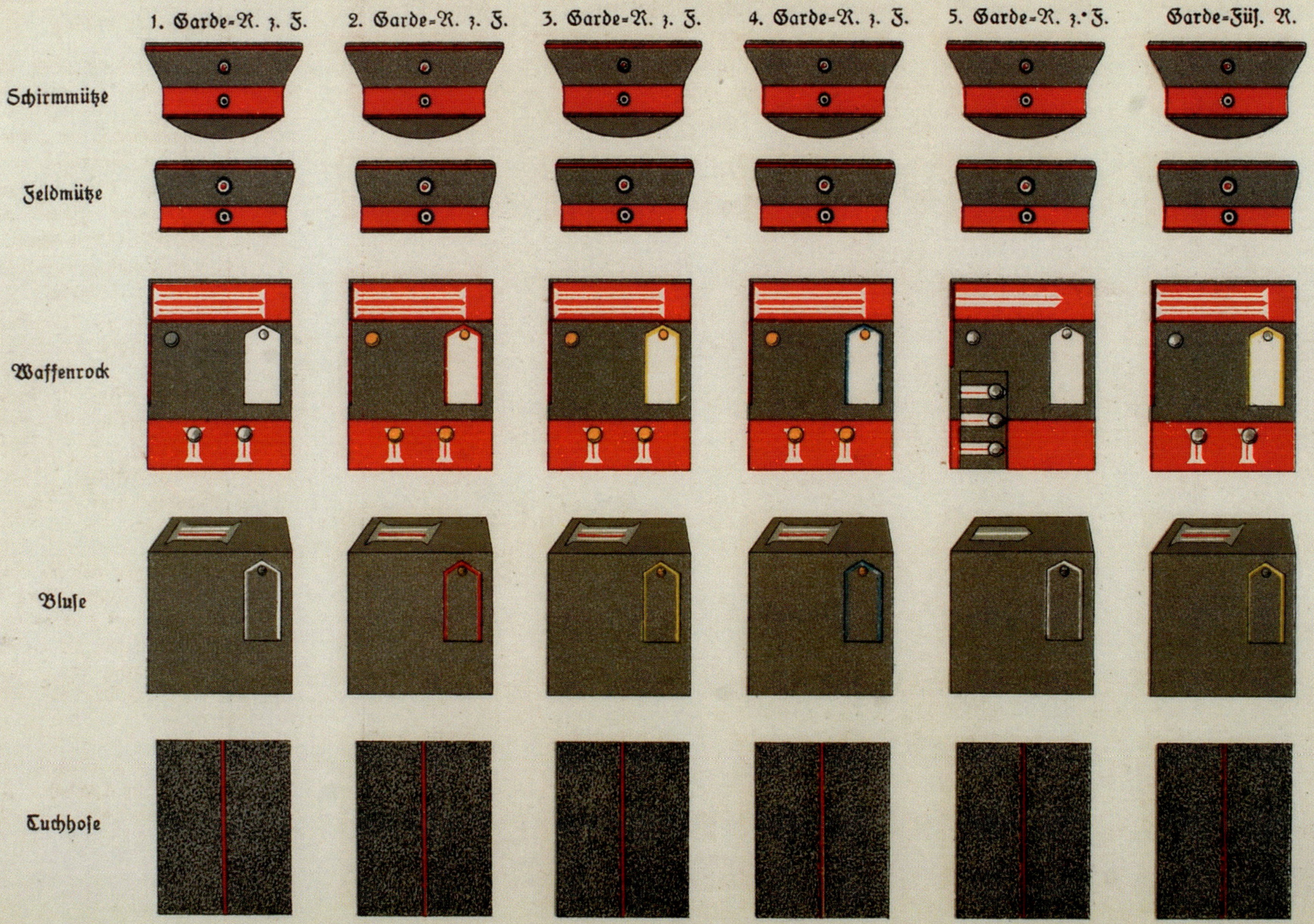

Infanterie.

Infanterie-Regimenter.

Gardekorps.

Garde-Gren. R. 1 | Garde-Gren. R. 2 | Garde-Gren. R. 3 | Garde-Gren. R. 4 | Garde-Gren. R. 5

Anmerkung.

1. Am Waffenrock sind die Vorstöße vorn herunter und an den Taschenleisten (bei den Kürassieren auch in den Ärmel-, Armloch- u. Rückennähten):
   - a) Infanterie, Pioniere, Verkehrstruppen, Feld- und Fußartillerie: ponceaurot,
   - b) Jäger (Schützen) und Jäger zu Pferde: hellgrün,
   - c) Kürassiere und Dragoner: von der Farbe der Ärmelaufschläge (Ausnahmen: Kürassier-Rgt. 1: weiß, Dragoner-Rgt. 22: ponceaurot),
   - d) Train: kaliblau,
   - e) Krankenwärter: kornblumenblau.
2. An der Ulanka sind die Vorstöße an den Taschenleisten, in den Ärmel- und Rückennähten sowie Farbe um die Schöße von der Farbe der Brustklappen-Vorstöße auf Seite 24—26.
3. Reithosen und Stiefelhosen grau (wie die Tuchhose), jedoch allgemein ohne Vorstoß. Husaren siehe Seite 21—23.

Infanterie-Regimenter
des
I., II., IX. u. X. Armeekorps.

— Schirmmütze, Feldmütze u. Tuchhose wie beim Gardekorps —

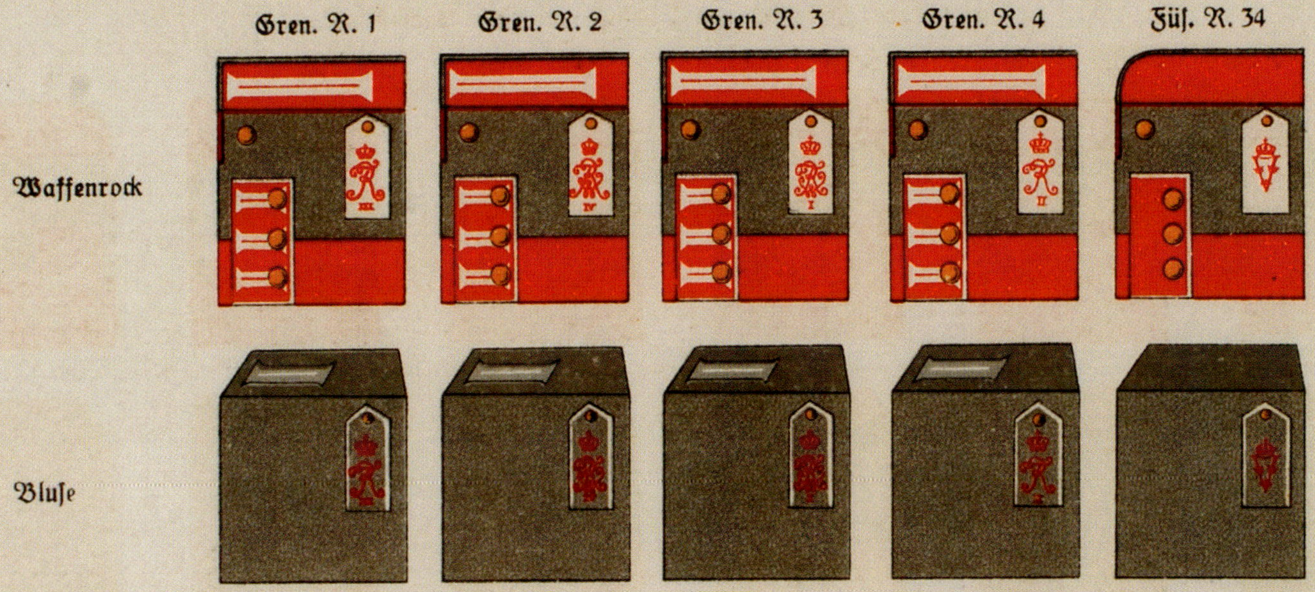

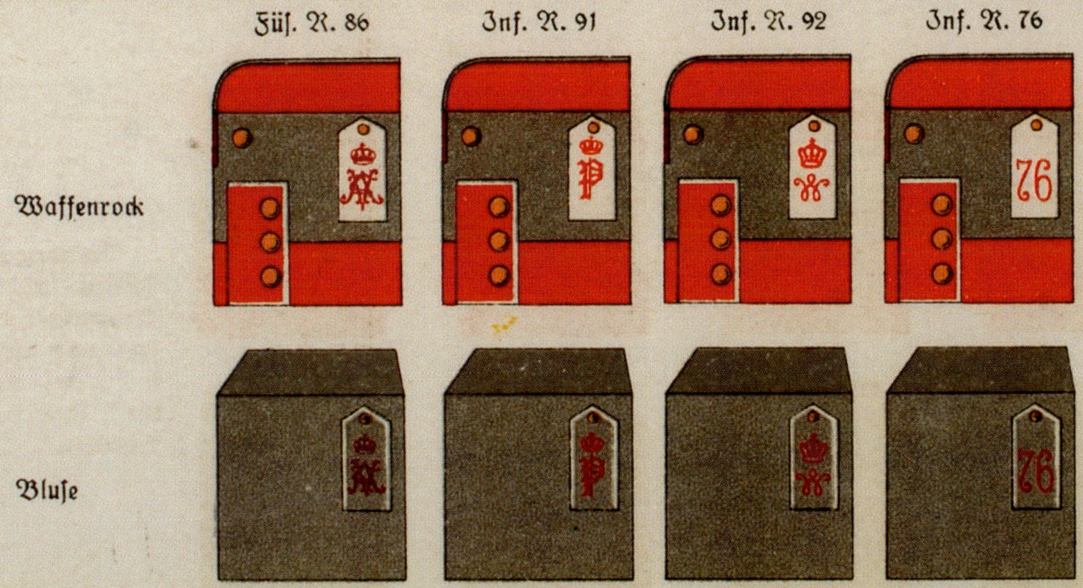

Die übrigen Grenadier-, Füsilier- und Infanterie-Regimenter dieser 4 Armeekorps wie: Inf. Rgt. 76 mit ihrer Regimentsnummer.

Infanterie-Regimenter
des
III., IV., XI., XIV. und XV. Armeekorps.

— Schirmmütze, Feldmütze und Tuchhose wie beim Gardekorps. —

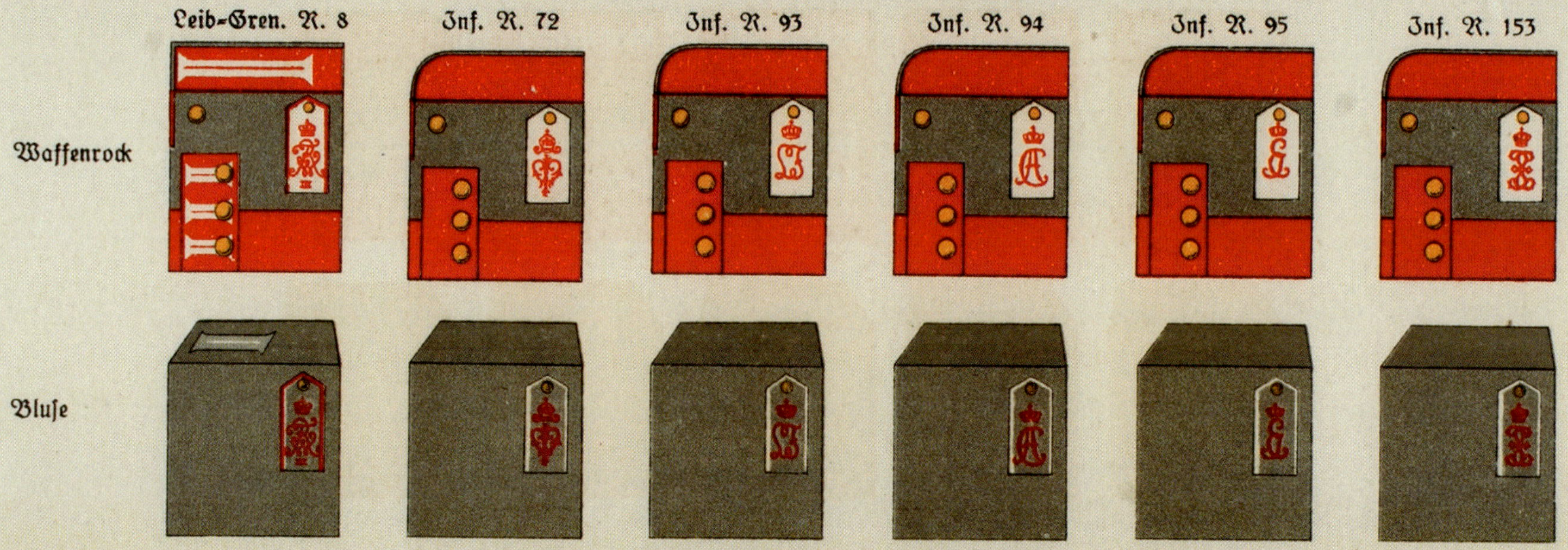

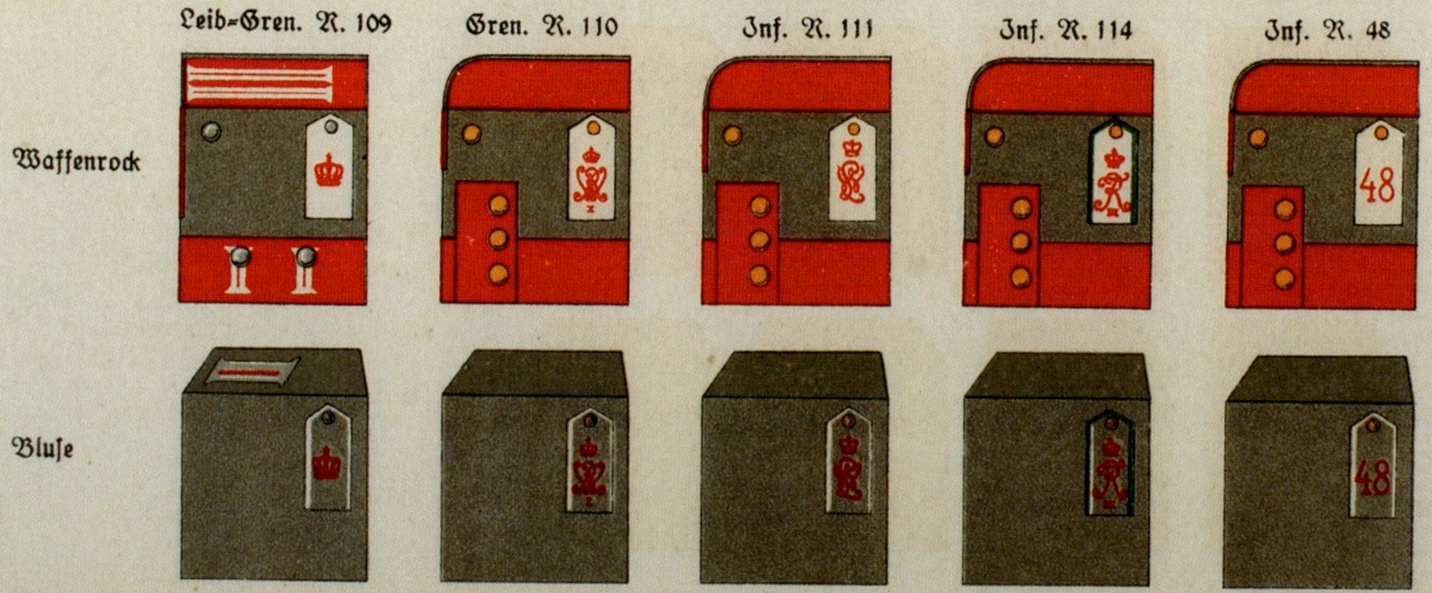

Die übrigen Grenadier-, Füsilier- und Infanterie-Regimenter dieser 5 Armeekorps wie:
Inf.-Rgt. 48
mit ihrer Regiments-Nummer.

Infanterie-Regimenter
des
V., VI., XVI. u. XVII. Armeekorps.

— Schirmmütze, Feldmütze u. Tuchhose wie beim Gardekorps —

Gren. R. 5 | Gren. R. 6 | Gren. R. 7 | Gren. R. 10

Waffenrock

Bluse

Gren. R. 11 | Inf. R. 47 | Königs-Inf. R. 145 | Inf. R. 21

Waffenrock

Bluse

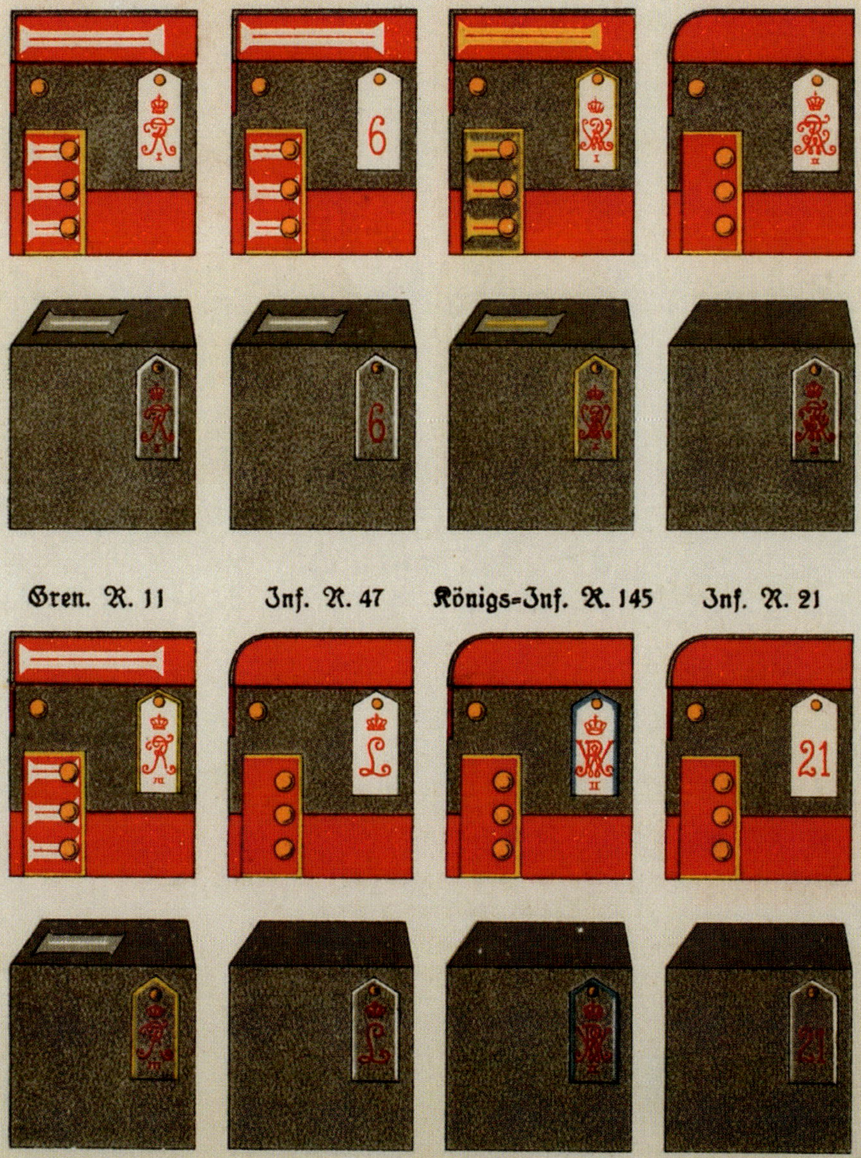

Die übrigen Füsilier- und Infanterie-Regimenter dieser 4 Armeekorps wie:
Inf. Rgt. 21
mit ihrer Regimentsnummer.

Infanterie-Regimenter
des
VII., VIII., XVIII. u. XX. Armeekorps.

— Schirmmütze, Feldmütze u. Tuchhose wie beim Gardekorps —

Inf. R. 53 | Füs. R. 80 | Inf. R. 88 | Inf. R. 25

Waffenrock

Bluse

Die übrigen Grenadier-, Füsilier- und Infanterie-Regimenter dieser 4 Armeekorps wie:
Inf. Rgt. 25
mit ihrer Regimentsnummer.

XXI. Armeekorps.

Inf. R. 17

Waffenrock

Bluse

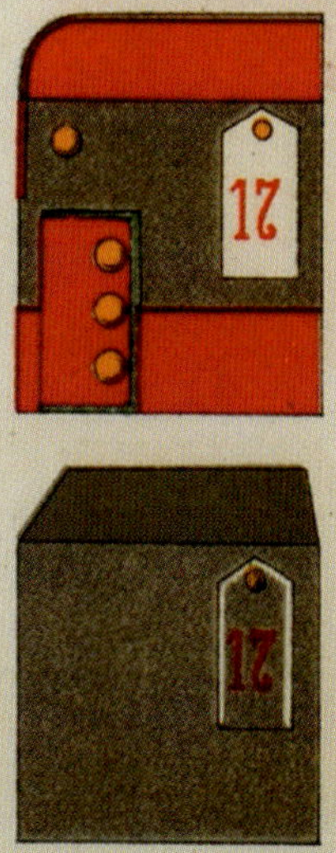

Die übrigen Infanterie-Regimenter des XXI. Armeekorps wie:
Inf. Rgt. 17
mit ihrer Regimentsnummer.

Unteroffizierschulen.

Schirmmütze, Feldmütze und Tuchhose wie Garde-Infanterie.

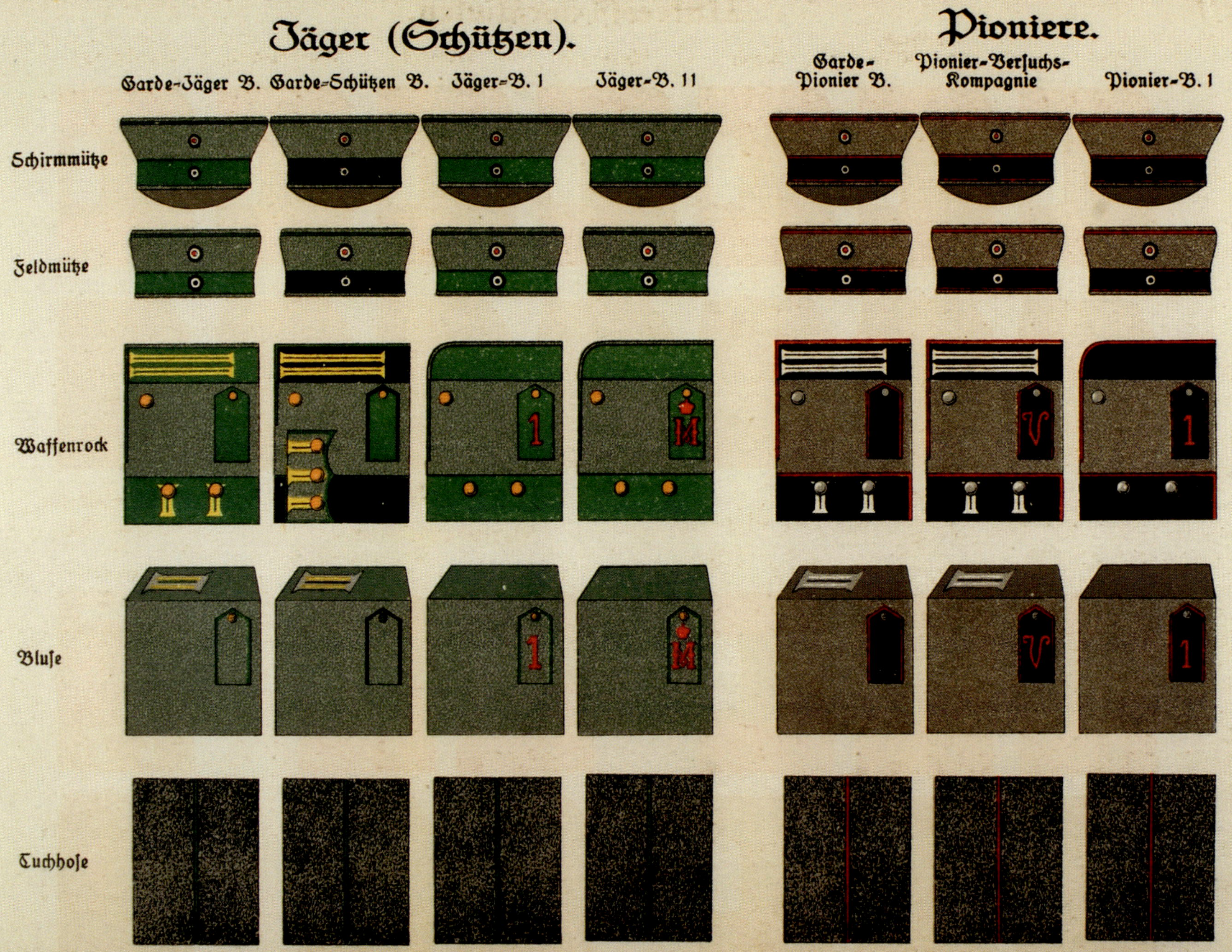

Die übrigen Jäger-Bataillone wie Jäger-Bataillon 1 mit ihrer Bataillons-Nummer.

Die übrigen Pionier-Bataillone und -Regimenter wie Pionier-Bataillon 1 mit ihrer Bataillons- bezw. Regiments-Nummer.

Verkehrstruppen.

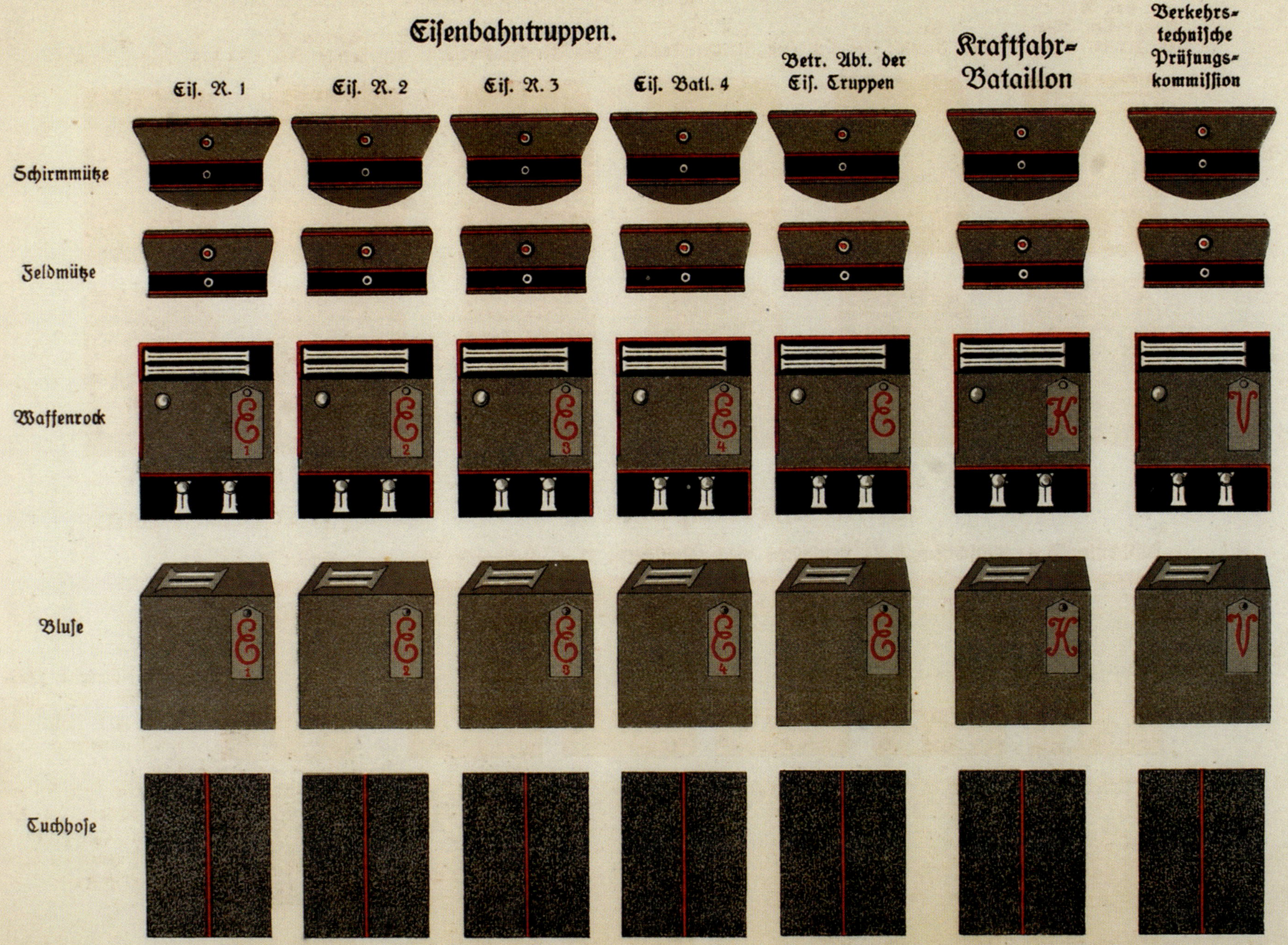

Telegraphentruppen.

Tel. B. 1 Kriegs-Tel. Schule Fest. Fernspr. Komp. 1 — Tel. B. 2 Fest. Fernspr. Komp. 2 — Tel. B. 3 Fest. Fernspr. Komp. 3 — Tel. B. 4 Fest. Fernspr. Komp. 4 — Tel. B. 5 Fest. Fernspr. Komp. 5 — Tel. B. 6 Fest. Fernspr. Komp. 6

Waffenrock

Bluse

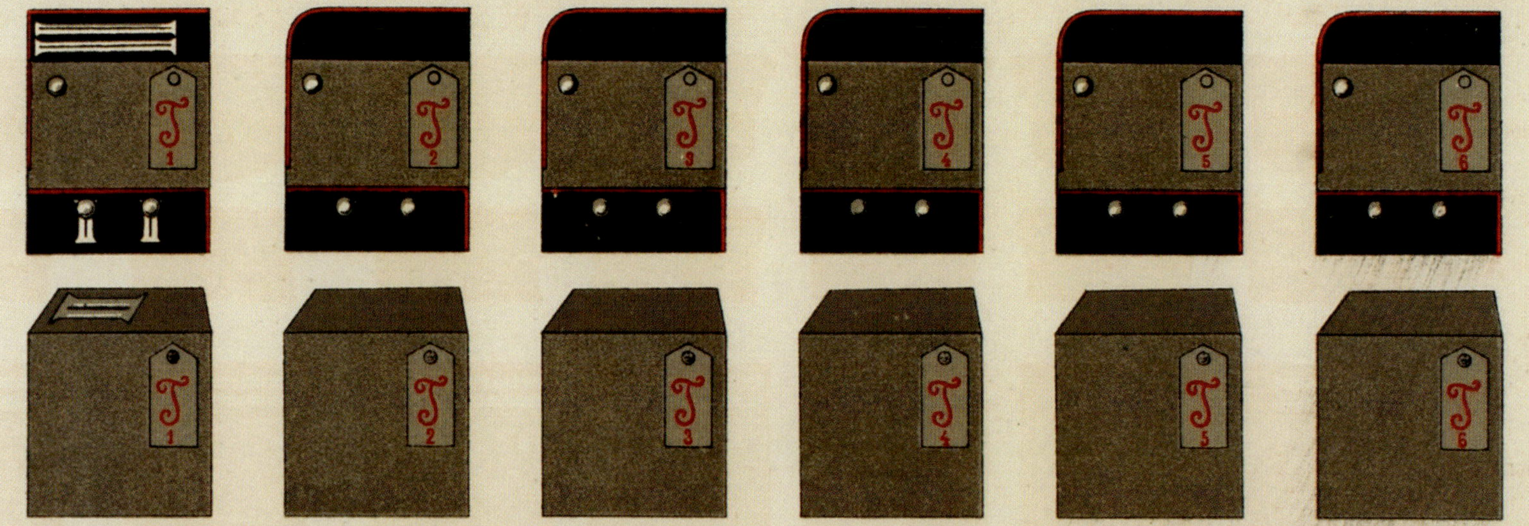

Luftschiffertruppen.

Luftschiffer B. 1 — Luftschiffer B. 2 — Luftschiffer B. 3 — Luftschiffer B. 4 — Luftschiffer B. 5

Fliegertruppen.

Flieger B. 1

Waffenrock

Bluse

Die übrigen Flieger-Bataillone wie Flieger-Bataillon 1 mit ihrer Bataillonsnummer.

Schirmmütze, Feldmütze und Tuchhose der Telegraphen-, Luftschiffer- und Fliegertruppen wie bei den Eisenbahntruppen.

Kürassiere.

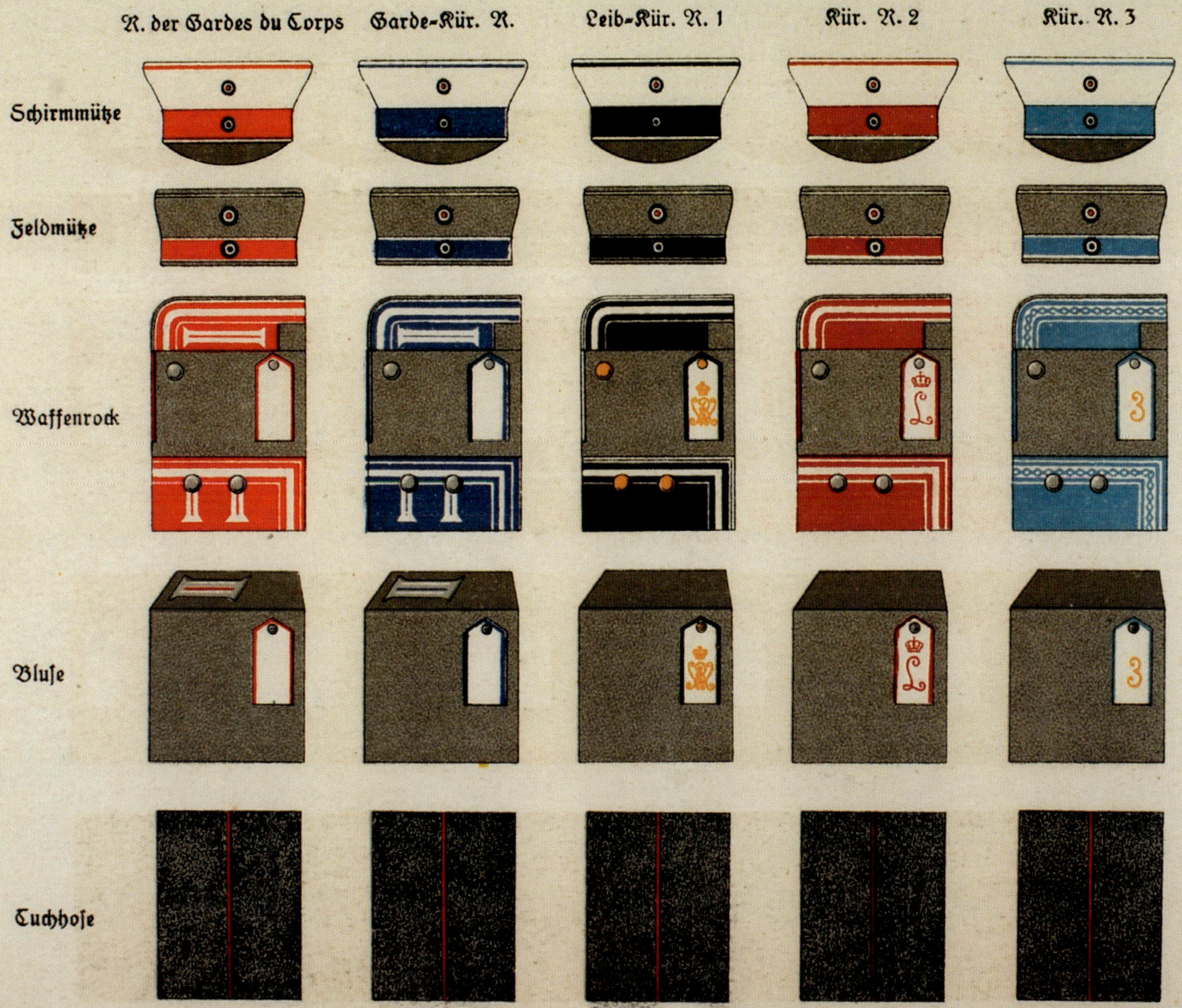
R. der Gardes du Corps
Garde-Kür. R.
Leib-Kür. R. 1
Kür. R. 2
Kür. R. 3
Schirmmütze
Feldmütze
Waffenrock
Bluse
Tuchhose

Kürassiere.

Kür. N. 4
Kür. N. 5
Kür. N. 6
Kür. N. 7
Kür. N. 8
Schirmmütze
Feldmütze
Waffenrock
Bluse
Tuchhose
4
5
7
4
5
7

Dragoner.

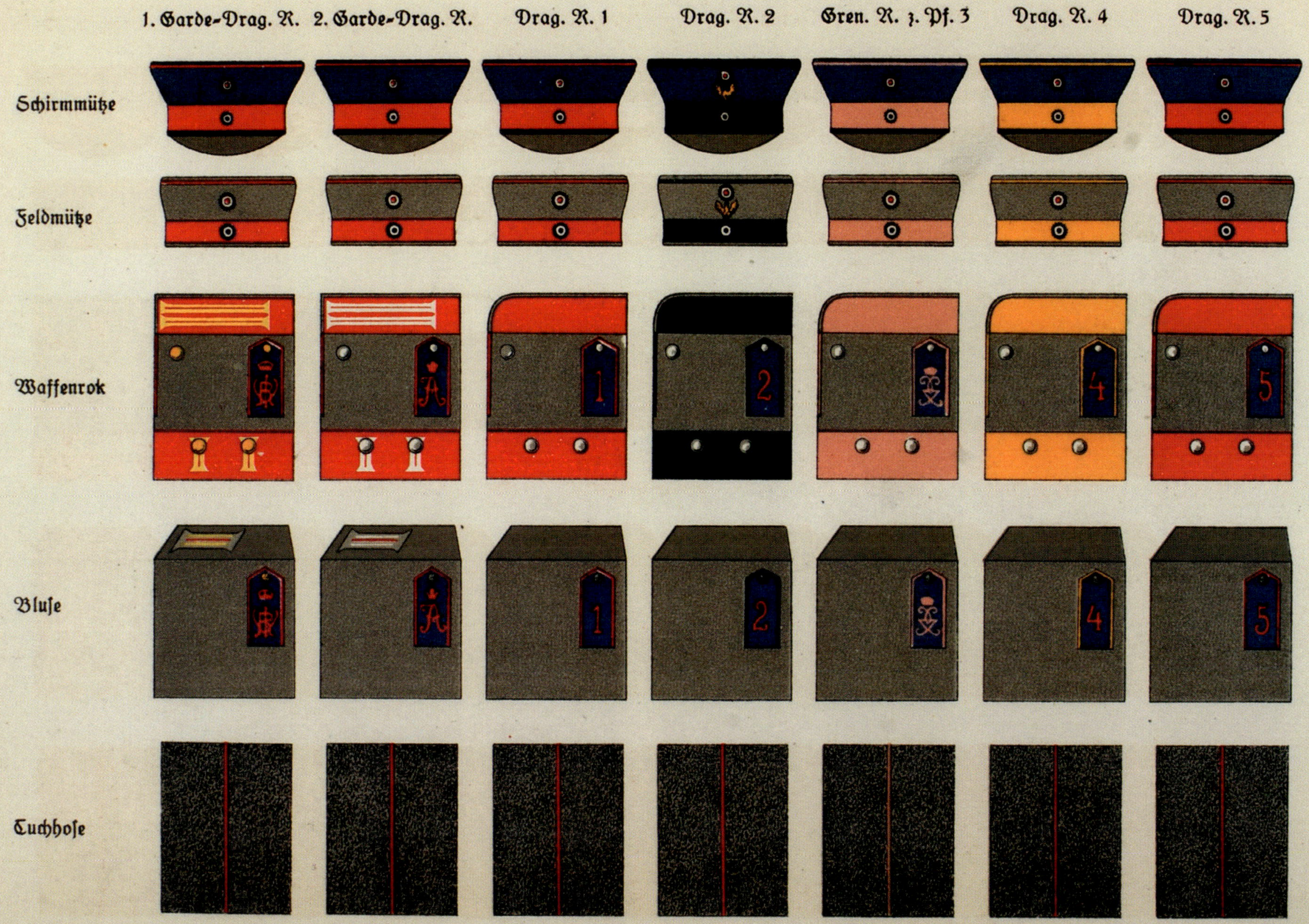
1. Garde-Drag. R.
2. Garde-Drag. R.
Drag. R. 1
Drag. R. 2
Gren. R. z. Pf. 3
Drag. R. 4
Drag. R. 5
Schirmmütze
Feldmütze
Waffenrok
Bluse
Tuchhose

Dragoner.

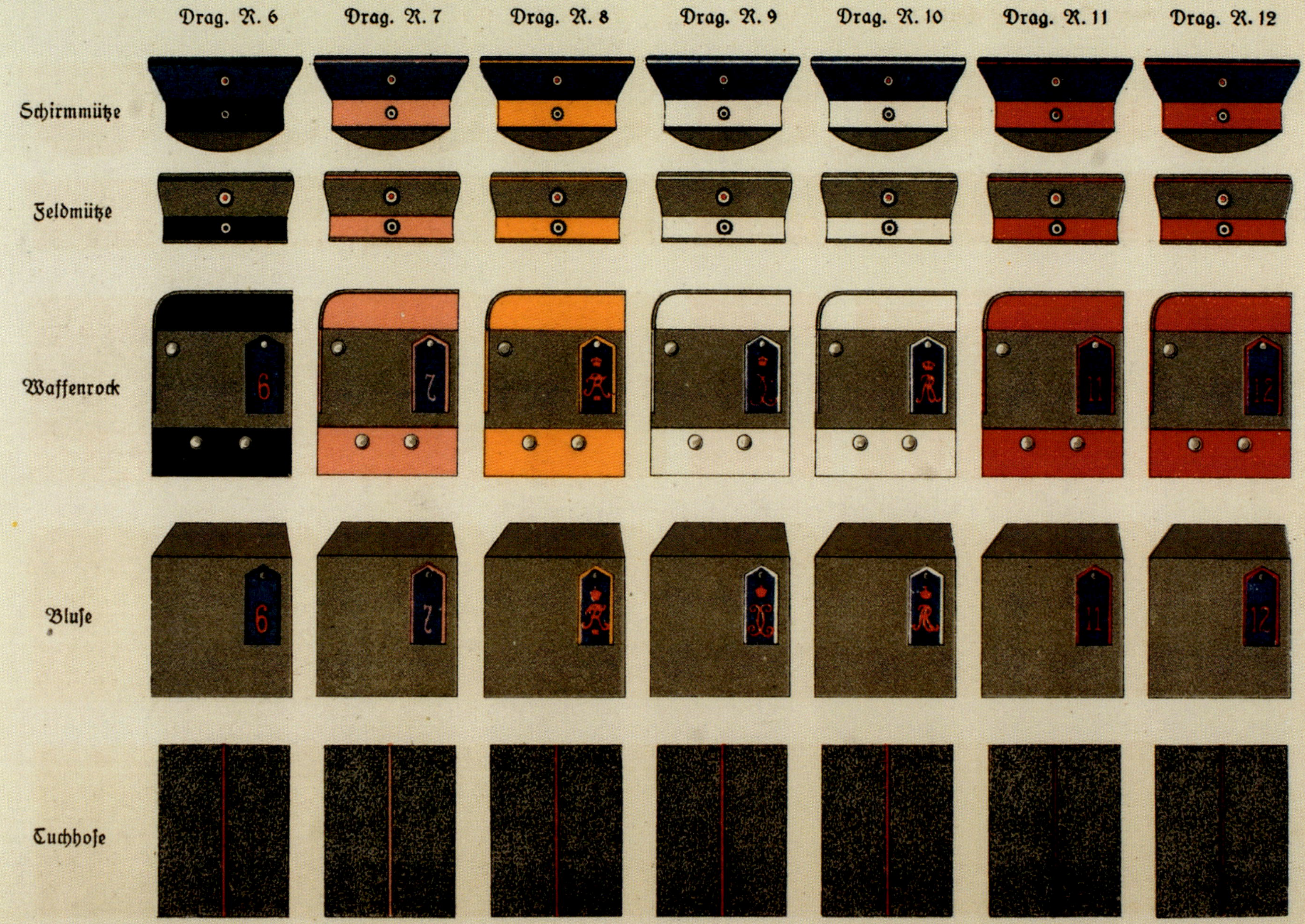
Drag. R. 6
Drag. R. 7
Drag. R. 8
Drag. R. 9
Drag. R. 10
Drag. R. 11
Drag. R. 12
Schirmmütze
Feldmütze
Waffenrock
Bluse
Tuchhose

Dragoner.

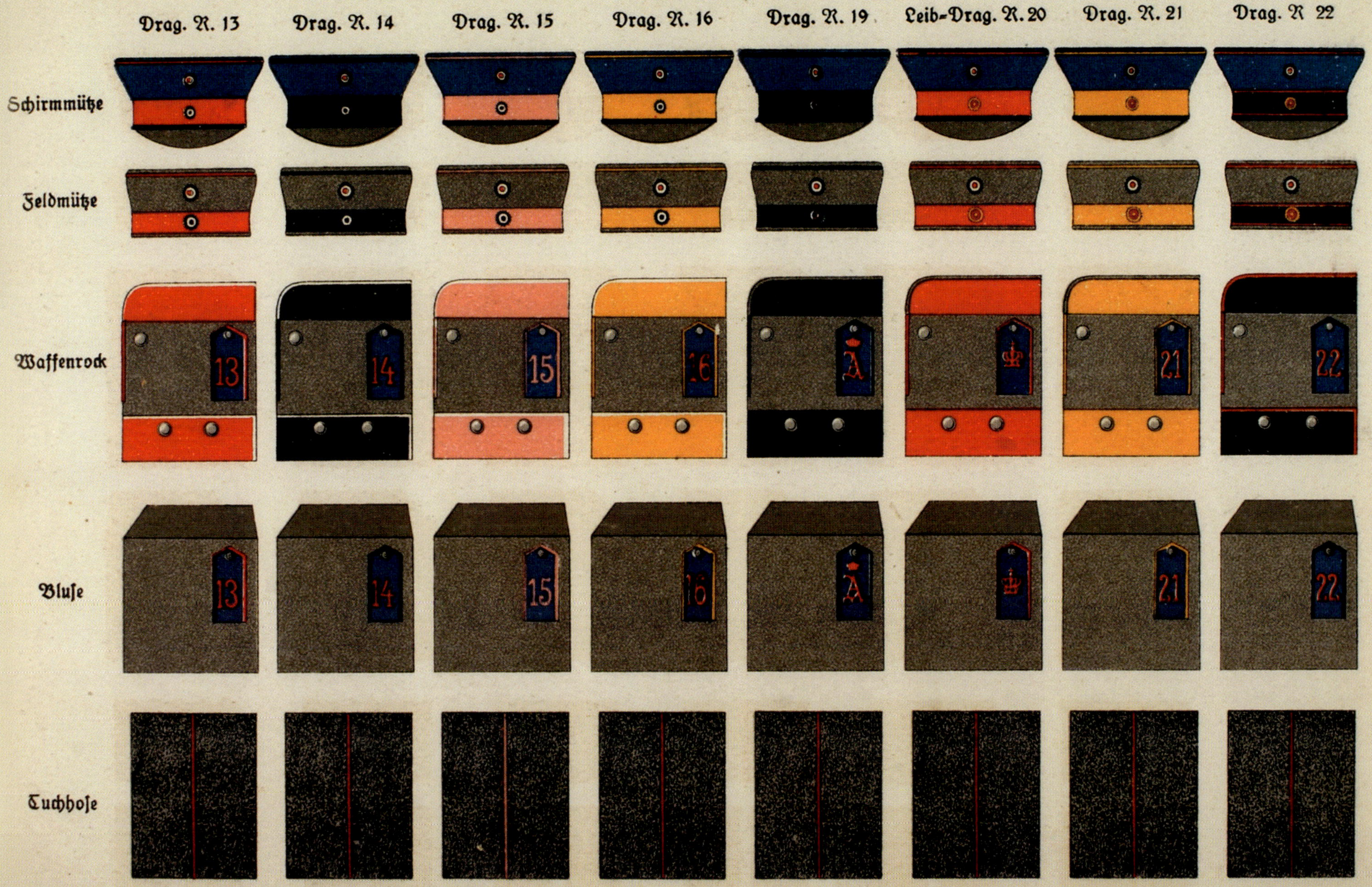
Drag. R. 13
Drag. R. 14
Drag. R. 15
Drag. R. 16
Drag. R. 19
Leib-Drag. R. 20
Drag. R. 21
Drag. R 22
Schirmmütze
Feldmütze
Waffenrock
Bluse
Tuchhose
13
14
15
16
21
22

Husaren.

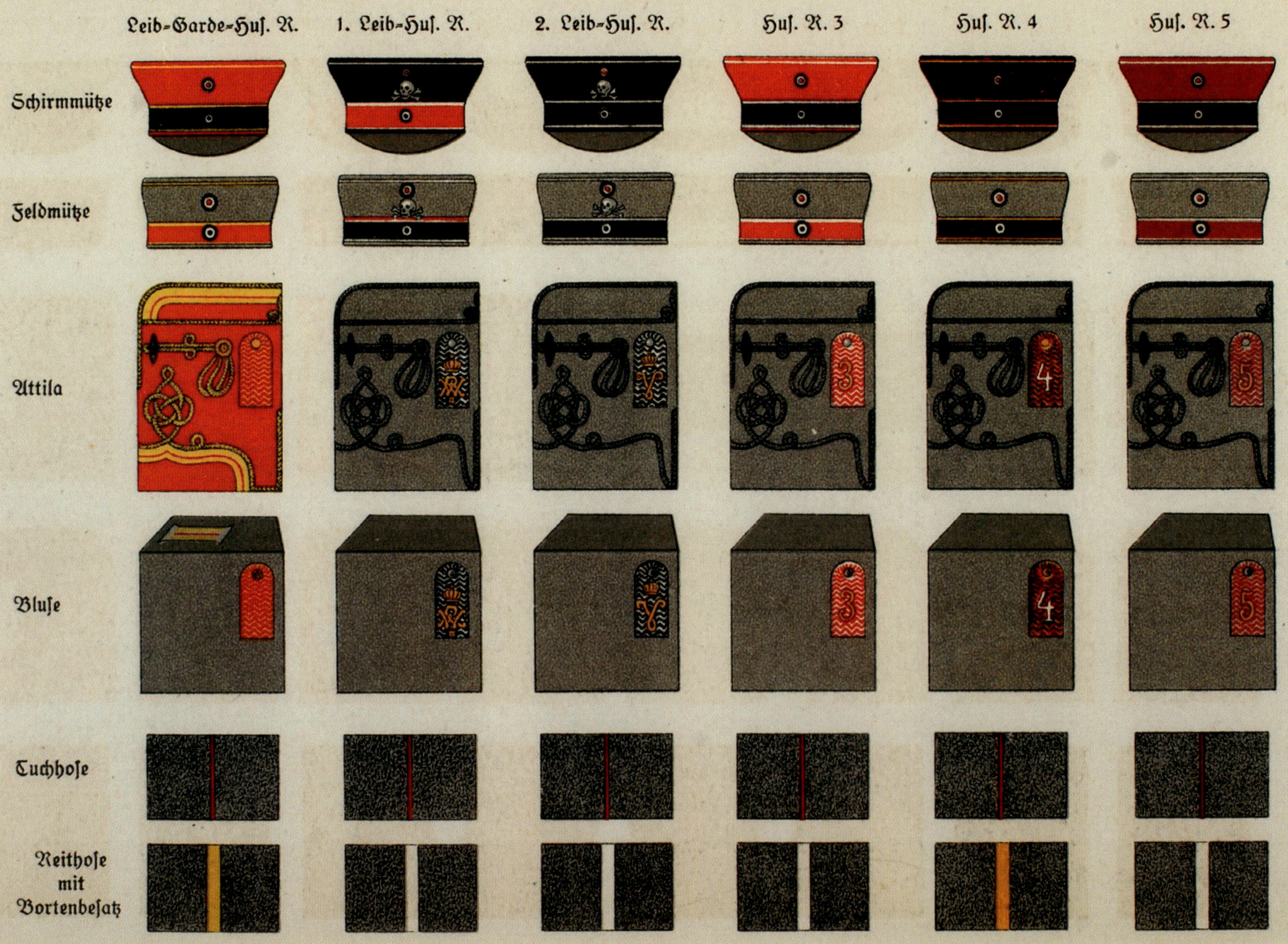
Leib-Garde-Hus. R.
1. Leib-Hus. R.
2. Leib-Hus. R.
Hus. R. 3
Hus. R. 4
Hus. R. 5
Schirmmütze
Feldmütze
Attila
Bluse
Tuchhose
Reithose mit Bortenbesatz

Husaren.

Hus. R. 6
Hus. R. 7
Hus. R. 8
Hus. R. 9
Hus. R. 10
Hus. R. 11
Schirmmütze
Feldmütze
Attila
Bluse
Tuchhose
Reithose mit Bortenbesatz

Husaren.

Hus. R. 12
Hus. R. 13
Hus. R. 14
Hus. R. 15
Hus. R. 16
Hus. R. 17
Schirmmütze
Feldmütze
Attila
12
14
16
17
Bluse
12
14
16
17
Tuchhose
Reithose
mit
Bortenbesatz

Ulanen.

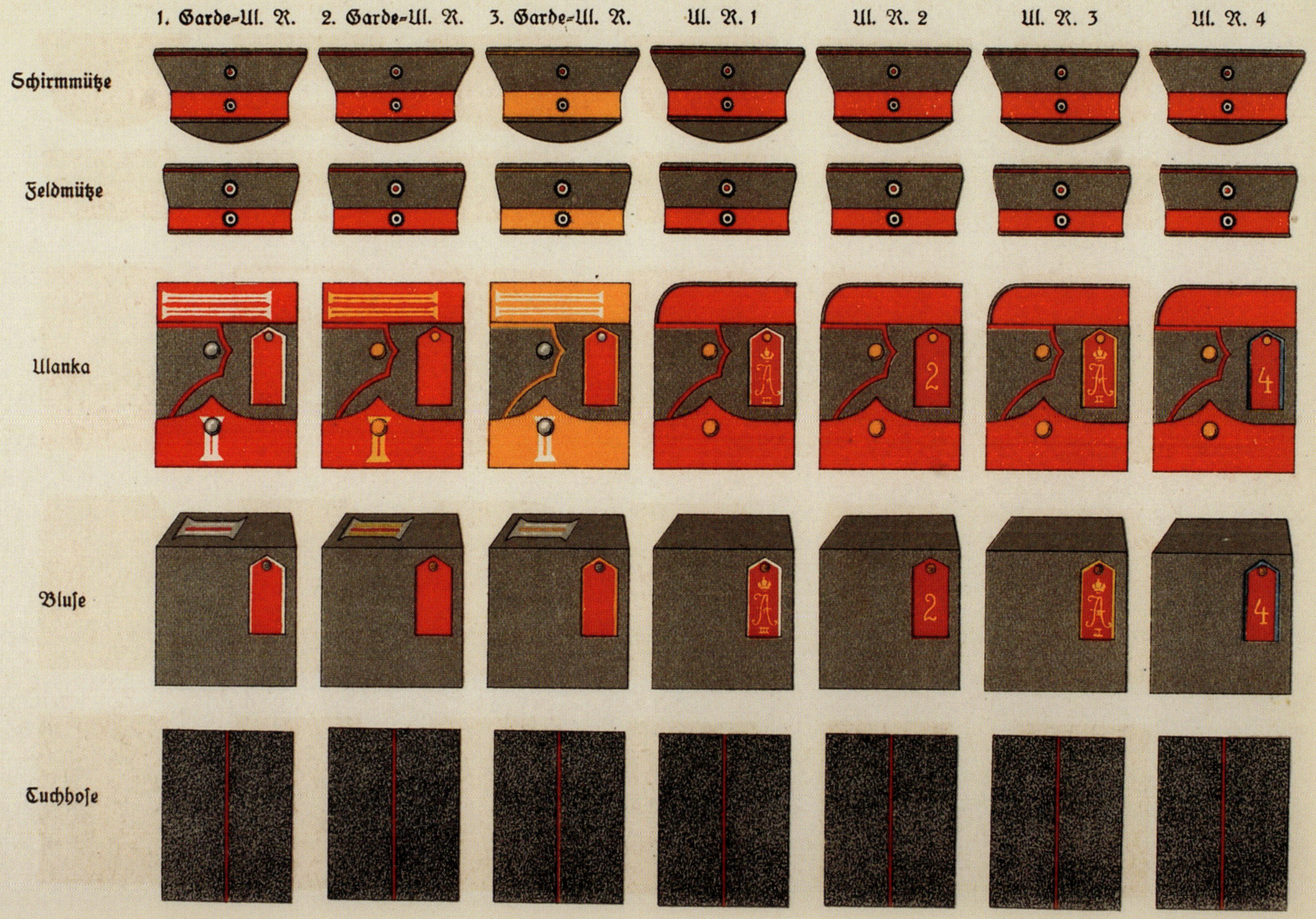
1. Garde-Ul. R.
2. Garde-Ul. R.
3. Garde-Ul. R.
Ul. R. 1
Ul. R. 2
Ul. R. 3
Ul. R. 4
Schirmmütze
Feldmütze
Ulanka
Bluse
Tuchhose

Ulanen.

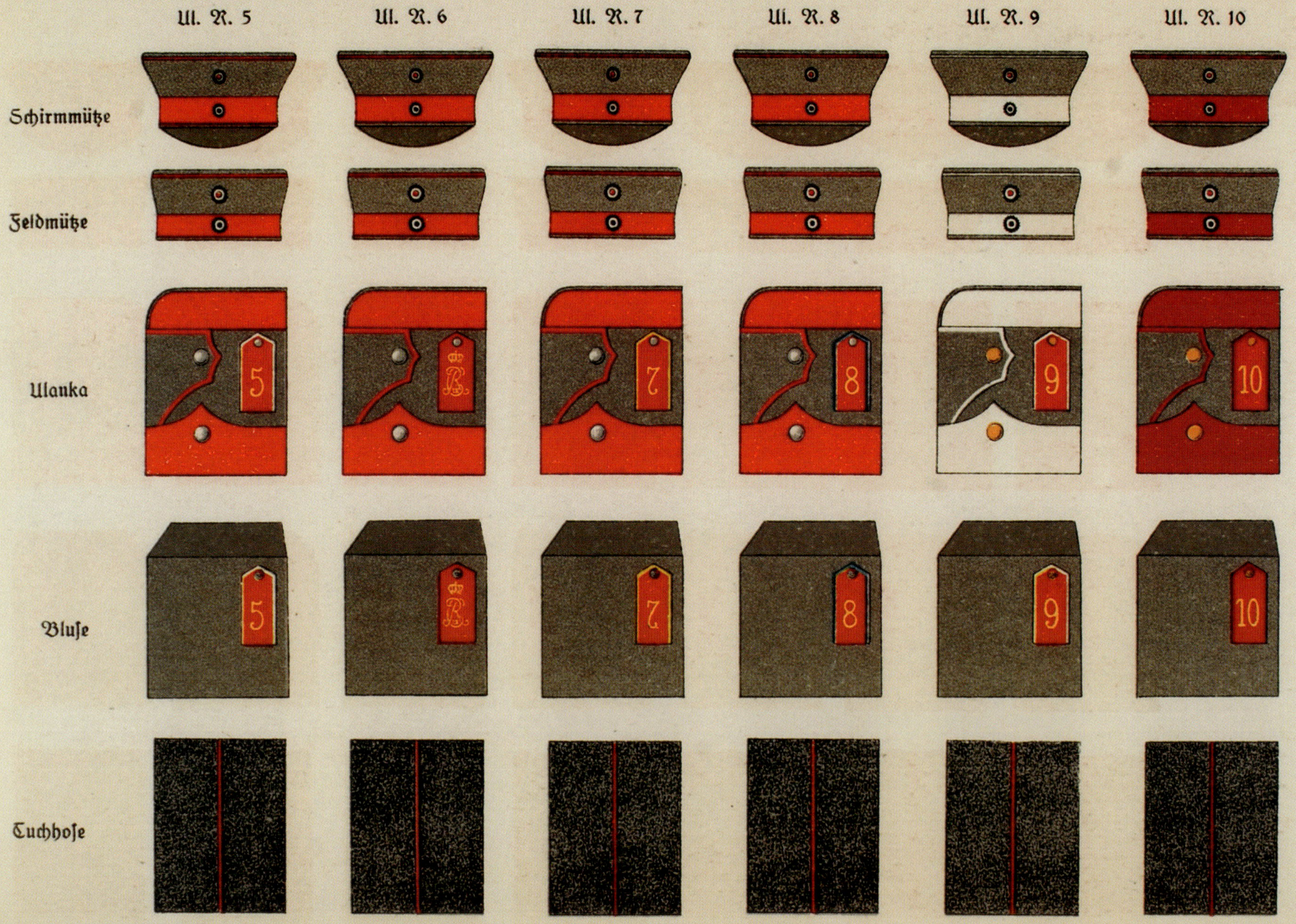
Ul. N. 5
Ul. N. 6
Ul. N. 7
Ul. N. 8
Ul. N. 9
Ul. N. 10
Schirmmütze
Feldmütze
Ulanka
5
7
8
9
10
Bluse
5
7
8
9
10
Tuchhose

Ulanen.

Ul. R. 11 — Ul. R. 12 — Ul. R. 13 — Ul. R. 14 — Ul. R. 15 — Ul. R. 16

Schirmmütze

Feldmütze

Ulanka

Bluse

Tuchhose

Jäger zu Pferde.

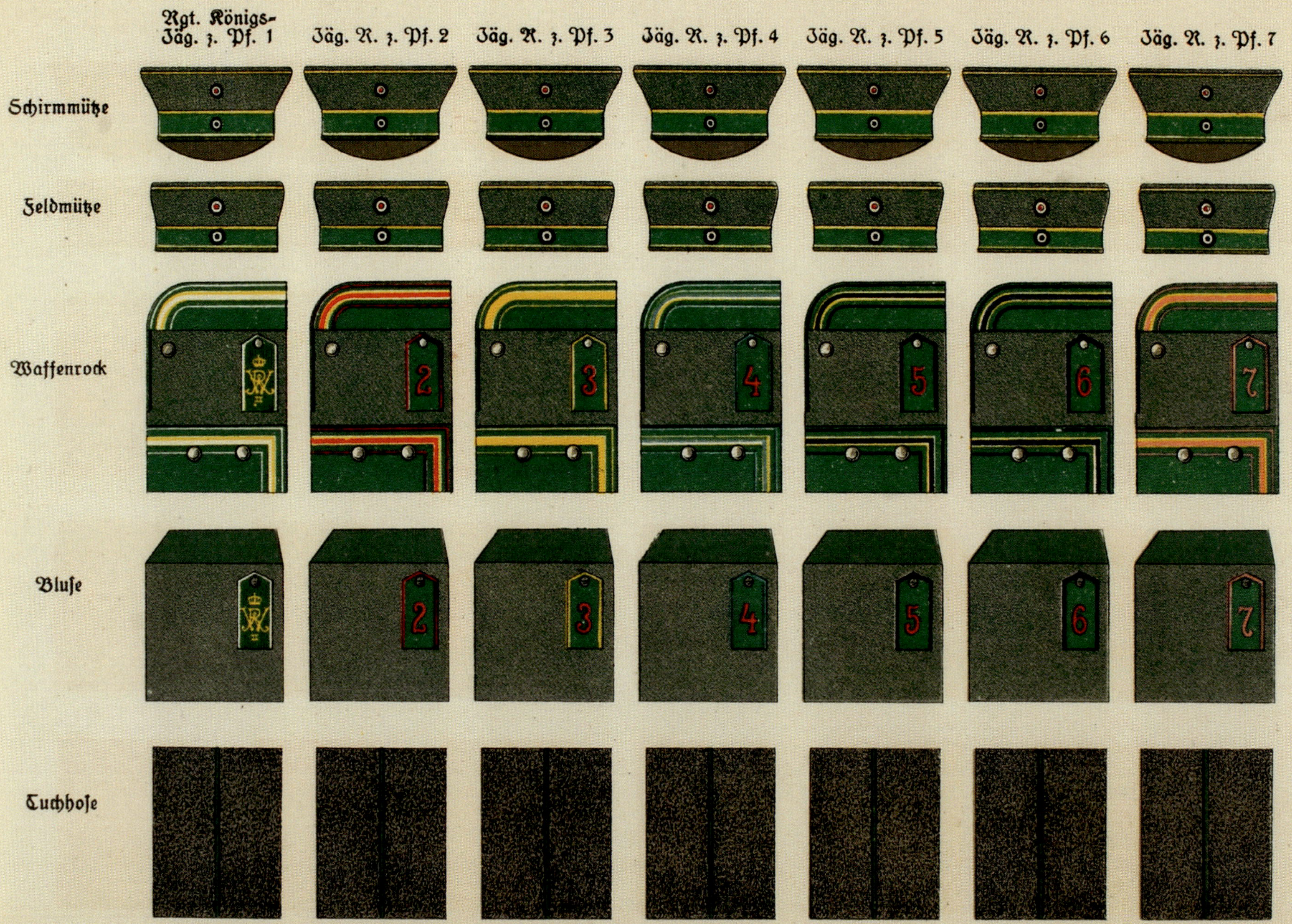

Jäger zu Pferde.

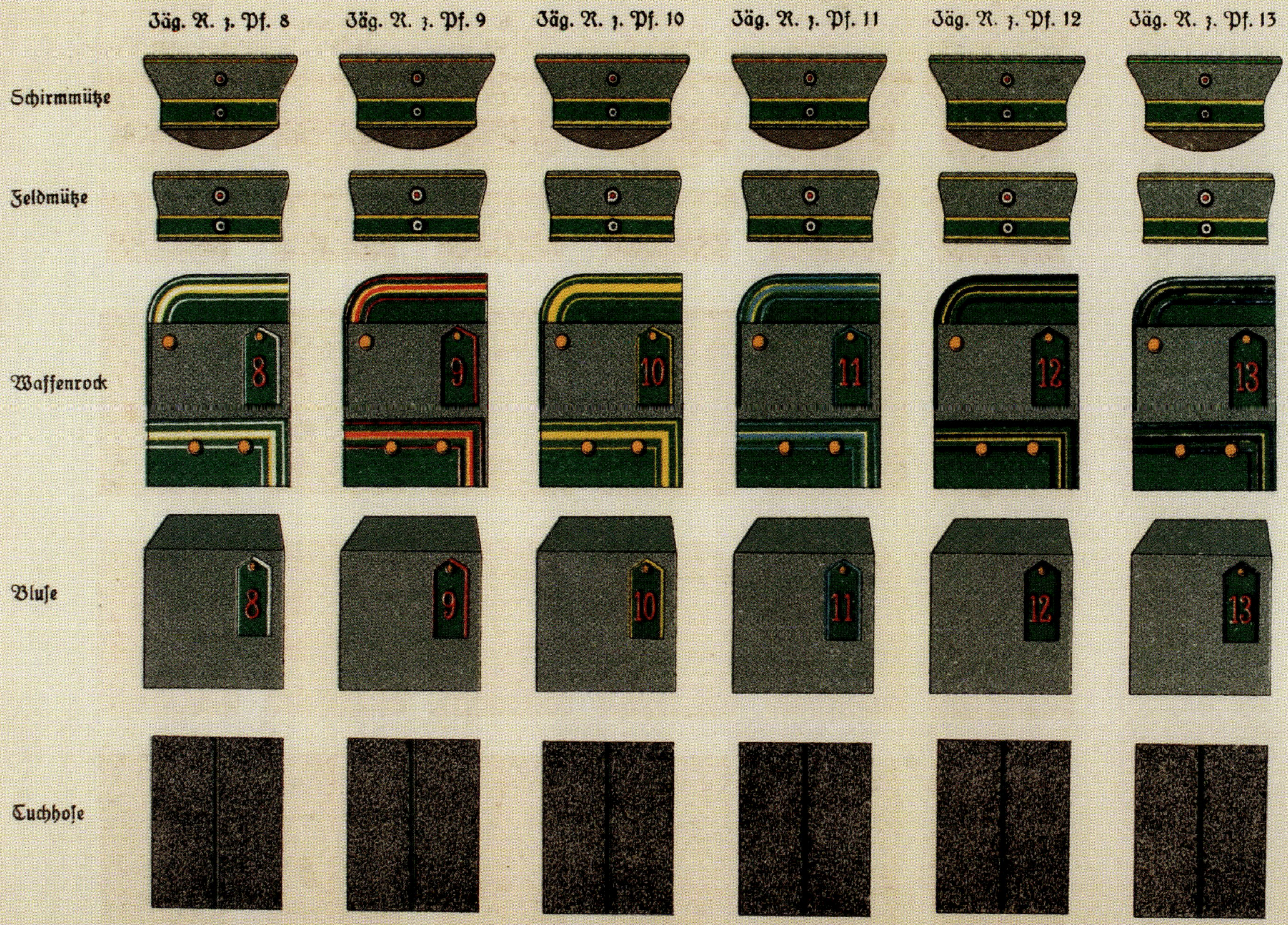

Feldartillerie.

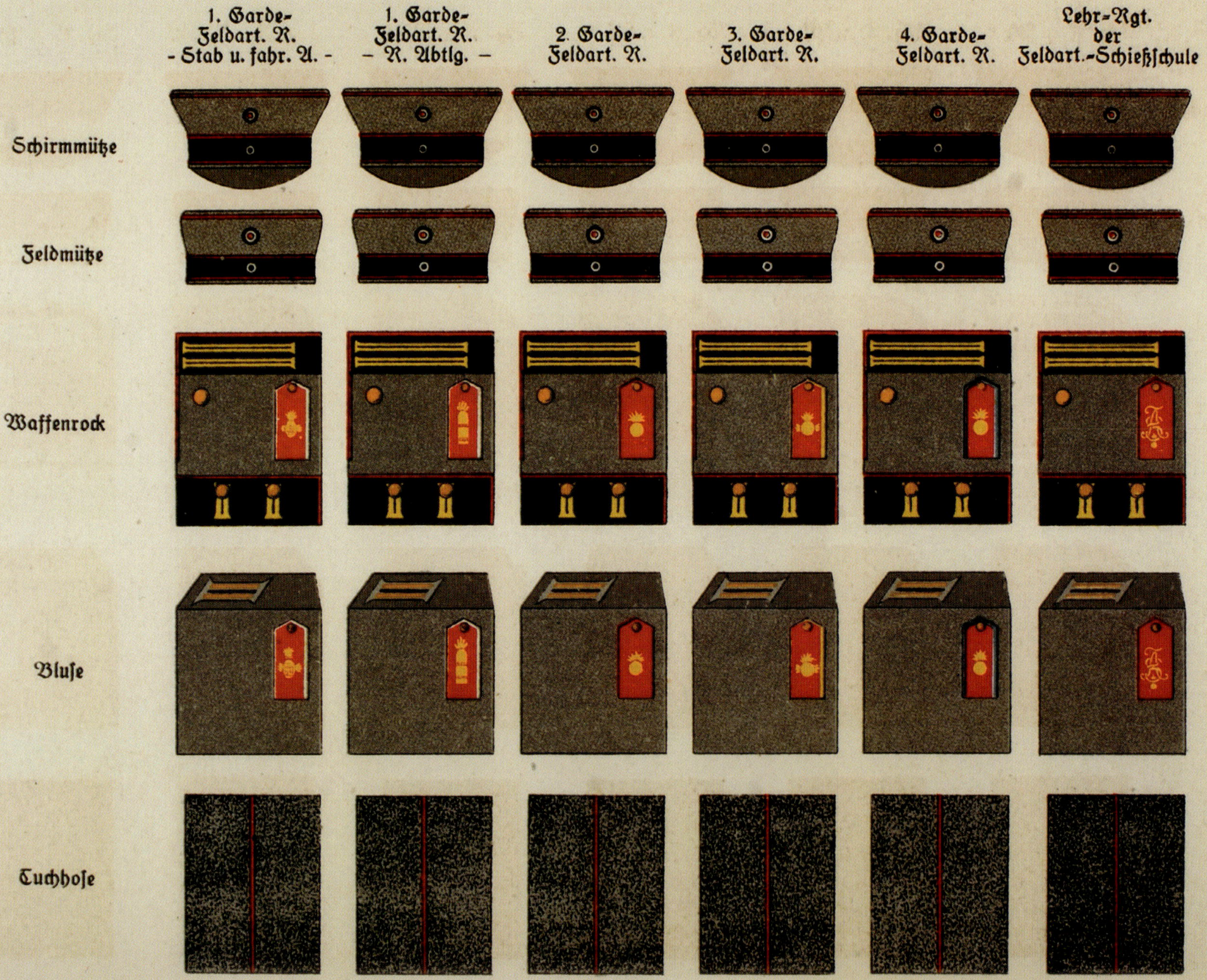

Feldartillerie.

Feldart. R. 4 — Feldart. R. 14 — 2. u. 3. Batt. Feldart. R. 62 — Feldart. R. 6

Waffenrock

Bluse

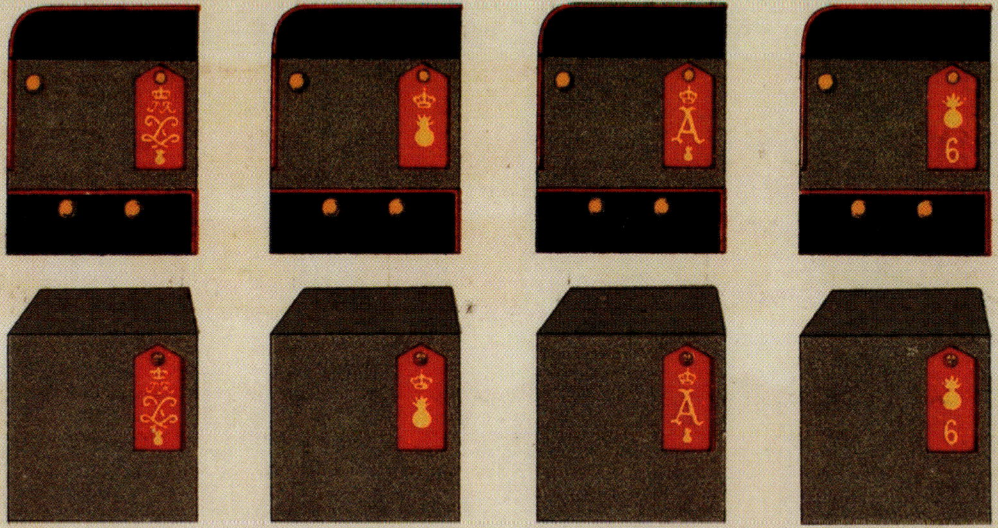

Die übrigen Feldartillerie-Regimenter sämtlicher Armeekorps wie:

Feldart. Rgt. 6

mit ihrer Regimentsnummer.

Schirmmütze, Feldmütze und Tuchhose wie Garde-Feldartillerie.

Fußartillerie.

Garde-Fußart. R. — Lehr-R. d. Fußart. Schießschule — Vers. Batt. der Art. Prüf. Komm. — Fußart. R. 9

Waffenrock

Bluse

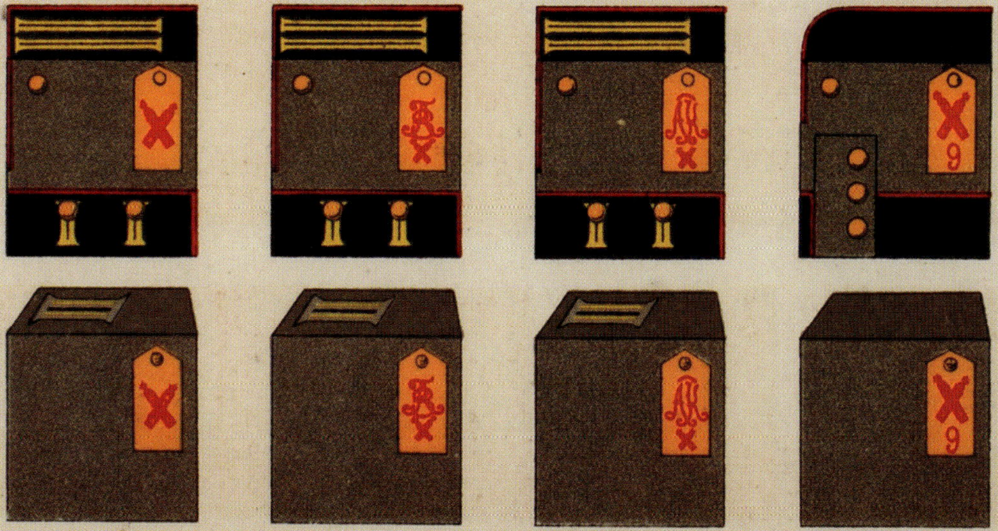

Die übrigen Fußartillerie-Regimenter wie:
Fußartillerie Rgt. 9 mit ihrer Regimentsnummer.

Schirmmütze, Feldmütze und Tuchhose wie Garde-Feldartillerie.

Train.

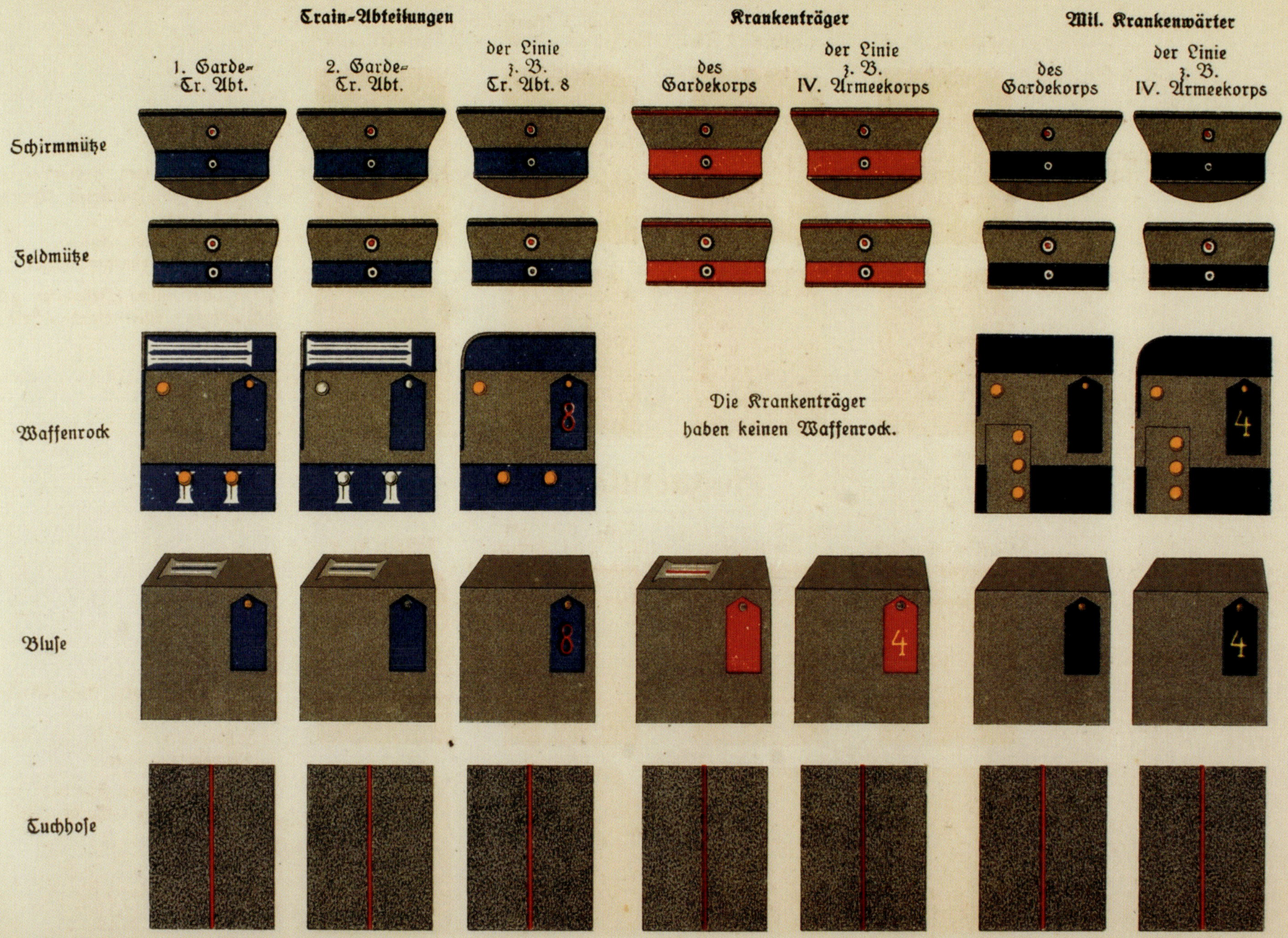
Train-Abteilungen
Krankenträger
Mil. Krankenwärter
1. Garde-Tr. Abt.
2. Garde-Tr. Abt.
der Linie z. B. Tr. Abt. 8
des Gardekorps
der Linie z. B. IV. Armeekorps
des Gardekorps
der Linie z. B. IV. Armeekorps
Schirmmütze
Feldmütze
Waffenrock
Die Krankenträger haben keinen Waffenrock.
Bluse
Tuchhose
8
8
4
4
4

Mantel.

Kragen allgemein von feldgrauem Abzeichentuch ohne Litzen.
Farbe der Knöpfe wie an Waffenrock und Bluse.

Inf.-Rgter. u. Unteroffizierschulen.

Schulterklappen feldgrau mit weißem oder farbigem Vorstoß wie an der Bluse, z. B. Garde-Gren. R. 3.

Bezirkskommandos.

Schulterklappen feldgrau ohne Vorstoß, z. B. Bezirkskommandos Berlin, Bromberg und Breslau usw.

Handwerker-Abteilungen
der Bekleidungsämter.

Schulterklappen feldgrau ohne Vorstoß, z. B. III. Armeekorps.

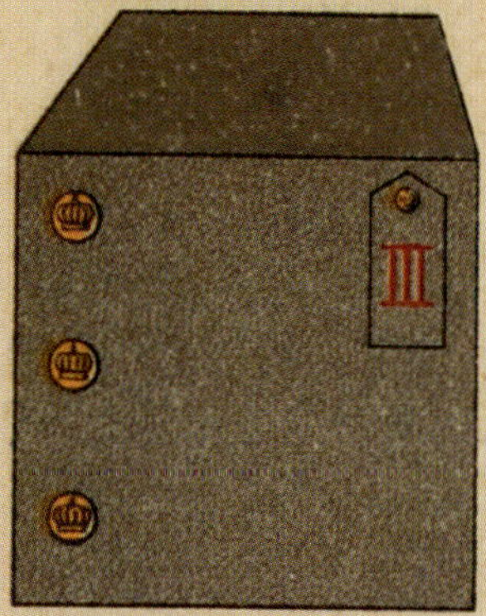

Halbinvaliden-Abteilung
des Gardekorps.

Schulterklappen feldgrau ohne Vorstoß und ohne Abzeichen.

Jäger (Schützen)

Schulterklappen feldgrau mit hellgrünem (Garde-Schützen schwarzem) Vorstoß, z. B. Jäger-Batl. 1.

Alle Übrigen und zwar:

Pioniere, Verkehrstruppen, Kavallerie, Feldartillerie, Fußartillerie und Train: farbige Schulterklappen (Husaren: Schulterschnüre) wie an der Bluse, z. B. 1. Garde-Ulanen-Rgt.

Feldgrau in Krieg u. Frieden

II. Teil

Offiziere und Beamte

4. Auflage.

Uniformtafeln

nach der Allerhöchsten Kabinettsordre vom 21. September 1915 mit Genehmigung des Königl. Preuß. Kriegsministeriums herausgegeben von

Otto Weiß

Berlin 1916 · Druck u. Verlag von H. G. Hermann · Preis 3.50 Mark

Wegen Beschaffung aus amtlichen Mitteln — Unkosten — siehe
Preuß. A. V. Bl. 1916 S. 417 Nr. 640
Württbg. V. Bl. 1916 S. 550 Nr. 808

Feldgrau in Krieg und Frieden

II. Teil

Uniformtafeln für Offiziere und Beamte

der Kgl. Preuß. Armee / ausschl. des Mecklenburgischen und Hessischen Kontingents / nach der Allerh. Kabinettsordre vom 21. September 1915

Mit Genehmigung des Kgl. Preuß. Kriegsministeriums herausgegeben von

Otto Weiß

Ob. Mil. Intendantursekretär kdt. zur Bekleidungs-Abteilung des Kgl. Preuß. Kriegsministeriums

Druck und Verlag von H. S. Hermann in Berlin SW 19, Beuth-Straße 8

Inhaltsverzeichnis

Linien-Infanterie-Regimenter:

Fortsetzung des Inhaltsverzeichnisses.

Regimentierte Offiziere.

Nichtregimentierte Offiziere.

Beamte.

Vorbemerkungen.

[1]) An welchen Bekleidungsstücken Samt zur Verwendung kommt, ergeben die Erläuterungen. Alle übrigen Besätze und Vorstöße bestehen aus Tuch.

[2]) Besatz der Feldmütze und Kragenpatten der Bluse sind durchweg von Tuch, auch wenn Schirmmütze und Waffenrock Besatz von Samt haben.

[3]) Stiefelhosen haben nur dann Vorstöße in den Seitennähten, wenn Besatzstreifen zu ihnen gehören.

Mantel.

Gendarmerie mit dunkelgrünem Kragen (oben und unten) u. mit ponc. rotem Vorstoss

Generale u. San. Off. im Generalsrang mit ponc. roten Vorstössen vorn herunter an beiden Seiten, um die Aermelumschläge, an den Taschenklappen ringsherum und am Rückengurt.

Räte I. Kl. Vorstösse wie Generale, jedoch karmesinrot.

Sämtliche Beamten — auch Räte I. Kl. — um den Kragen kornblumenblauen Vorstoss.

Waffenrock.

(Infanterie)

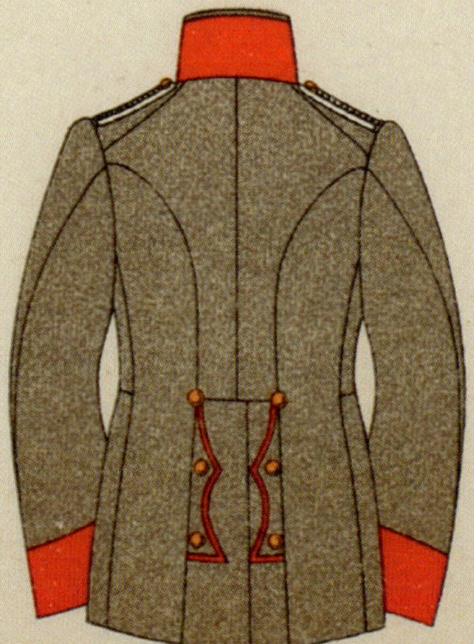

Attila.

Ulanka.

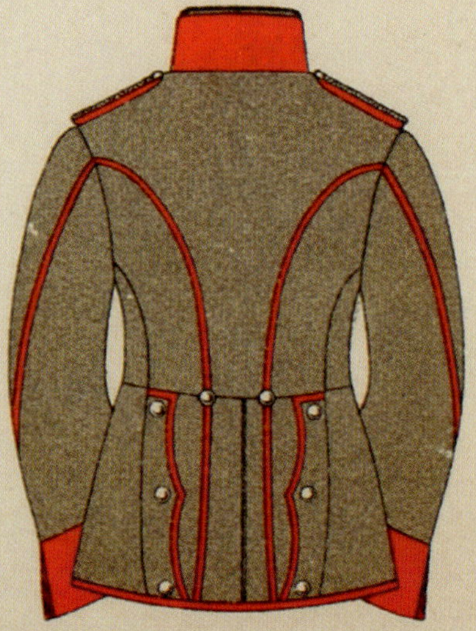

Offizieruniformen.

Kleiner Rock

für Offiziere und obere Beamte, letztere mit kornblumenblauen Vorstössen um Kragen, Aermelumschläge und vornherunter.

Kleiner Rock

für Generale, San. Off. im Generalsrang und Räte I. Kl.

Wegen der abweichenden Kragenpatten, Vorstösse und des Brustklappen-Futters s. Tafeln auf Seite 27 u. 28.

Bluse.

Gendarmerie mit dunkelgrünem Kragen (oben u. unten) u. mit ponc. rotem Vorstoss

Generale u. San. Off. im Generalsrang mit Brusttaschen u. ponc. rotem Vorstoss am Kragen u. Aermelumschläge.

Räte 1. Kl. mit Brusttaschen und karmesinrotem Vorstoss um die Aermelumschläge.

Sämtliche Beamten – auch Räte I. Kl. – um den Kragen kornblumenblauen Vorstoss.

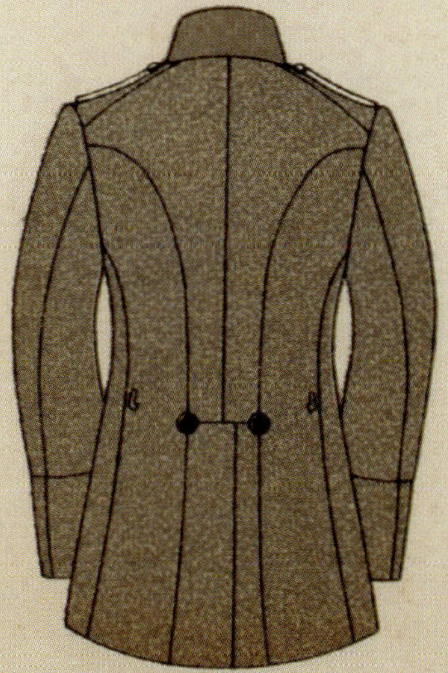

Mantel.

Rückansicht.

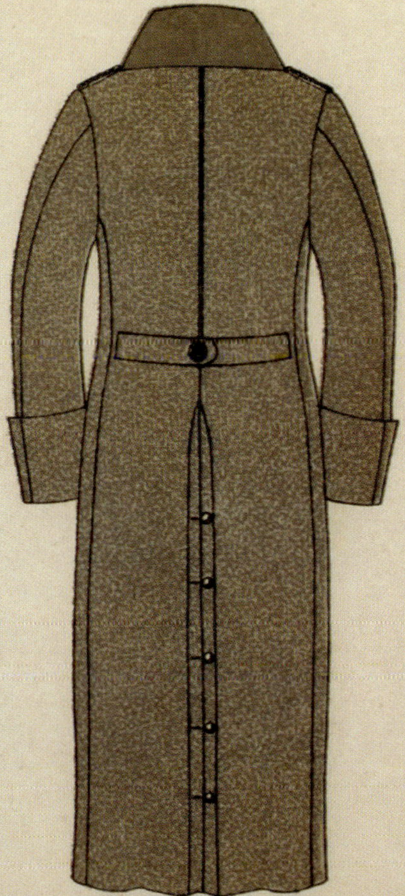

Infanterie-Regimenter.

Gardekorps.

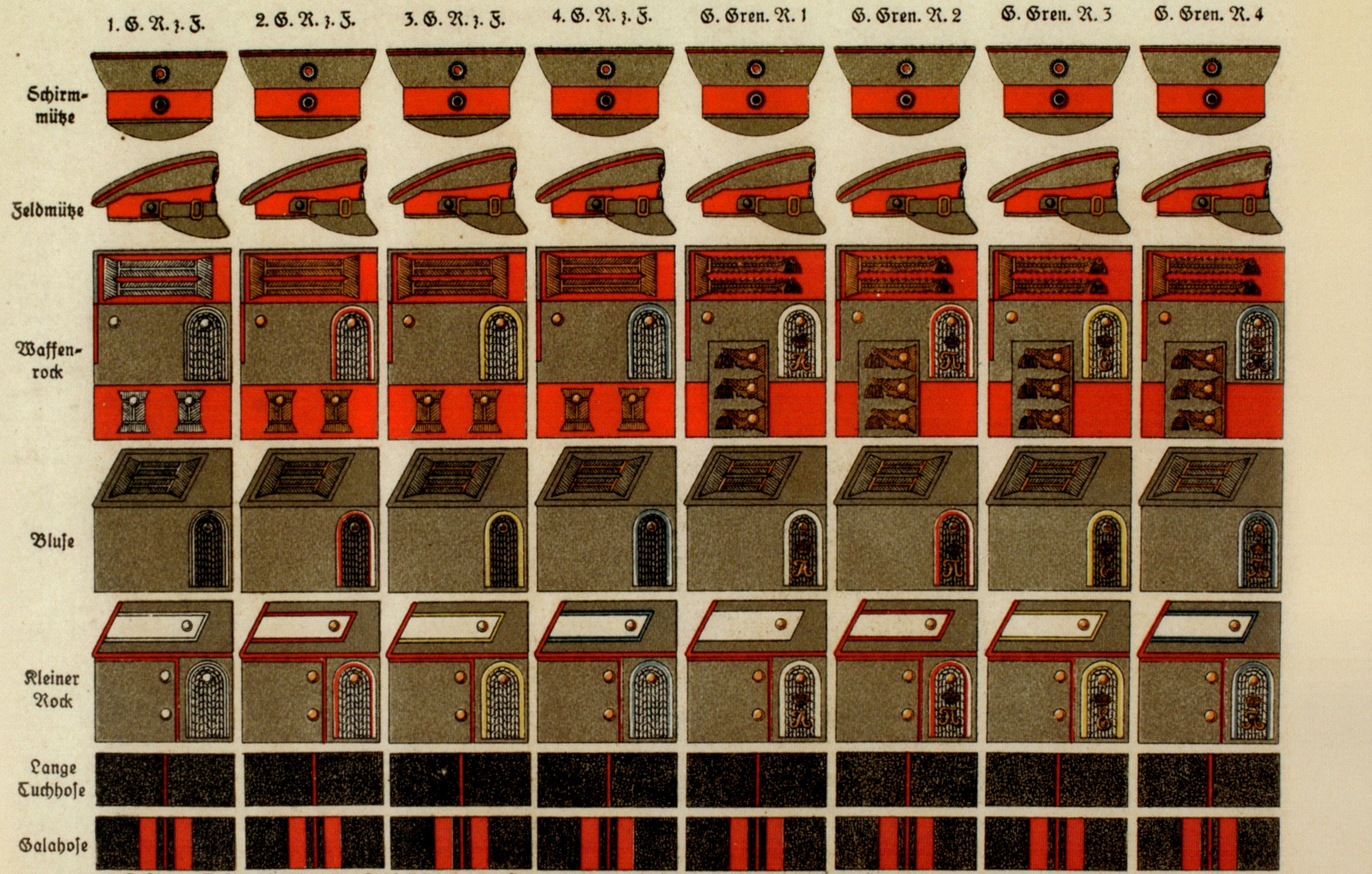

1. G. Rgt. z. F. Randstreifen der Achselstücke und Kragenpattenvorstoß am Kl. Rock: Silbertresse.

Infanterie-Regimenter
des I., II., IX. und X. Armeekorps.

Gardekorps.

5. G. R. z. F. | G. Gren. R. 5 | G. Füs. R. | Gren. R. 1 | Gren. R. 2 | Gren. R. 3 | Gren. R. 4 | Füs. R. 34

Die übrigen Regimenter dieser 4 Armeekorps wie Füs. R. 34 mit ihrer Regiments-nummer, Regimenter 86, 91 u. 92 mi Namenszug:

86

91

92

Rgt. 92 mit Totenkopf an der Mütze.

Infanterie-Regimenter

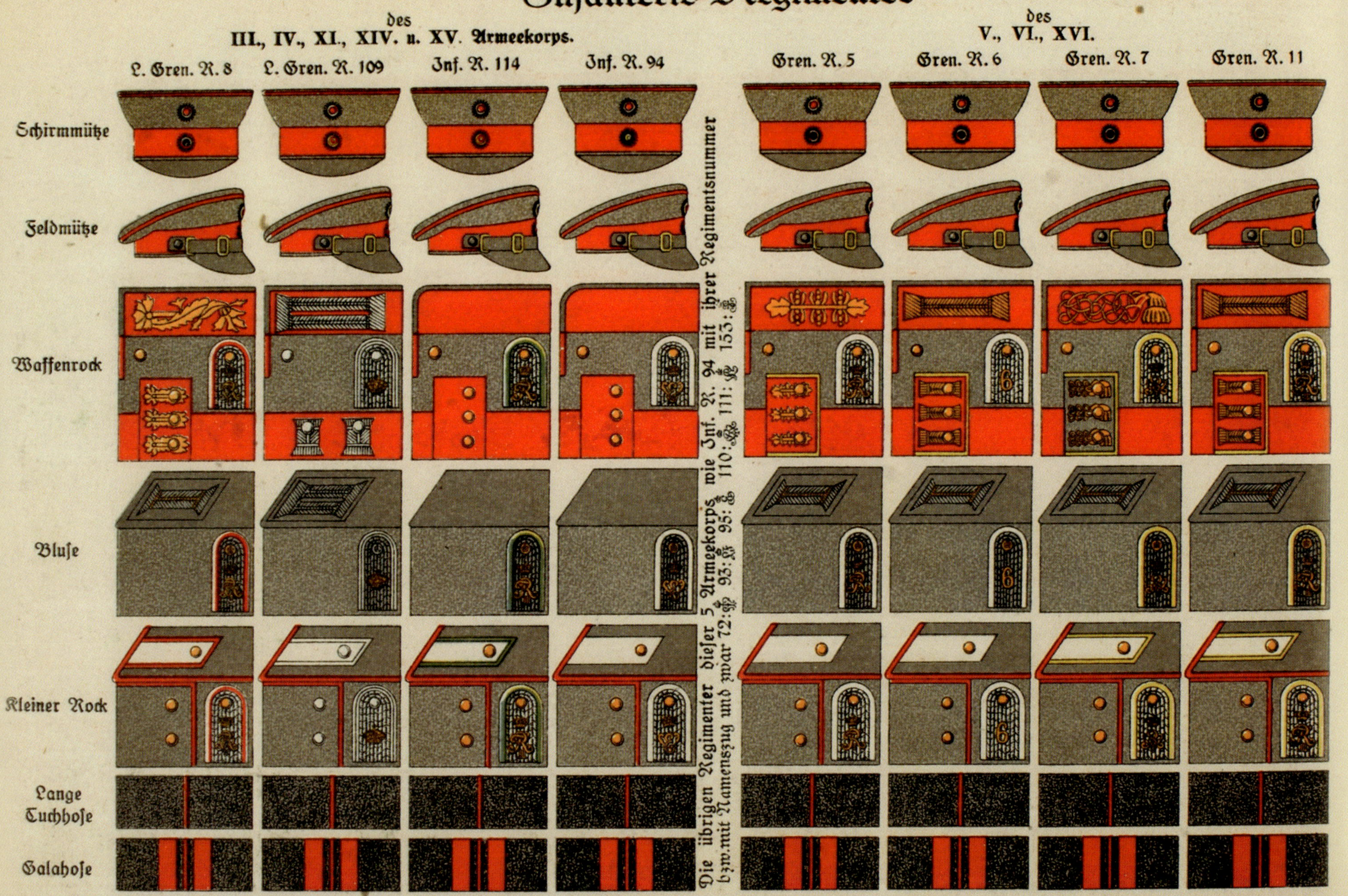

L. Gren. R. 109: Pattenvorstoß am Kl. Rock und Randstreifen der Achselstücke: Silbertresse.

Infanterie-Regimenter

Jäger (Schützen).

u. XVII. Armeekorps — des VII., VIII., XVIII. u. XX. A. K. — des XXI. A. K.

Königs-J. R. 145 | Gren. R. 10 | Füs. R. 80 | Inf. R. 88 | Inf. R. 17 | G.-Jäg. B. | G.-Schützen B. | Jäg. B. 11

Die übrigen Regimenter dieser 4 Armeekorps wie Gren. R. 10 mit ihrer Regimentsnummer (J. R. 47 Namenszug: L)

Die übrigen Regimenter dieser 4 Armeekorps wie Inf. R. 88 mit ihrer Regimentsnummer (J. R. 53 mit Krone ohne Nummer).

Die übrigen Regimenter des XXI. Armeekorps wie J. R. 17 mit ihrer Regimentsnummer.

Die übrigen Jäger-Bataillone wie Jäger-B. 11 mit ihrer Bataillonsnummer

G.-Schützen B. Schwarzer Samt: Besatzstreifen der Schirmmütze u. Galahose, Kragen u. Aufschläge am Waffenrock, Pattenvorstoß am Kleinen Rock und Randstreifen der Achselstücke; Schwarzes Tuch: Besatzstreifen der Feldmütze.

Pioniere.

Sämtliche Eisenbahn-, Telegraphen-, Luftschiffer-Truppen.

zum Beispiel:

Fliegertruppen.

Besatzstreifen der Schirmmütze u. Galahose, Kragen und Ärmelaufschläge am Waffenrock (Pioniere auch Kragenpatten am Kleinen Rock und Unterlage der Achselstücke): schwarzer **Samt**. Besatzstreifen der Feldmütze · schwarzes **Tuch**.

Kürassiere.

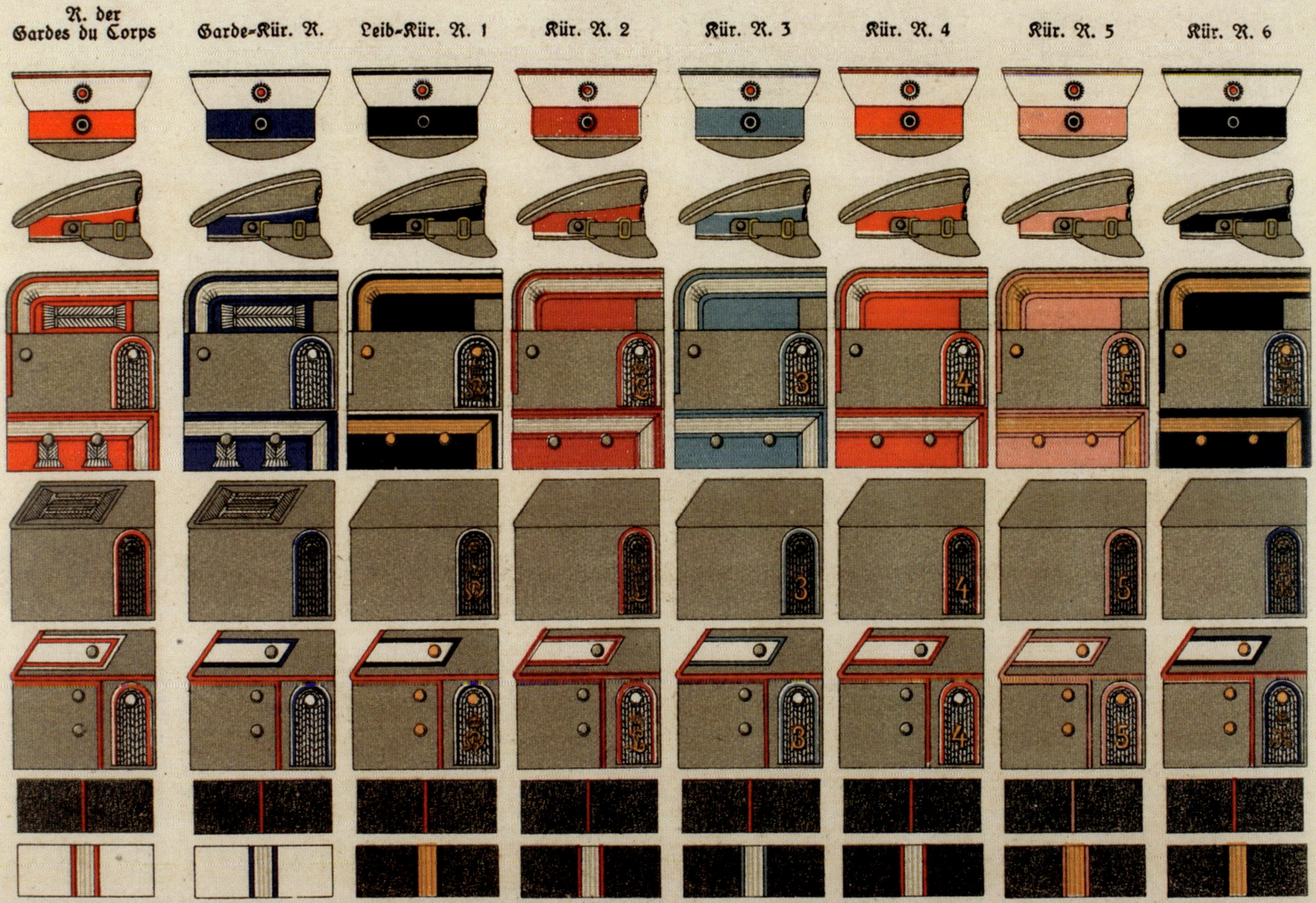

Beim Kür. R. 1: Besatzstreifen und Deckelvorstoß der Schirmmütze, Kragenpatten u. Ärmelaufschläge am Waffenrock, Pattenvorstoß am Kleinen Rock u. Randstreifen der Achselstücke: schwarzer Samt; Besatzstreifen der Feldmütze: schwarzes Tuch.

Kürassiere. Dragoner.

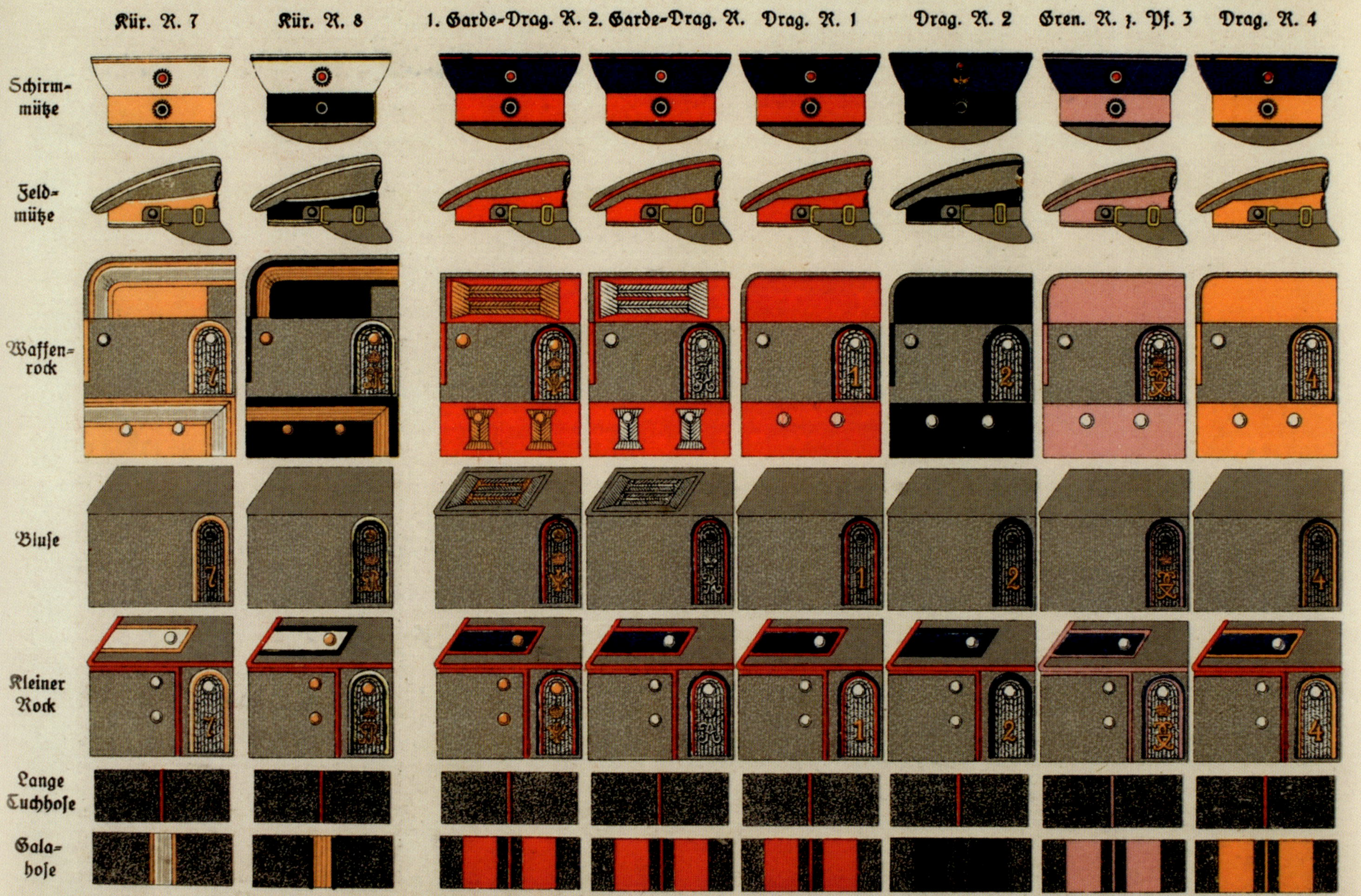

Beim Drag. R. 2: Besatzstreifen u. Vorstoß der Schirmmütze u. der Galahose, Kragen u. Ärmelaufschläge am Waffenrock, Kragenpattenvorstoß am Kleinen Rock u. Randstreifen der Achselstücke: schwarzer Samt; Besatzstreifen u. Vorstoß der Feldmütze: schwarzes Tuch.

Dragoner.

Drag. R. 5 | Drag. R. 6 | Drag. R. 7 | Drag. R. 8 | Drag. R. 9 | Drag. R. 10 | Drag. R. 11 | Drag. R. 12

Drag. R. 6, 11 u. 12. Von **Samt:** Besatzstreifen u. Vorstoß der Schirmmütze u. der Galahose, Kragen u. Ärmelaufschläge am Waffenrock, Pattenvorstoß am Kleinen Rock, u. Randstreifen der Achselstücke; von **Tuch:** Besatzstreifen u. Vorstoß der Feldmütze. **Drag. 11 u. 12** auch Vorstöße vorn u. an den Taschenleisten des Waffenrocks von **Samt.**

Dragoner.

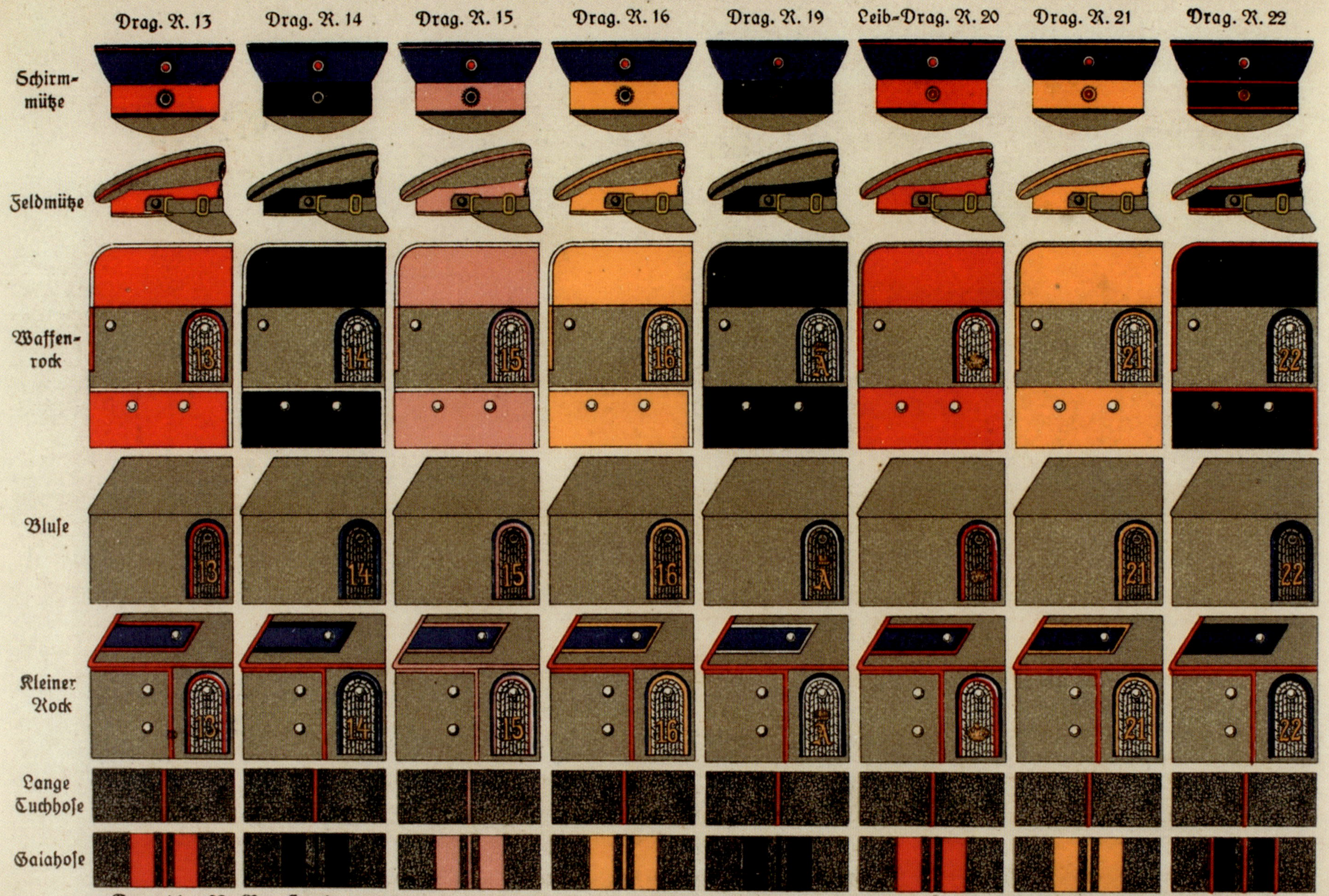

Drag. 14 u. 22: Von Samt: Besatz (Drag. 14 auch Vorstoss) der Schirmmütze, Kragen und Aufschläge am Waffenrock, Besatz (Drag. 14 auch Vorstoss) der Galahose, Randstreifen der Achselstücke und Pattenvorstoss am Kl. Rock.
Von Tuch: Besatz und Vorstoss der Feldmütze

Drag. 19: Randstreifen der Achselstücke und Kragenpattenvorstoss am Kl. Rock: Silbertresse. Besatz der Schirmmütze, Kragen und Aufschläge am Waffenrock, Besatz u. Vorstoss der Galahose von Samt.

Husaren.

Leib-Garde-Hus. R. | 1. Leib-Hus. R. | 2. Leib-Hus. R. | Hus. R. 3 | Hus. R. 4 | Hus. R. 5 | Hus. R. 6

Attila

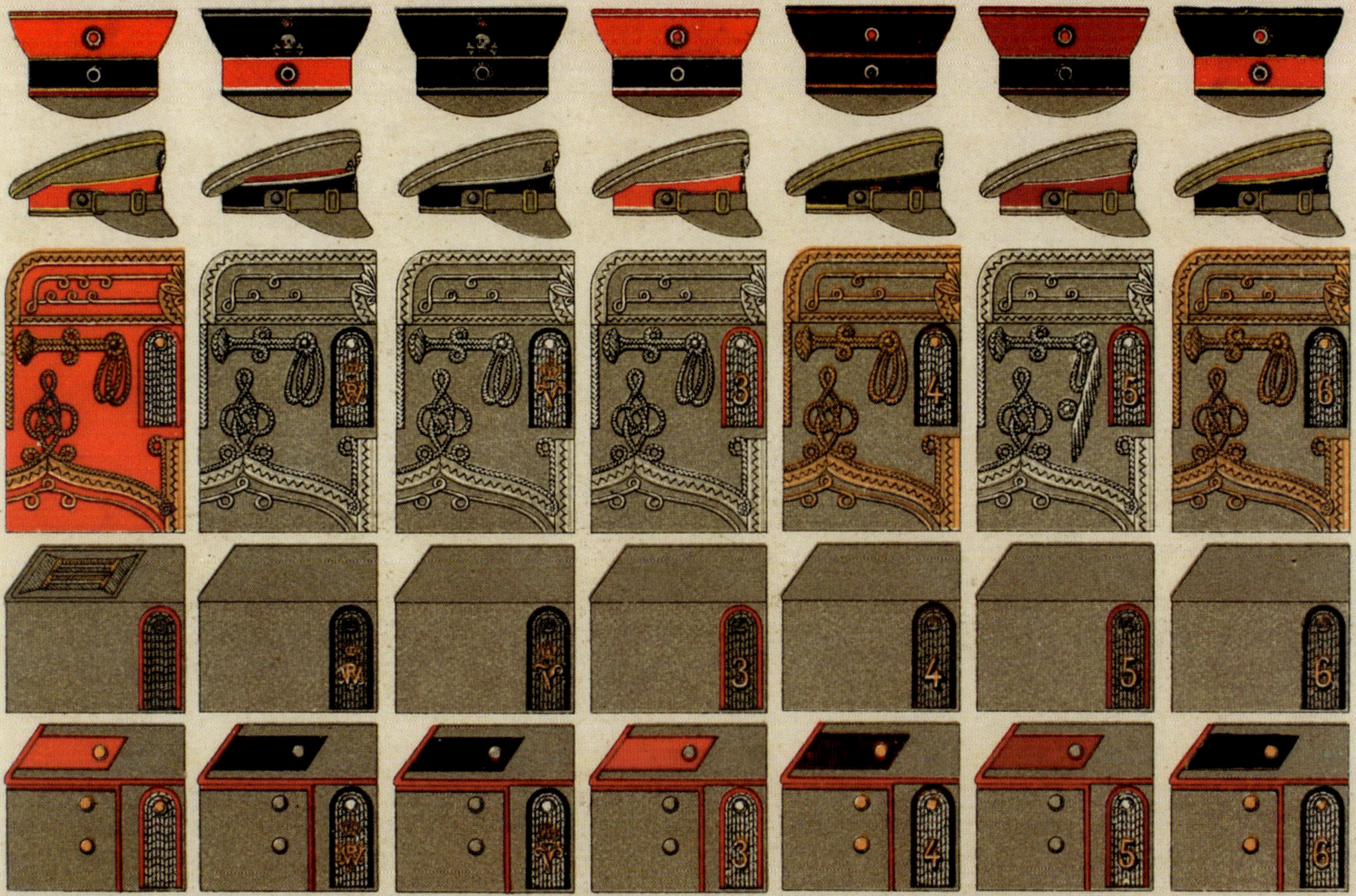

1. Hus. 1, 2 u. 17 tragen als Paradeattila den bisherigen schwarzen Attila.

2. Leib-G. Hus. R. trägt als Interimsattila einen feldgrauen Attila.

3. Pelze haben das Leib-G. Hus. R. u. die Hus. Rgter: 1, 2, 3, 8, 12, 13, 15 u. 16.

Husarenoffiziere haben keine lange Tuchhose.

Galahosen haben nur die Offiziere des Leib-Garde-Hus. Rgts.

Stiefelhose

Beim Hus. R. 2 u. 5: Besatzstreifen der Schirmmütze: Samt; Besatzstreifen der Feldmütze: Tuch.

Husaren.

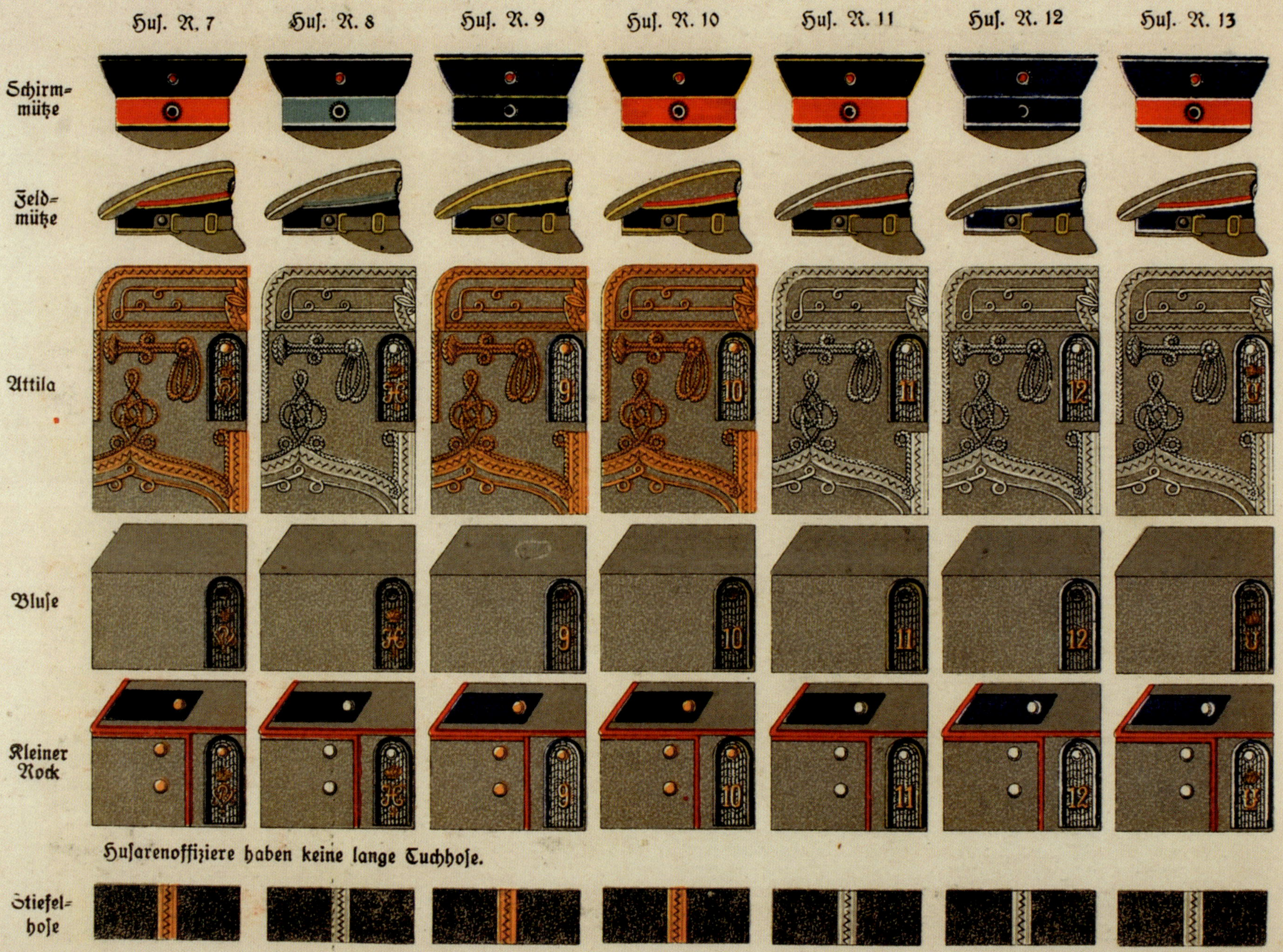
Hus. N. 7
Hus. N. 8
Hus. N. 9
Hus. N. 10
Hus. N. 11
Hus. N. 12
Hus. N. 13
Schirmmütze
Feldmütze
Attila
Bluse
Kleiner Rock
Husarenoffiziere haben keine lange Tuchhose.
Stiefelhose

Husaren. — Ulanen.

Hus. R. 14 | Hus. R. 15 | Hus. R. 16 | Hus. R. 17 | 1. Garde-Ul. R. | 2. Garde-Ul. R. | 3. Garde-Ul. R.

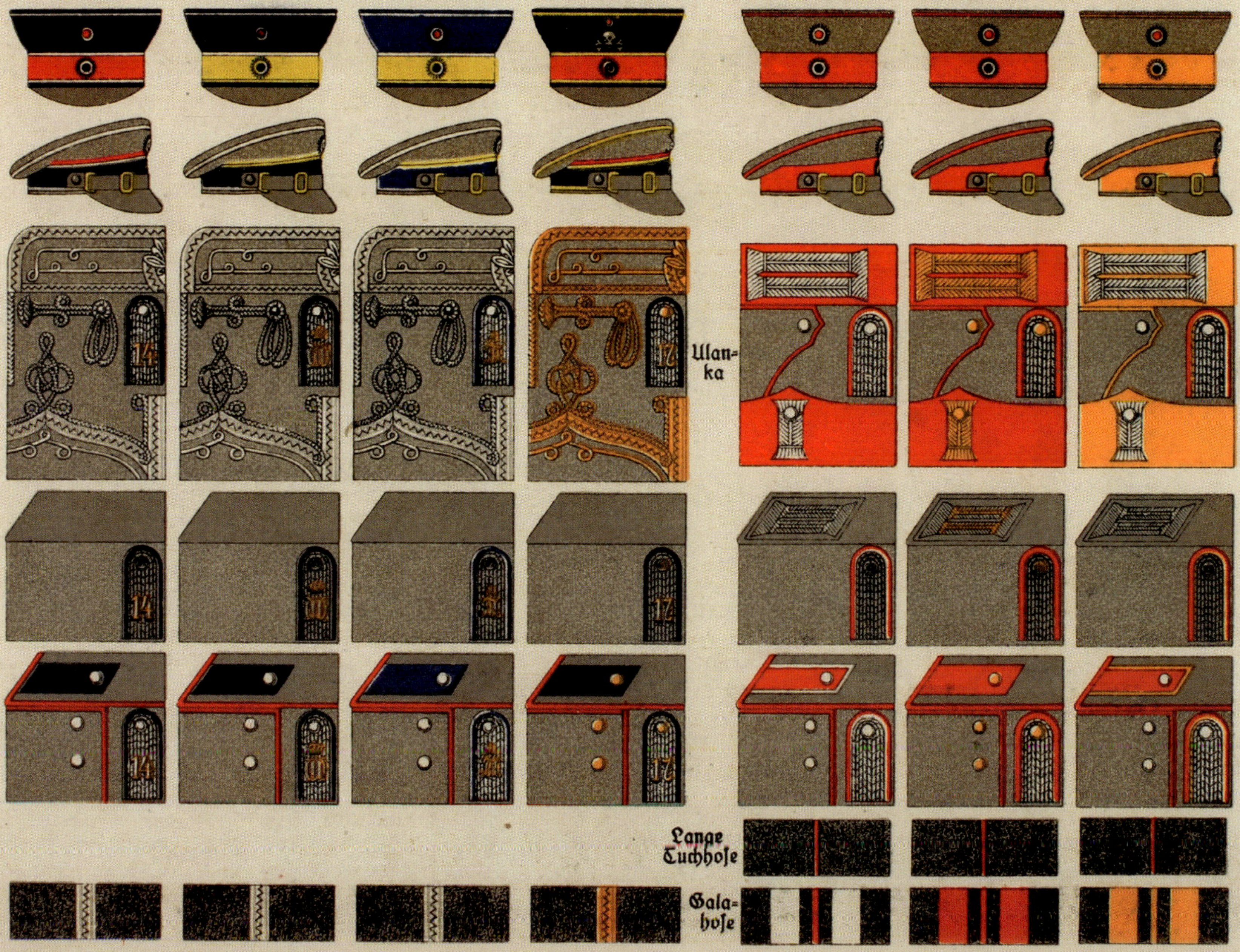

Ulanen.

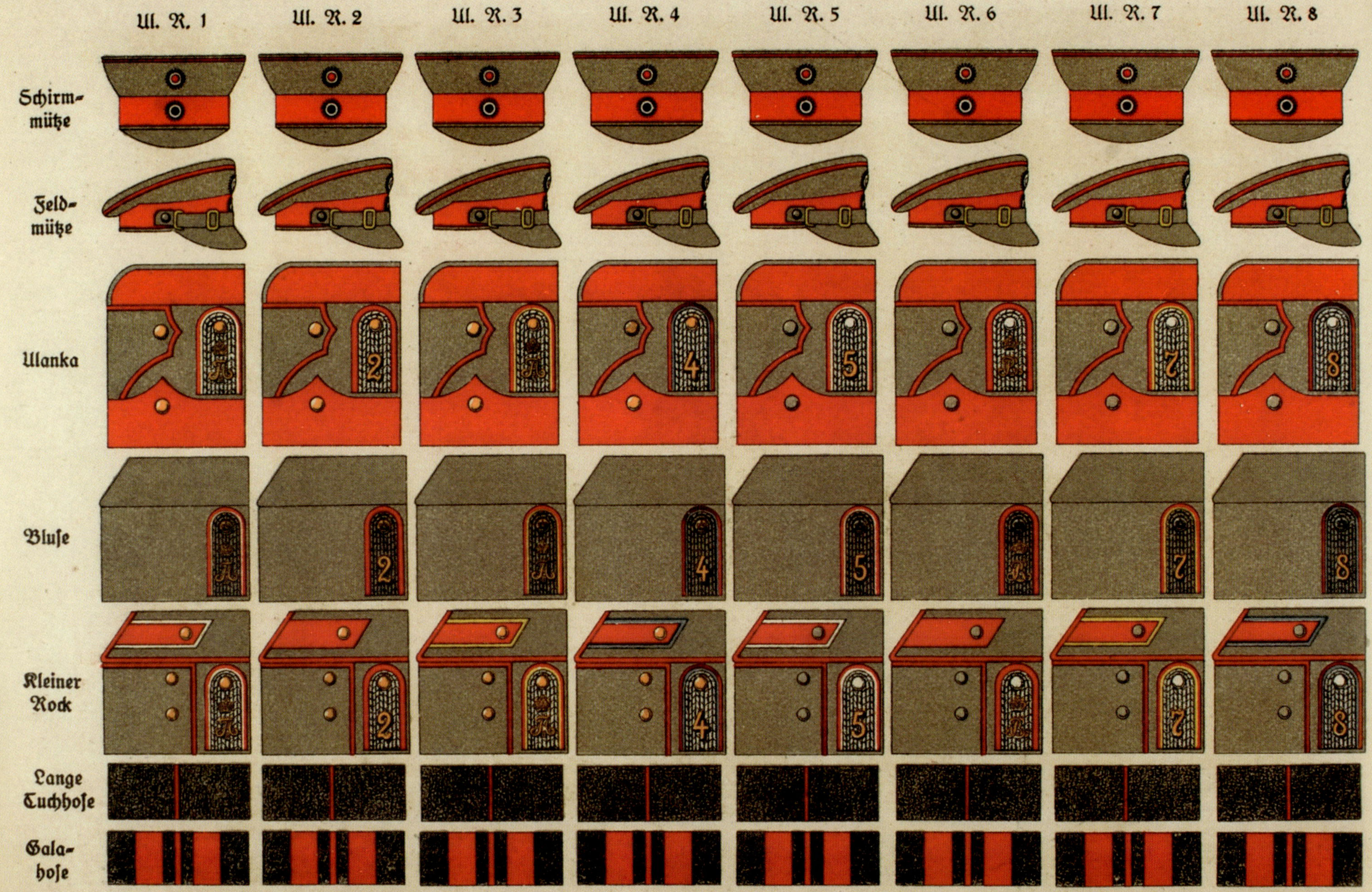
Ul. R. 1
Ul. R. 2
Ul. R. 3
Ul. R. 4
Ul. R. 5
Ul. R. 6
Ul. R. 7
Ul. R. 8
Schirm-mütze
Feld-mütze
Ulanka
Bluse
Kleiner Rock
Lange Tuchhose
Gala-hose

Ulanen.

Ul. R. 9	Ul. R. 10	Ul. R. 11	Ul. R. 12	Ul. R. 13	Ul. R. 14	Ul. R. 15	Ul. R. 16

Jäger zu Pferde.

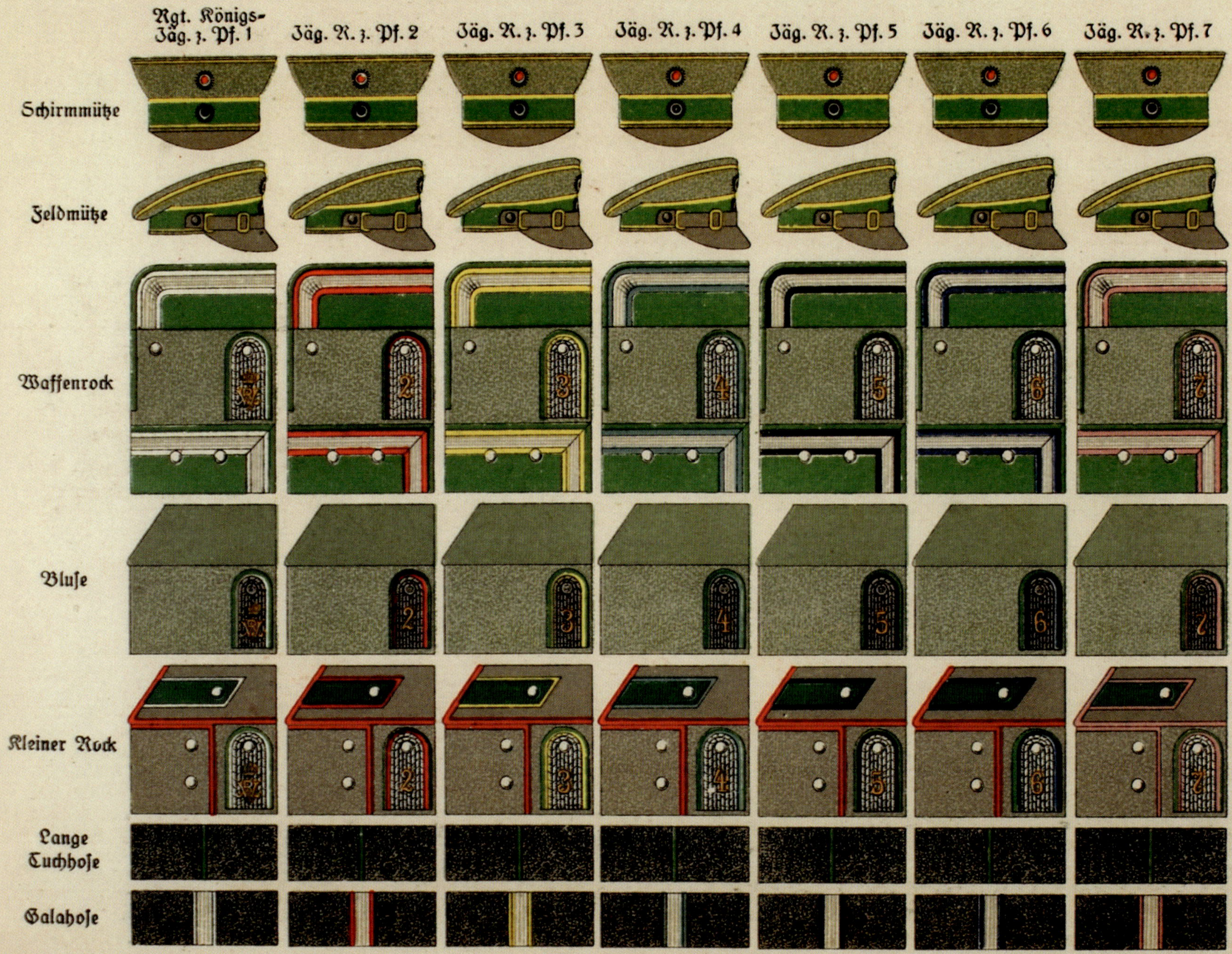

Rgter. 8—13 allgemein vergoldete Knöpfe und goldenen Tressenbesatz um Kragen und Ärmelaufschläge und an der Galahose, sonst:

Rgt. 8 wie Rgt. 1
„ 9 „ „ 2
„ 10 „ „ 3
„ 11 „ „ 4
„ 12 „ „ 5
„ 13 „ „ 6

Auf den Achselstücken Regimentsnummer.

Feldartillerie.

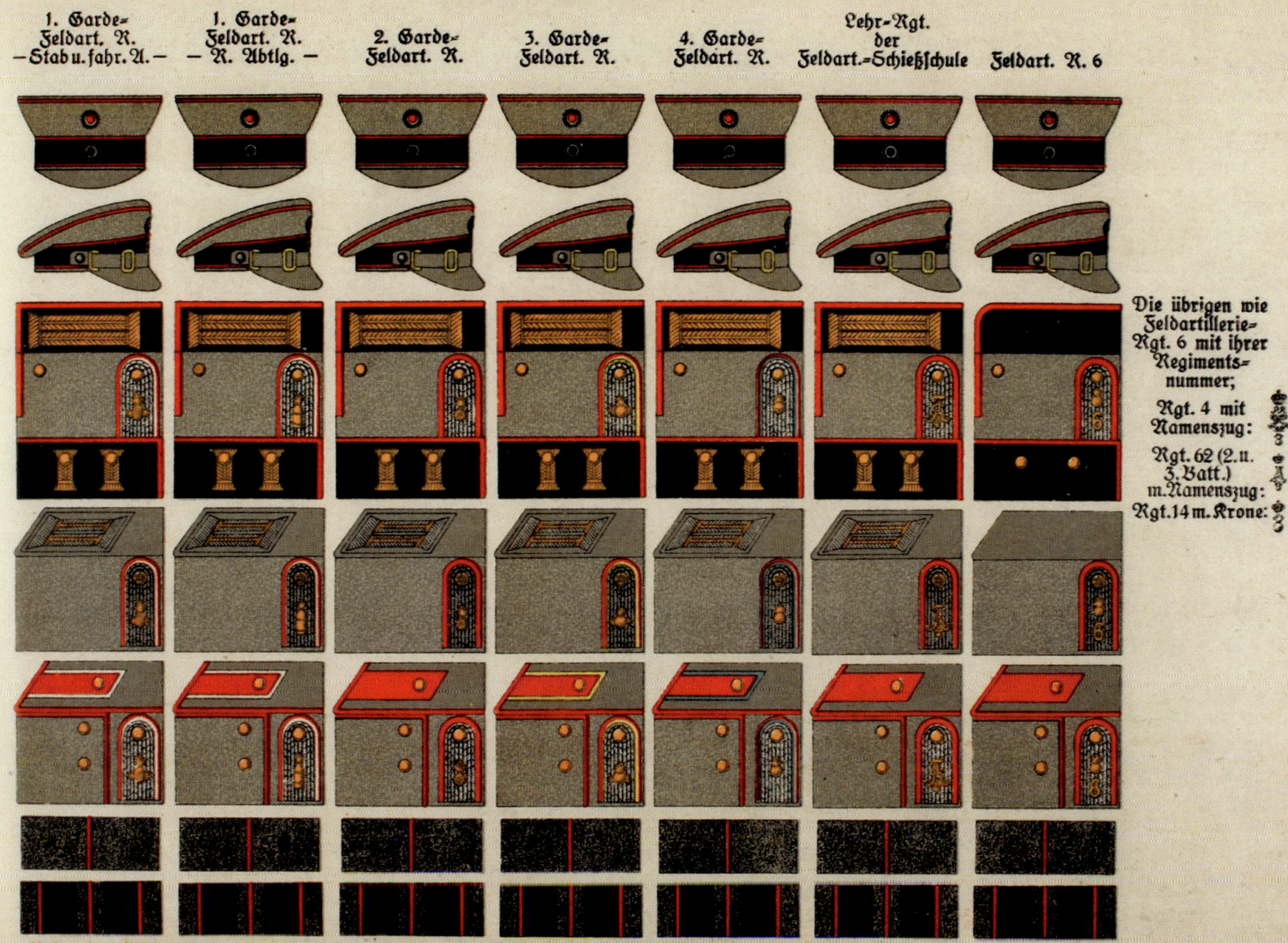

Besatz der Schirmmütze und Galahose, Kragen und Aufschläge des Waffenrocks: schwarzer Samt;
Besatz der Feldmütze: schwarzes Tuch.

Fußartillerie. | Train.

G. Fußart. R. — Fußart. Schieß-schule — Artillerie-Prüfungs-Kommission — Fußart. R. 9 — 1. Garde-Tr. Abt. — 2. Garde-Tr. Abt. — der Linie z. B. Tr. Abt. 8

Schirm-mütze

Feld-mütze

Waffen-rock

Bluse

Kleiner Rock

Lange Tuchhose

Galahose

Fußartillerie: Besatzstreifen der Schirmmütze, Waffenrockkragen und Aufschläge sowie Besatzstreifen der Galahose: schwarzer Samt; Besatz der Feldmütze: schwarzes Tuch.

Nichtregimentierte Offiziere.

General	Generaladjutant Sr. Majestät	General à la suite Sr. Majestät	Flügeladjutant Sr. Majestät	Adjutant der Kgl. Prinzen	Kriegsministerium	Militärkabinett	Generalstab

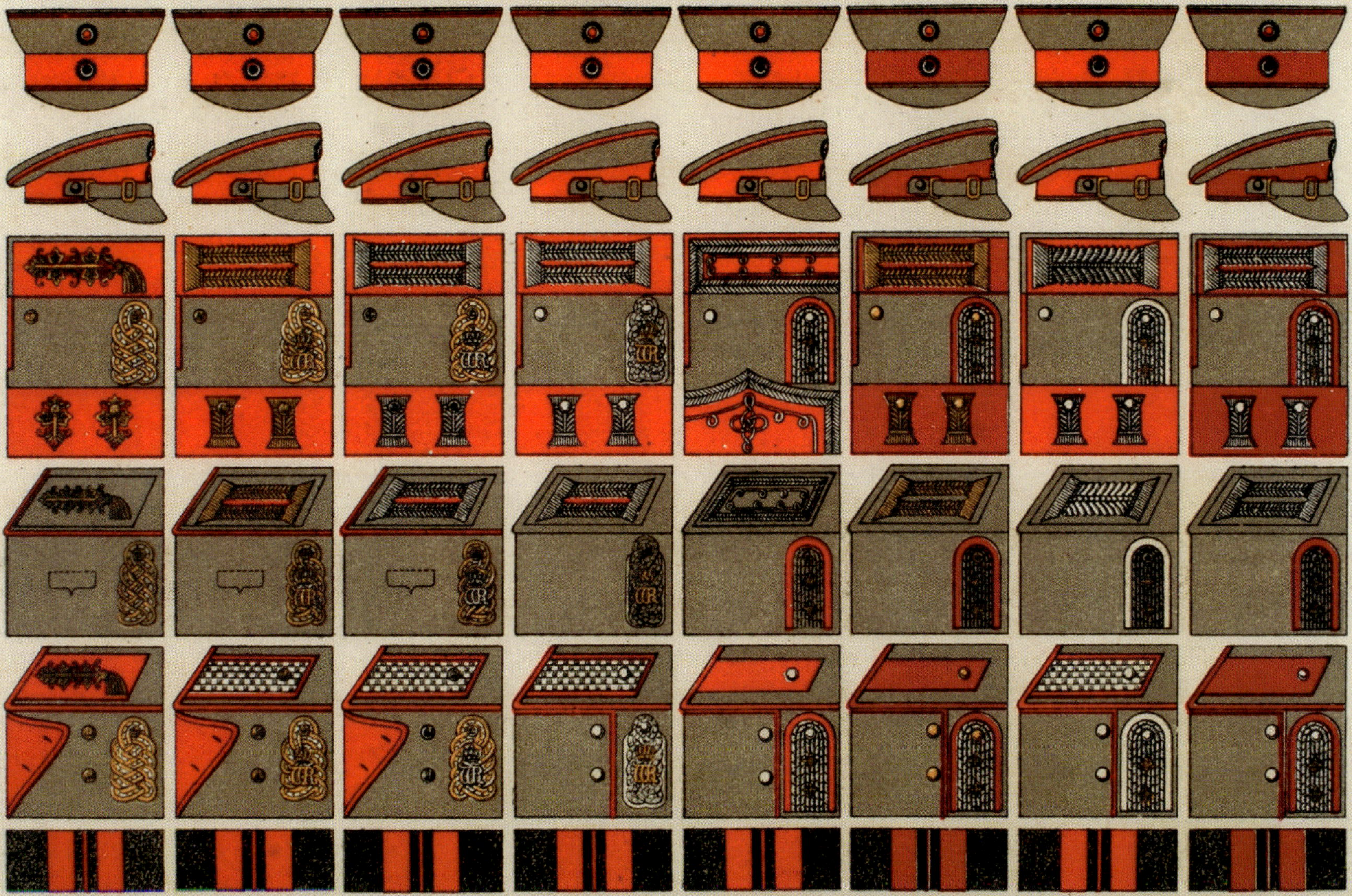

Keine Galahose	Keine Galahose	Keine Galahose	Keine Galahose	Keine Galahose	Keine Galahose	Keine Galahose	Keine Galahose

General- und Flügeladjutanten, Generale à la suite Sr. M. und Offiziere des Militärkabinetts: Silberne Kragenpatten am Kleinen Rock. Flügeladjutanten um die weiße Tuchunterlage der Achselstücke silberner Vorstoß.

Invalidenhäuser.

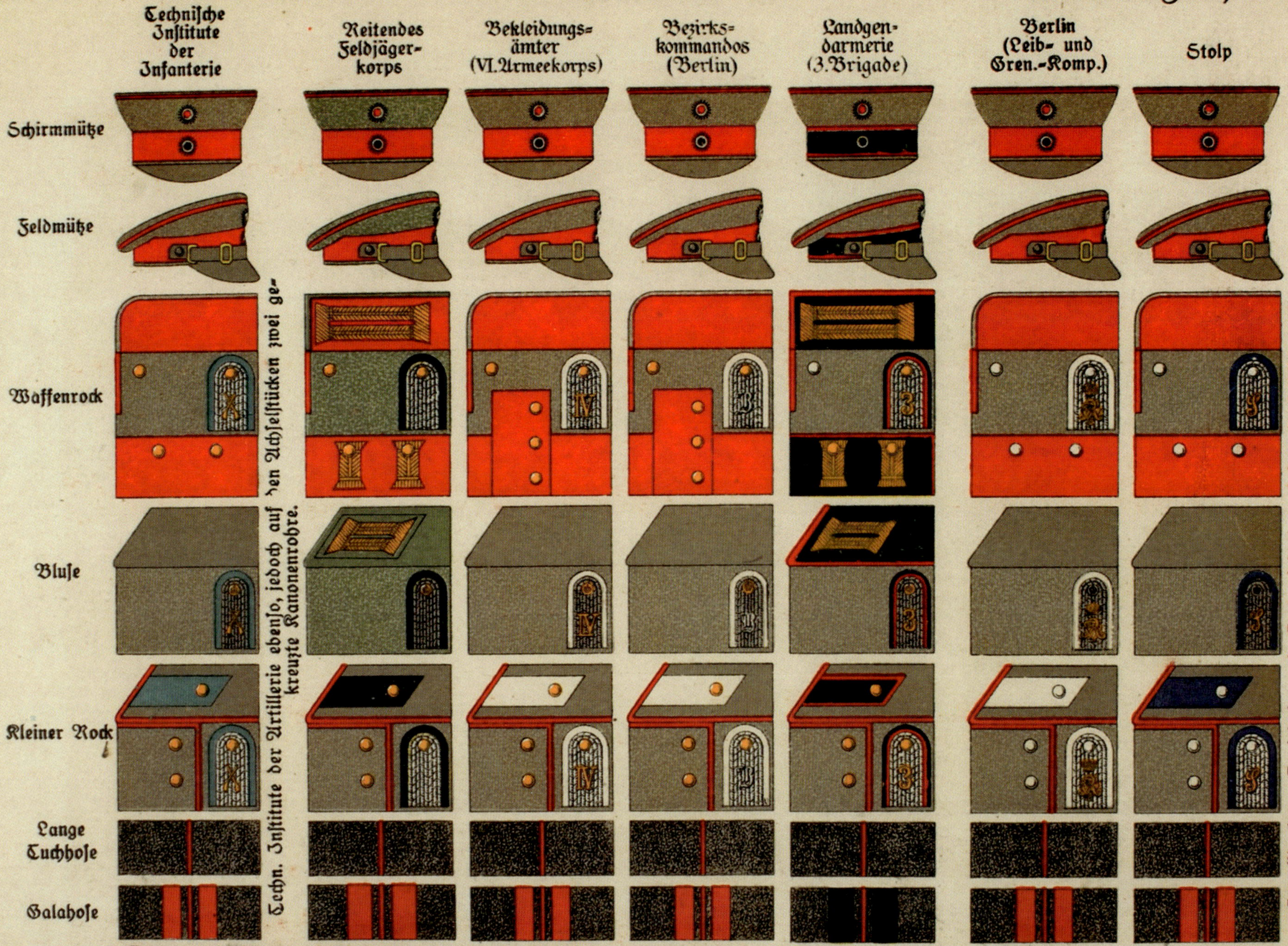

Techn. Inſtitute der Artillerie ebenſo, jedoch auf den Achſelſtücken zwei gekreuzte Kanonenrohre.

Invalidenhaus Carlshafen wie Stolp, jedoch auf den Achſelſtücken ein: [monogram]
Beim Invalidenhaus Berlin trägt die 3. bis 8. Komp. den Namenszug: [monogram]

Gendarmerieoffiziere: Bluſenkragen dunkelgrün.

Kadettenkorps.

Kadettenhäuser:

Haupt-Kadettenanstalt Berlin-Lichterfelde	Köslin	Potsdam	Wahlstatt	Bensberg	Plön	Naumburg	Karlsruhe

Oranienstein wie Bensberg, jedoch mit zitronengelbem Vorstoß an den Aufschlägen.

Armeeuniform Landwehr-Kavallerie.

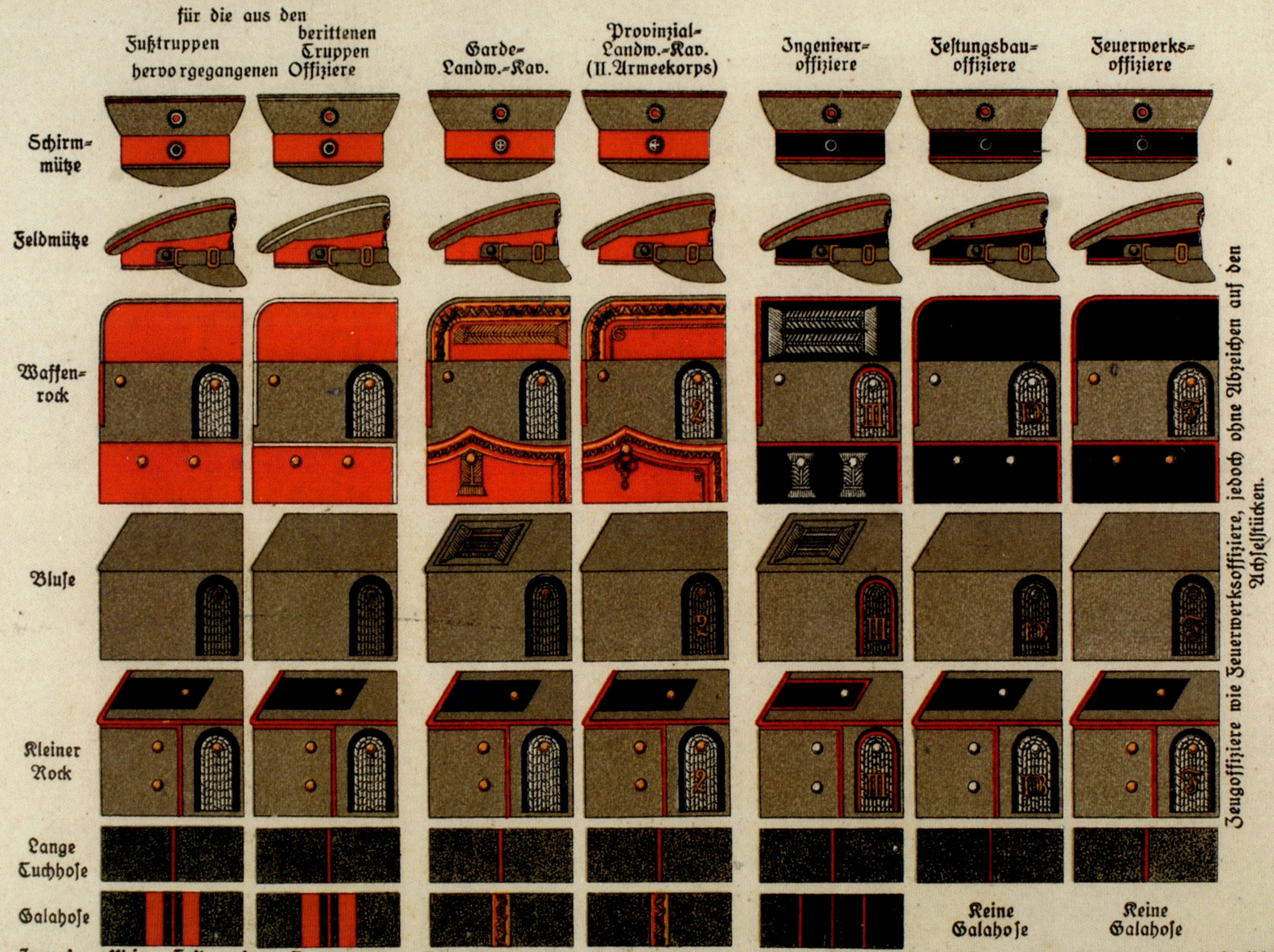

Ingenieuroffiziere, Festungsbau-, Feuerwerks- u. Zeugoffiziere: Besatzstreifen der Schirmmütze (Ingenieuroffiziere auch der Galahose), Kragen und Aufschläge am Waffenrock, Achselstückunterlage u. Kragenpatten am Kleinen Rock von Samt; Besatzstreifen der Feldmütze von schwarzem Tuch.

Sanitätsoffiziere.

Ober-generalarzt | Oberstabsarzt | Assistenzarzt

Generaloberarzt wie Oberstabsarzt mit 1 Stern;
Generalarzt " " " 2 Sternen;
Oberarzt " Assistenzarzt " 1 Stern;
Stabsarzt " " " 2 Sternen.

Sanitätsoffiziere: Achselstückunterlage von Samt.

Veterinäroffiziere.

Korpsstabs- und Oberstabsveterinär | Stabsveterinär

Generalveterinär wie Oberstabsveterinär mit 2 Sternen;
Oberveterinär " Stabsveterinär " 1 Stern;
Veterinär " " ohne Stern.

Kriegsministerium. Militär-

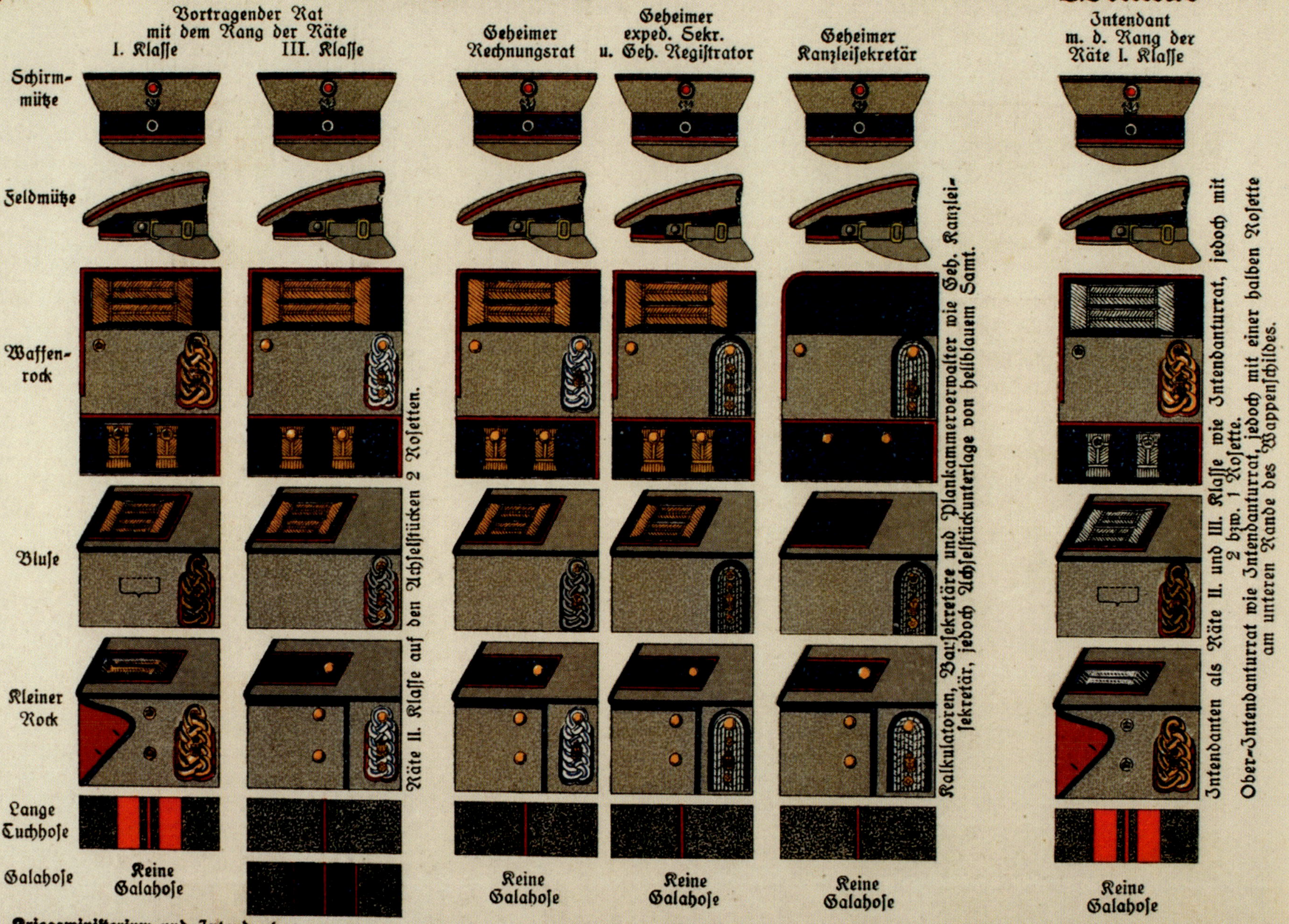

Kriegsministerium und Intendantur:
Dunkelblauer Samt: Besatz der Schirmmütze und Galahose, Kragen und Aufschläge am Waffenrock, Kragenpatten am Kl. Rock; Geh. Rechnungsräte, Geh. exp. Sekr. und Intendantursekr. auch Achselstückunterlage; **Dunkelblaues Tuch:** Besatz der Feldmütze und Kragenpatten der Bluse; Geh. Kanzleisekretäre auch Achselstückunterlage.

Intendantur.

Intendanturrat — Intendanturassessor — Ober-Intendantursekretär und -Registrator

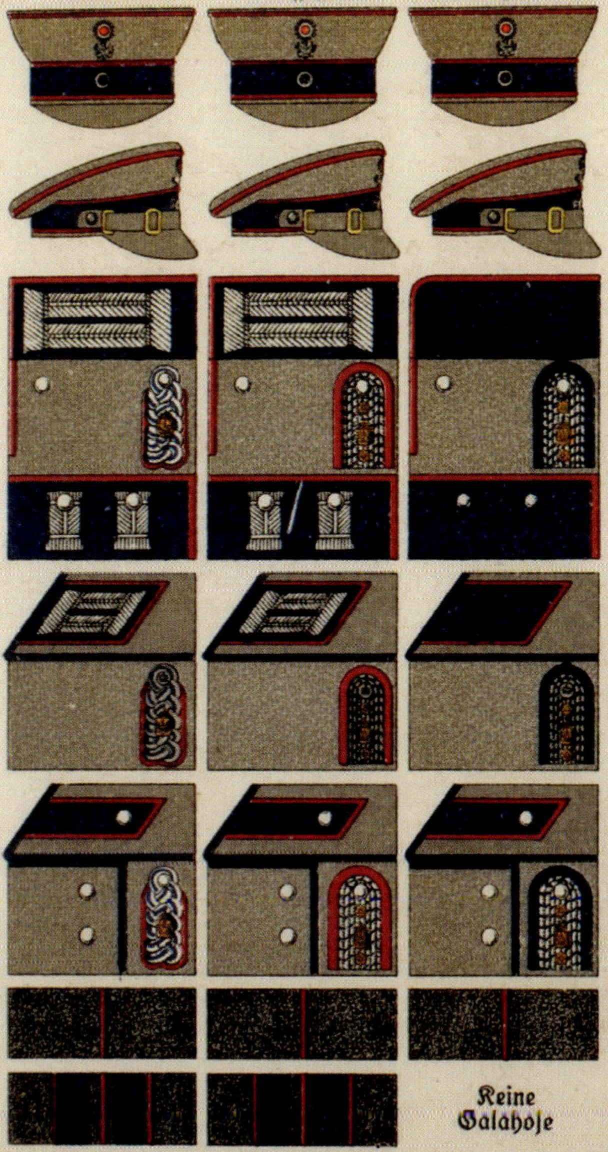

Mil. Int. Referendar wie Intendantursekretär, jedoch Achselstückunterlage von karmesinrotem Tuch.
Mil. Int. Diätar wie Intendantursekretär, jedoch ohne Rosette.

Militär-Gericht.

Kriegsgerichtsrat (mit dem Rang der Räte V. Kl.) — Kriegsgerichtssekretär

Oberkriegsgerichtsräte u. Kriegsgerichtsräte mit dem Rang der Räte IV. Kl. Achselstücke wie Intendanturräte, jedoch ponceaurote Tuchunterlage. Räte III. Kl. 1 Rosette, IV. Kl. ohne Rosette.
Oberkriegsgerichtssekretär: 2 Rosetten, Gerichtsassistent ohne Rosette.

Höhere Beamte der technischen Institute.

Betriebsleiter

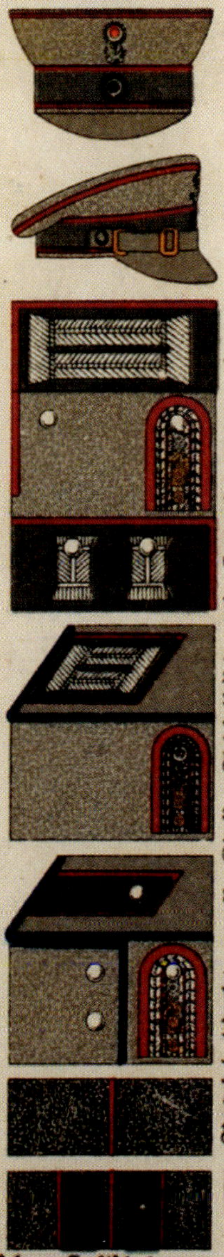

Betriebsdirektoren II. Klasse: Achselstücke wie Intendantur- und Bauräte, Betriebsdirektoren I. Klasse mit einer Rosette; Betriebsassistenten (Mil. Baumeister, -Chemiker und Physiker) wie Betriebsleiter, jedoch ohne Rosetten.

Kriegsgerichtsräte u. höhere Beamte der **technischen Institute:**
Von Samt: Besatz der Schirmmütze u. Galahose, Kragen u. Aufschläge am Waffenrock u. Kragenpatten am Kleinen Rock;
Von Tuch: Besatz der Feldmütze u. Kragenpatten der Bluse.

Militär-Baubeamte.

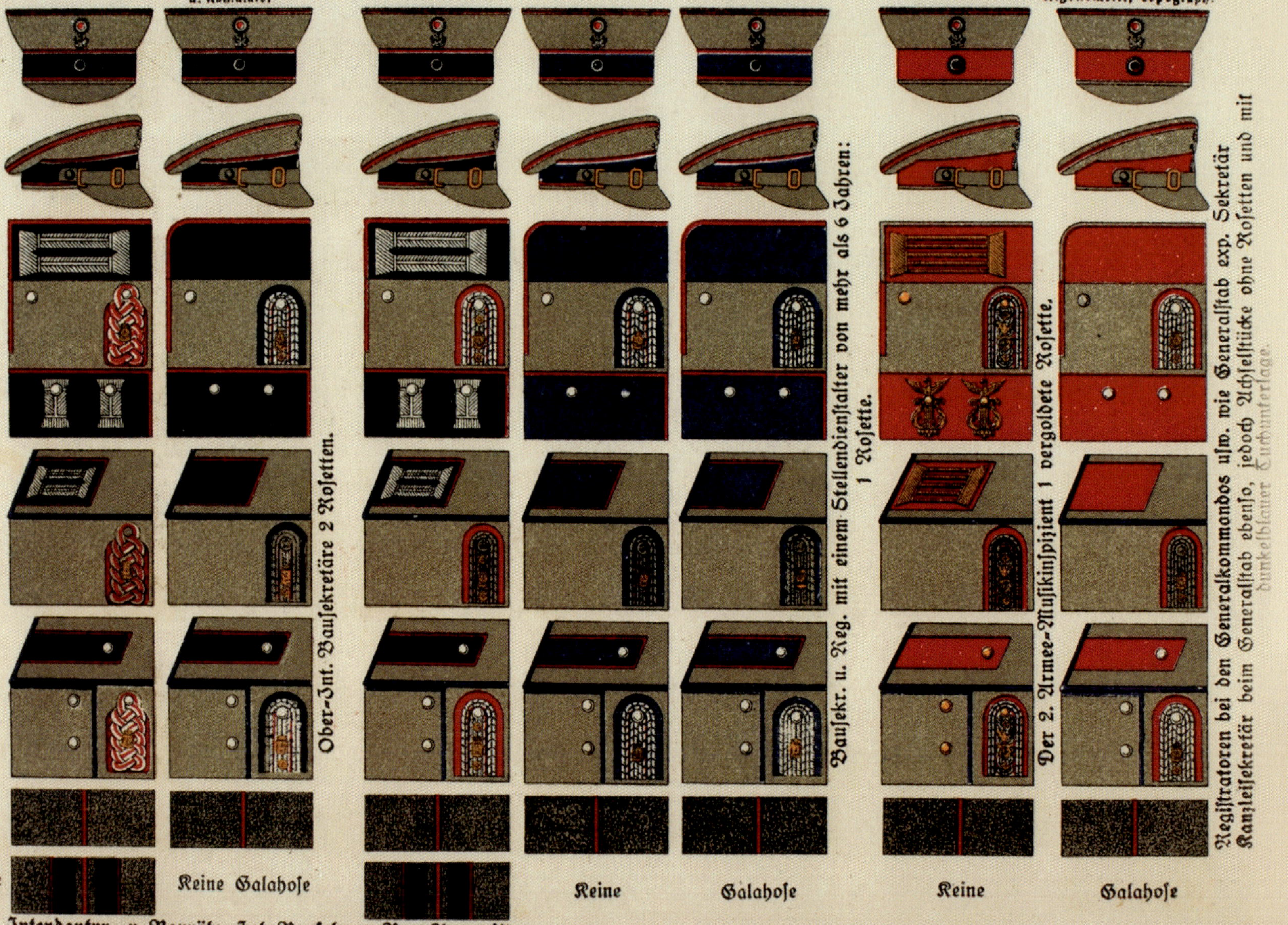

Intendantur- u. Bauräte, Int. Bausekr. u. Reg. Baumeister:

Von dunkelblauem **Samt**: Besatz der Schirmmütze u. Galahose, Kragen und Aufschläge am Waffenrock, Kragenpatten am Kl. Rock; Int. Bausekr. auch Achselstückunterlage.

Von dunkelblauem **Tuch**: Besatz der Feldmütze u. Kragenpatten der Bluse.

Militär-Apotheker.

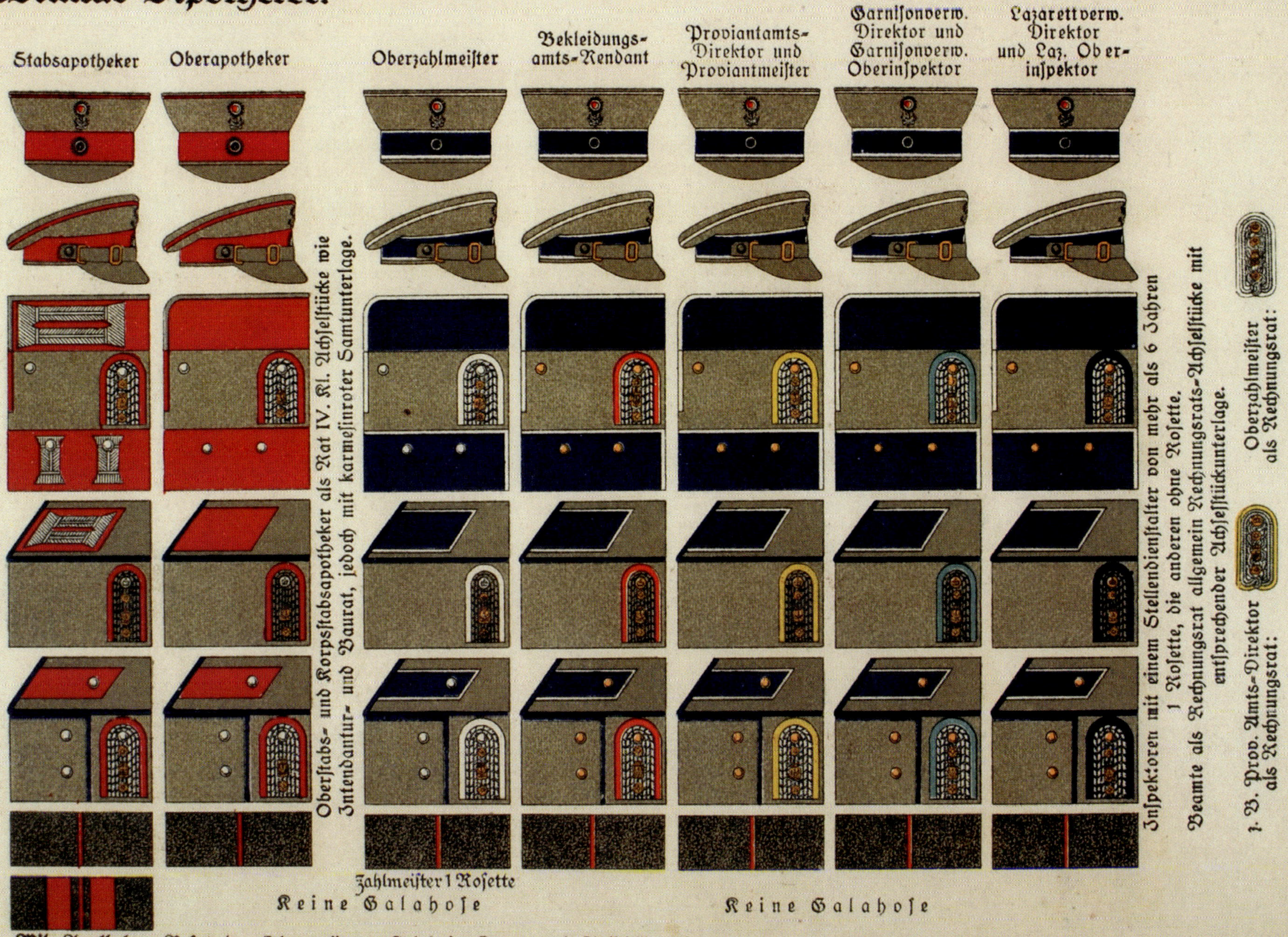

Mil.-Apotheker: Besatz der Schirmmütze u. Galahose, Kragen nnd Aufschläge, Kragenpatten am Kl. Rock: von Samt;
„ „ Feldmütze, Achselstückunterlage und Kragenpatten an der Bluse: von Tuch.

Telegraphen-Oberbauwart (Tel. Bauwart: 1 Rosette) | Werkstättenvorsteher, Materialienverwalter, Luftschiffhalleninspektor, Maschinenmeister bei den Verkehrstruppen | Kaiserliches Kraftfahr-Korps (Wehrpflichtiger Offizier, Offizier a la suite oder a. D.) | **Feldpost**: Armee-Postdirektor und Feld-Oberpostinspektor | Feld-Postmeister; Feld- u. Armee-Postinspektor | Feld-Postsekretär | Feldgeistliche

Schirmmütze — Feldmütze — Waffenrock — Bluse — Kleiner Rock — Lange Tuchhose

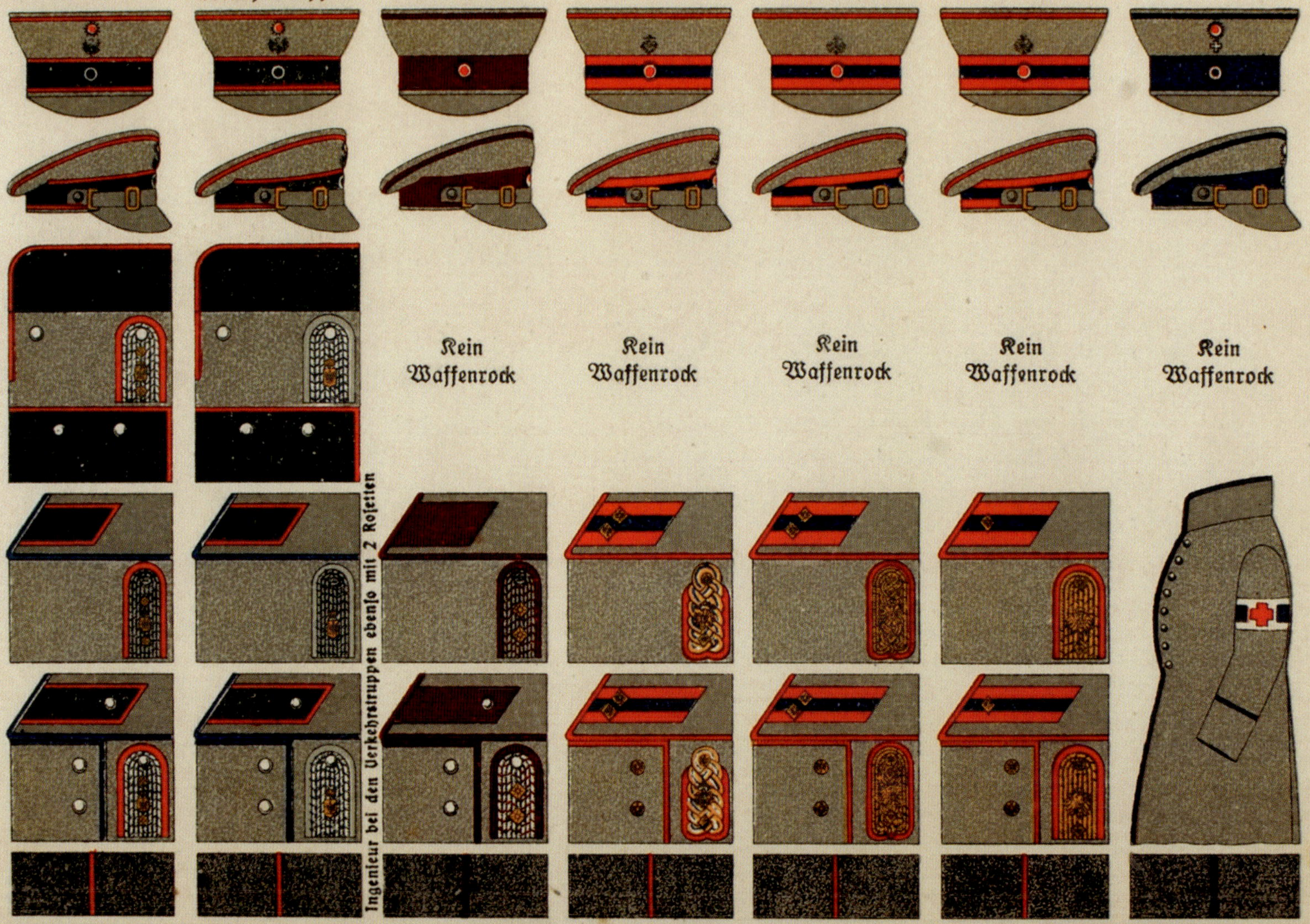

Zahnarzt: wie Oberapotheker (S. 31) ohne Rosette; Achselstückunterlage von **weißem** Tuch.
Feldbeamte der Kriegskassen: wie Zahlmeister (S. 31) mit vergoldeten Knöpfen.
Kriegszahlmeister: 2 Rosetten,
Kassier u. Buchhalter: 1 Rosette,
Assistent: ohne Rosette.

Tel. Bauwart: Besatzstreifen der Schirmmütze, Kragen und Aufschläge am Waffenrock und Kragenpatten am Kl. Rock von **Samt.**
Kais. Kraftfahr-Korps: Auf den Ärmeln silberne Kaiserkrone (3,5 cm Durchmesser)
Nichtwehrpflichtige: Achselband; Achselstücke ohne Abzeichen.
Feldpost: Blauer Mittelstreifen an der Schirmmütze und an der Kragenpatte des Kl. Rocks von **Samt.** — **Feldgeistliche:** Armbinde von Seide.

Die feldgraue Friedens- und Kriegs-Bekleidung der K. Bayerischen Armee

— 1916 —

Mit Genehmigung des K. Bayer. Kriegsministeriums herausgegeben

von

Helm,
Rechnungsrat

Ströbel,
Geheimer exped. Sekretär

im K. Bayer. Kriegsministerium.

Die feldgraue Friedens- und Kriegs-Bekleidung der K. Bayerischen Armee.

— 1916 —

Uniform-Tafeln

nach der Allerhöchsten Entschließung vom 31. März 1916 — V.-Bl. S. 325 ff. —

I. Offiziere und obere Beamte.
II. Mannschaften.
III. Einheitsmantel.

Mit Genehmigung des K. Bayer. Kriegsministeriums herausgegeben
von

Helm
Rechnungsrat

Ströbel
Geheimer exped. Sekretär

im K. Bayer. Kriegsministerium.

München / Selbstverlag der Herausgeber

I.

Uniformen für Offiziere und obere Beamte.

Inhaltsverzeichnis:

Regimentierte Offiziere:

Nicht regimentierte Offiziere:

Obere Beamte:

Ferner tragen

die Generalkommando-Registratoren die Uniform der Intendantur-Registratoren Seite 35

der Kanzleisekretär und Registrator des Generalstabes sowie der Registrator der Feldzeugmeisterei die Uniform der Geheimen Kanzleisekretäre des Kriegsministeriums Seite 32, Tuchunterlage der Achselstücke und Feldachselstücke jedoch aus dunkelblauem Tuch;

die Kanzleisekretäre
des Generalstabs u. d. zugehörig. Stellen,
der Intendanturen,
der General-Militär-Kasse und
der Militär-Bildungs-Anstalten
die Uniform der Kanzleisekretäre des Kriegsministeriums Seite 32

Vorbemerkungen: Soweit nicht anderes vermerkt ist, sind die Besätze und Vorstöße der Bekleidungsstücke aus Tuch.

Infanterie.

Infanterie-Leib-Regiment.

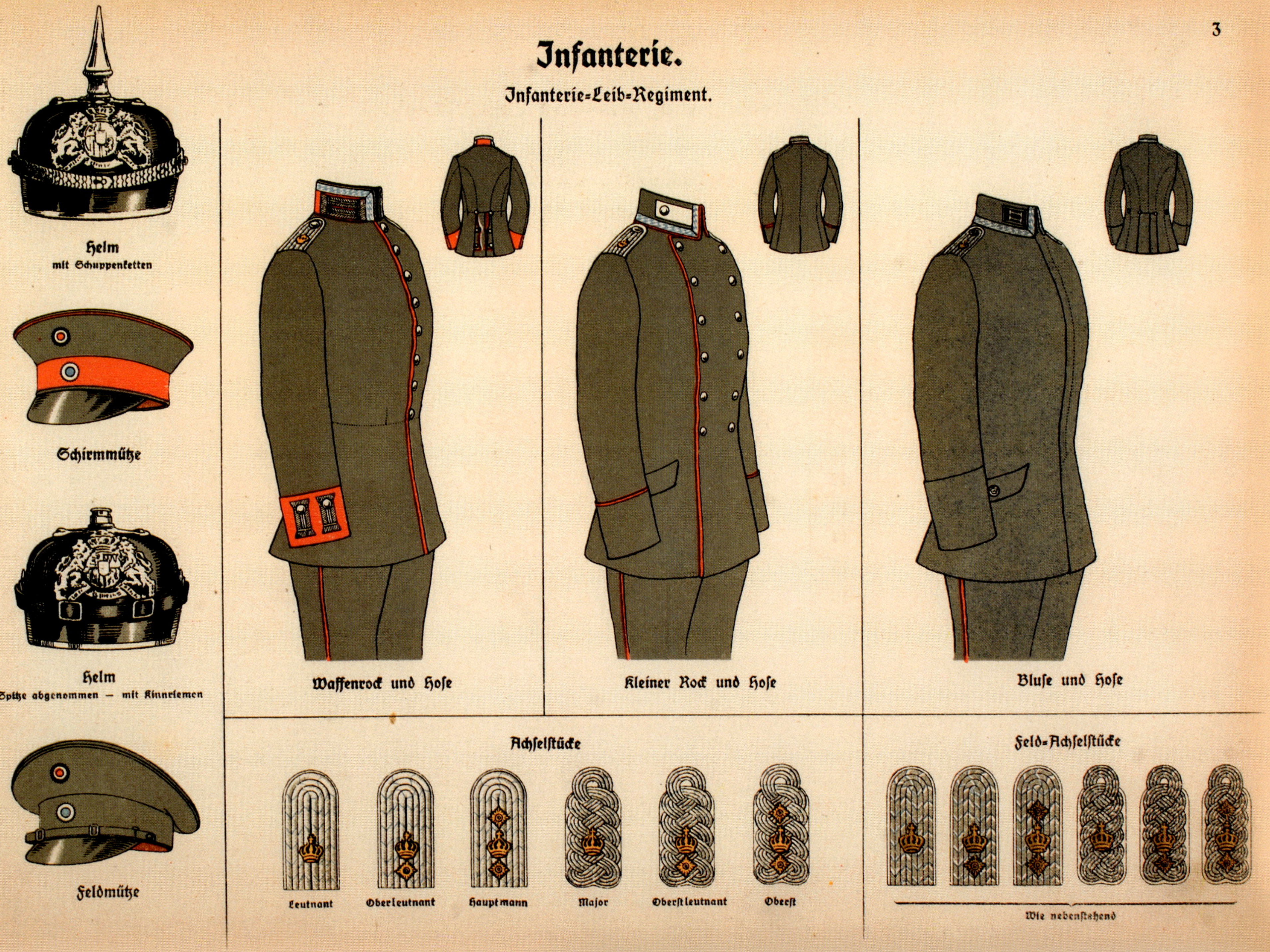

Infanterie.

Sämtliche übrigen Infanterie-Regimenter.

Helm
mit Schuppenketten

Schirmmütze

Helm
– Spitze abgenommen – mit Kinnriemen

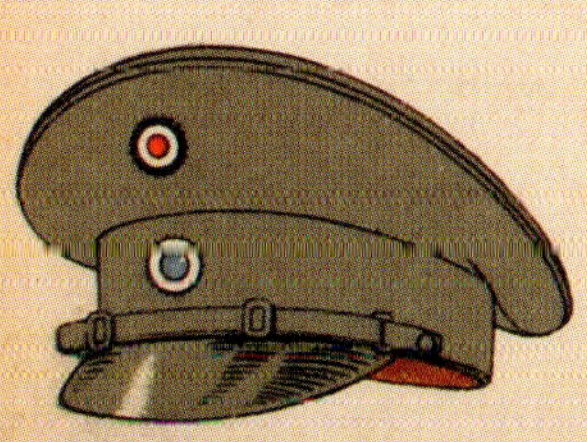

Feldmütze

Waffenrock und Hose

Kleiner Rock und Hose

Bluse und Hose

Achselstücke

1. Inf.-Reg. 2. Inf.-Reg. 3. Inf.-Reg. 6. Inf.-Reg. 10. Inf.-Reg.

Feld-Achselstücke

Wie nebenstehend

Jäger.

Tschako
mit Schuppenketten

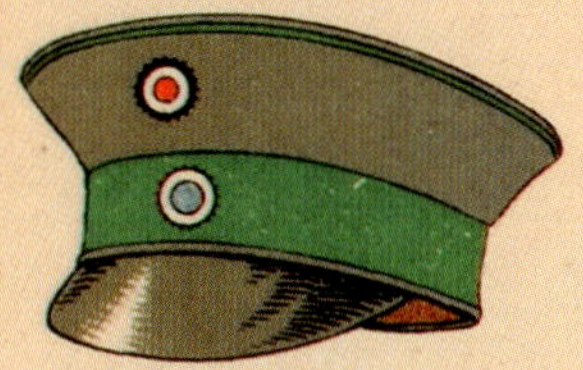

Schirmmütze

Tschako
— Feldzeichen abgenommen — mit Kinnriemen

Feldmütze

Waffenrock und Hose

Kleiner Rock und Hose

Bluse und Hose

Achselstücke

Feld-Achselstücke

Wie nebenstehend

Kavallerie.

1. und 2. Schweres Reiter=Regiment.

(Knöpfe und Helmbeschlag 1. Regiment: versilbert,
2. „ vergoldet).

Helm mit Schuppenketten
(Zum Paradeanzug mit Busch
aus weißem Büffelhaar)

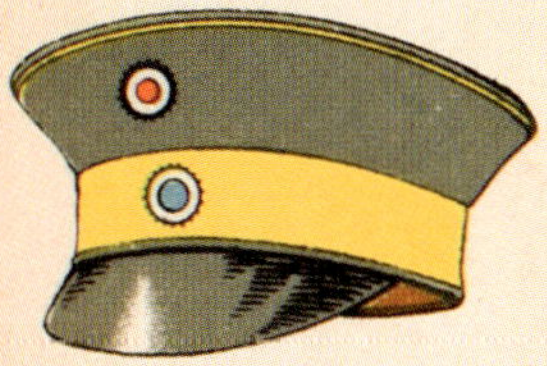

Schirmmütze

Helm
Spitze abgenommen — mit Kinnriemen

Feldmütze

Waffenrock und Hose
(Zum Paradeanzug mit Paraderabatte)

Kleiner Rock und Hose

Bluse und Hose

Achselstücke

Leutnant | Oberleutnant | Rittmeister | Major | Oberstleutnant | Oberst

Feld=Achselstücke

Wie nebenstehend

Kavallerie.

1. und 2. Ulanen-Regiment.

(Knöpfe und Tschapkabeschlag 1 Regiment: vergoldet,
2 „ versilbert).

Tschapka mit Schuppenketten
(Zum Paradeanzug mit Busch aus weißem Büffelhaar in Form eines Roßhaarschweifes, unten mit hellblauer Einfassung)

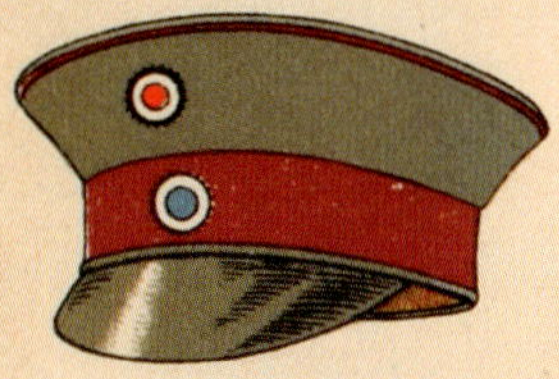

Schirmmütze

Tschapka
— Deckel abgenommen — mit Kinnriemen

Feldmütze

Waffenrock und Hose
(Zum Paradeanzug mit Paraderabatte)

Kleiner Rock und Hose

Bluse und Hose

Achselstücke

Leutnant | Oberleutnant | Rittmeister | Major | Oberstleutnant | Oberst

Feld-Achselstücke

Wie nebenstehend

Kavallerie.

1. und 2. Chevaulegers-Regiment.

(Knöpfe und Helmbeschlag 1. Regiment: vergoldet,
2. „ versilbert).

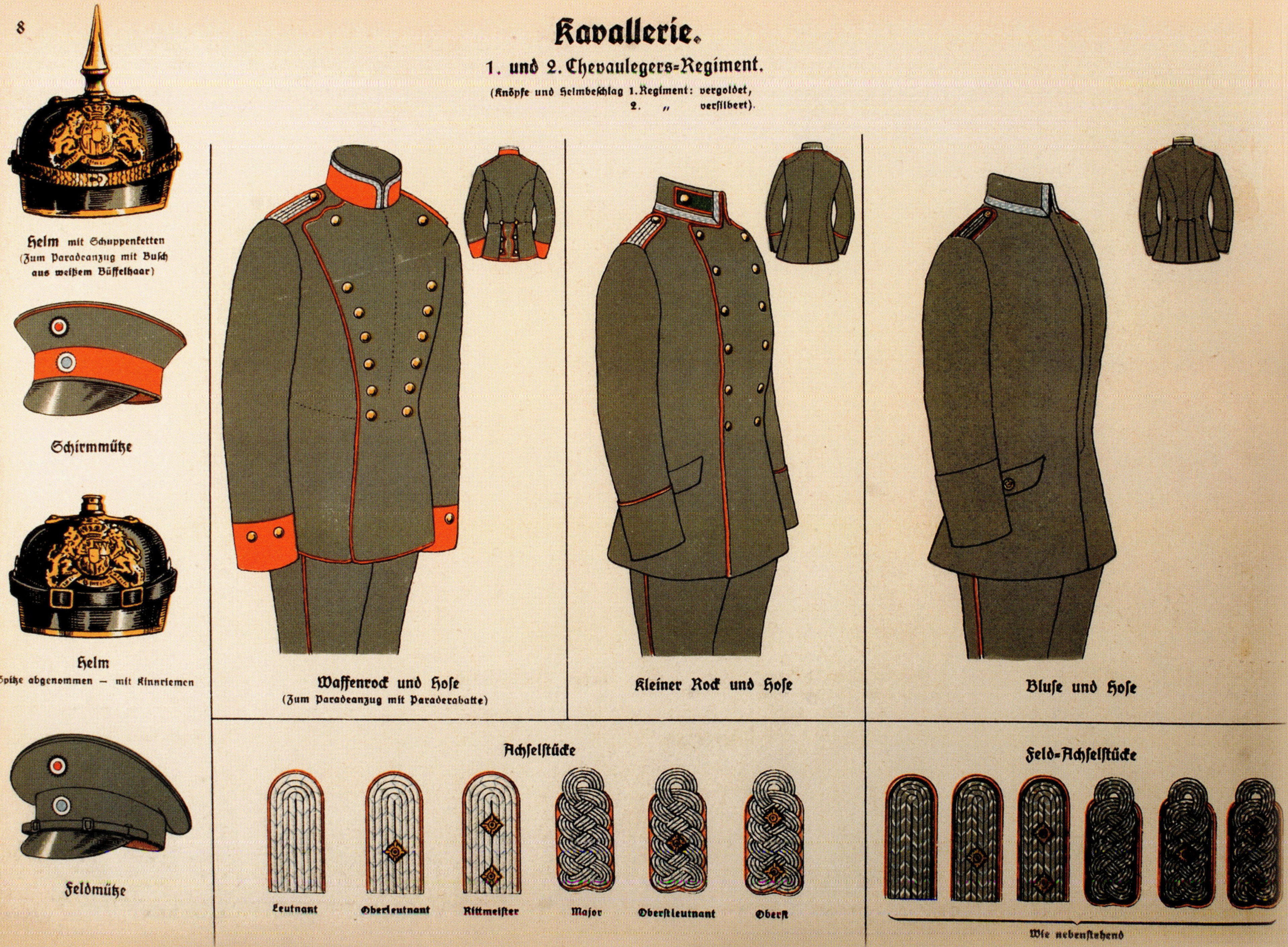

Kavallerie.

3. und 6. Chevaulegers=Regiment.

(Knöpfe und Helmbeschlag 3. Regiment: vergoldet,
6. „ versilbert).

Helm mit Schuppenketten
(Zum Paradeanzug mit Busch aus weißem Büffelhaar).

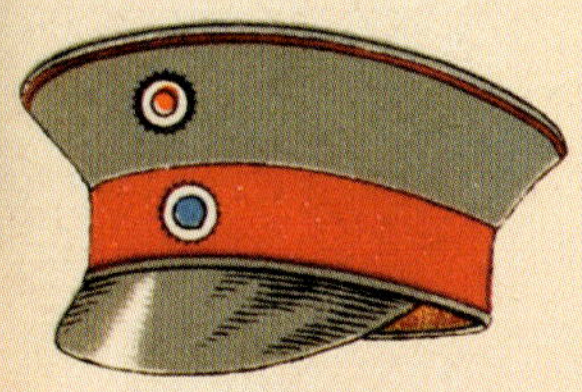

Schirmmütze

Helm
Spitze abgenommen — mit Kinnriemen

Feldmütze

Waffenrock und Hose
(Zum Paradeanzug mit Paraderabatte)

Kleiner Rock und Hose

Bluse und Hose

Achselstücke

Leutnant — Oberleutnant — Hauptmann — Major — Oberstleutnant — Oberst

Feld=Achselstücke

Wie nebenstehend

Kavallerie.

4. und 5. Chevaulegers-Regiment.

(Knöpfe und Helmbeschlag 4. Regiment: versilbert,
5. „ vergoldet).

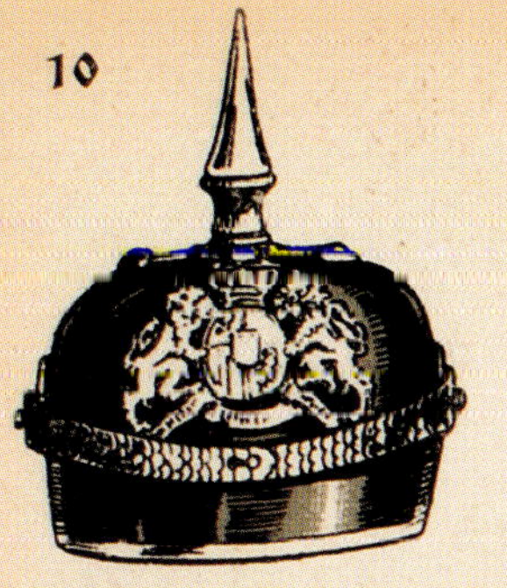

Helm mit Schuppenketten (Zum Paradeanzug mit Busch aus weißem Büffelhaar)

Schirmmütze

Helm
– Spitze abgenommen – mit Kinnriemen

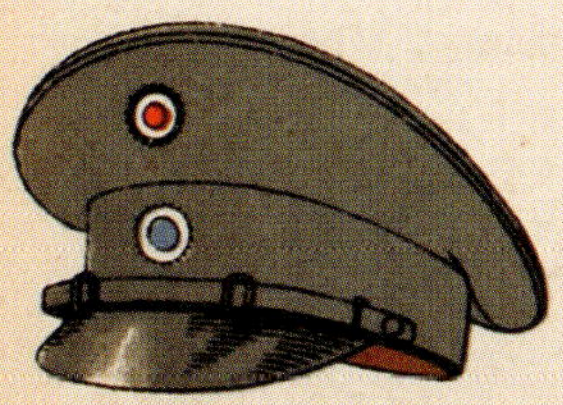

Feldmütze

Waffenrock und Hose
(Zum Paradeanzug mit Paraderabatte)

Kleiner Rock und Hose

Bluse und Hose

Achselstücke

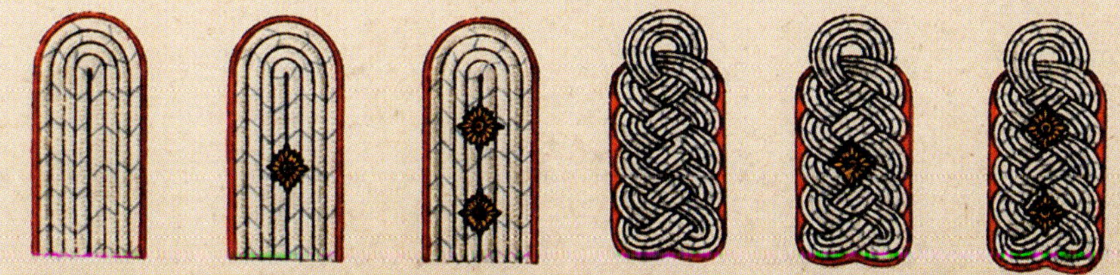

Feld-Achselstücke

Wie nebenstehend

Kavallerie.

7. und 8. Chevaulegers-Regiment.

(Knöpfe und Helmbeschlag 7. Regiment: vergoldet,
8. „ versilbert).

Helm mit Schuppenketten
(Zum Paradeanzug mit Busch
aus weißem Büffelhaar)

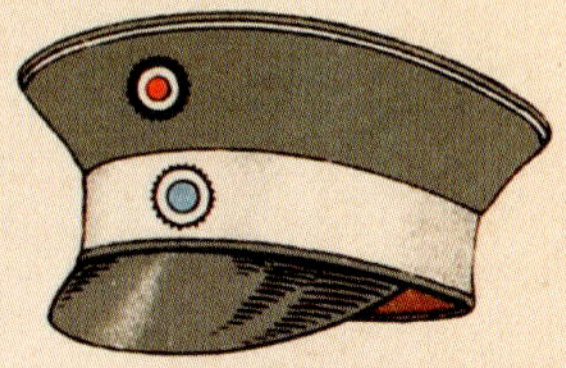

Schirmmütze

Helm
– Spitze abgenommen – mit Kinnriemen

Feldmütze

Waffenrock und Hose
(Zum Paradeanzug mit Paraderabatte)

Kleiner Rock und Hose

Bluse und Hose

Achselstücke

Leutnant | Oberleutnant | Rittmeister | Major | Oberstleutnant | Oberst

Feld-Achselstücke

Wie nebenstehend

Feldartillerie.

Helm
mit Schuppenketten

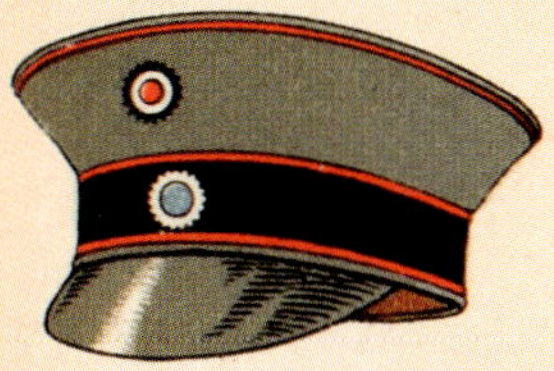

Schirmmütze
(Besatzstreifen aus Samt)

Helm
– Kugel abgenommen – mit Kinnriemen

Feldmütze

Waffenrock und Hose
(Kragen und Aufschläge aus Samt)

Kleiner Rock und Hose

Bluse und Hose

Achselstücke

1. Feld-Art.-Regiment

7. Feld-Art.-Regiment

Feld-Achselstücke

Wie nebenstehend

Fußartillerie.

Helm
mit Schuppenketten

Schirmmütze
(Besatzstreifen aus Samt)

Helm
– Kugel abgenommen – mit Kinnriemen

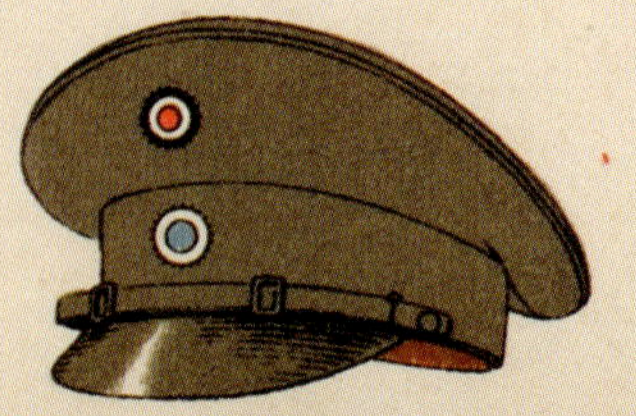

Feldmütze

Waffenrock und Hose
(Kragen und Aufschläge aus Samt)

Kleiner Rock und Hose

Bluse und Hose

Achselstücke

Leutnant — Ober-leutnant — Hauptmann — Major — Oberst-leutnant — Oberst

Feld-Achselstücke

Wie nebenstehend

Pioniere.

Helm
mit Schuppenketten

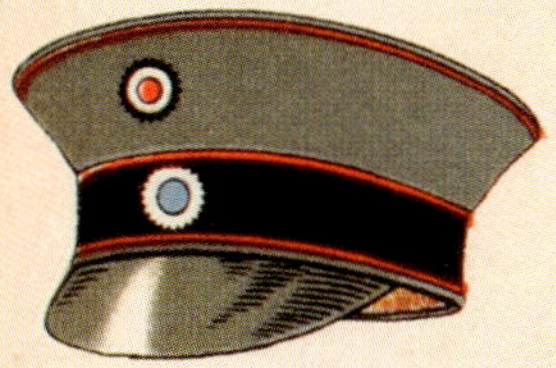

Schirmmütze
(Besatzstreifen aus Samt)

Helm
– Spitze abgenommen – mit Kinnriemen

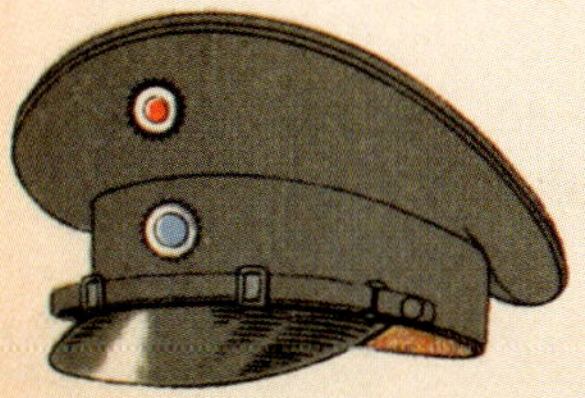

Feldmütze

Waffenrock und Hose
(Kragen und Aufschläge aus Samt)

Kleiner Rock und Hose
(Kragenpatten aus Samt)

Bluse und Hose

Achselstücke
(Unterlage aus Samt)

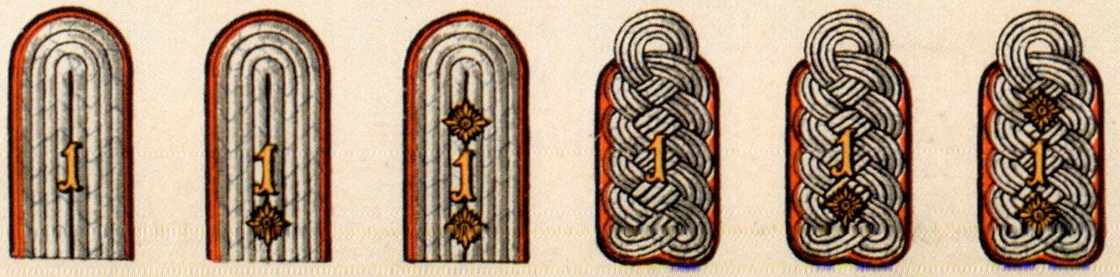

Leutnant — Oberleutnant — Hauptmann — Major — Oberstleutnant — Oberst

Feld-Achselstücke
(Unterlage aus Samt)

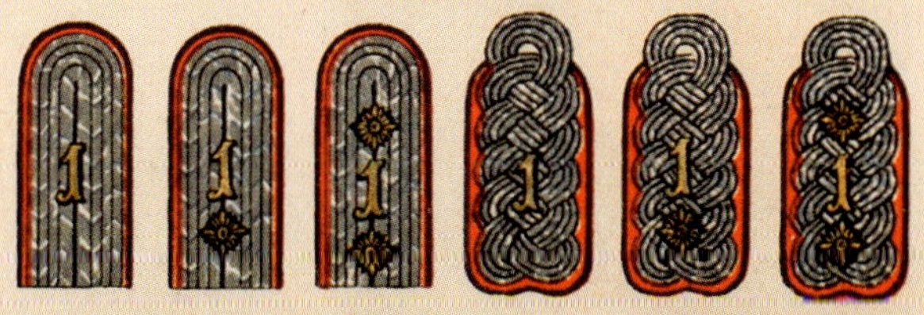

Wie nebenstehend

Verkehrstruppen.

Eisenbahn-, Luftschiffer-, Kraftfahr-, Telegraphen- und Flieger-Truppen.

Tschako
mit Schuppenketten

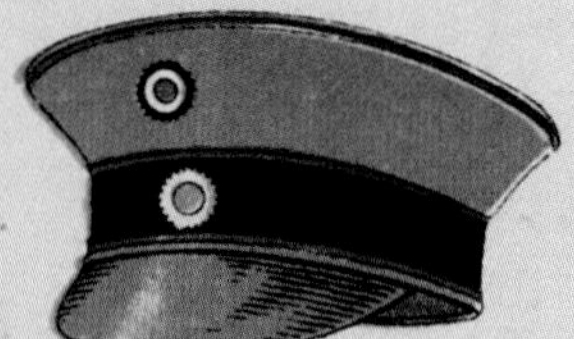

Schirmmütze
(Besatzstreifen aus Samt)

Tschako
– Feldzeichen abgenommen – mit Kinnriemen

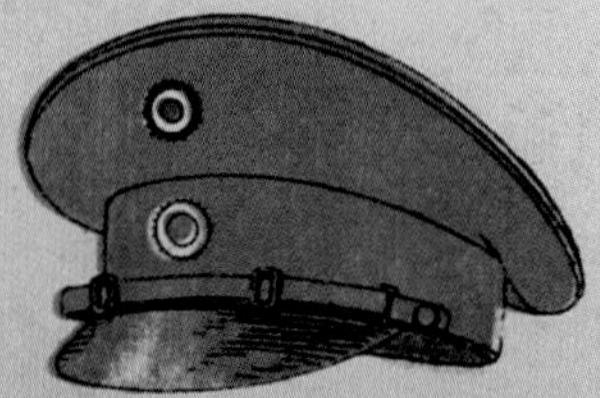

Feldmütze

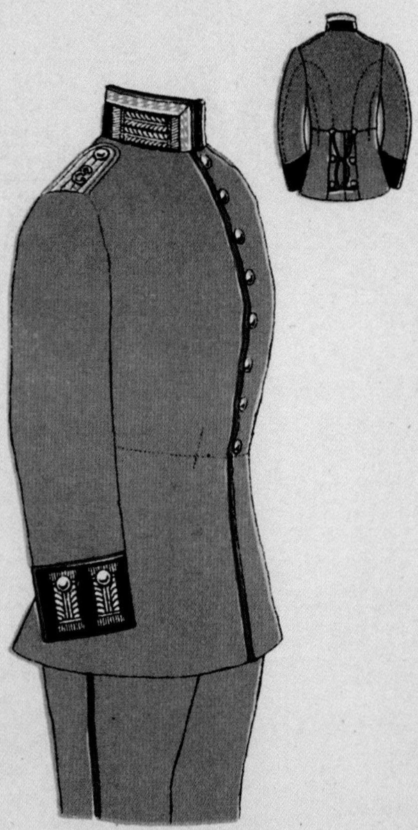

Waffenrock und Hose
(Kragen und Aufschläge aus Samt)

Kleiner Rock und Hose

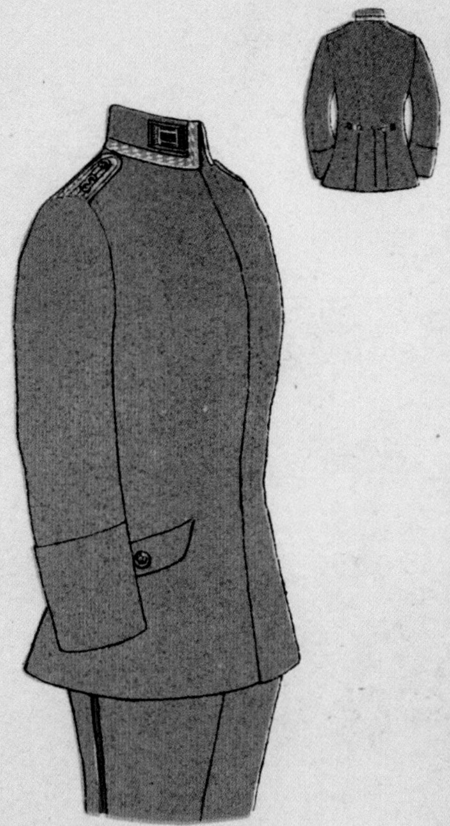

Bluse und Hose

Achselstücke

Eisenbahn-truppen

Luftschiffer

Kraftfahrer

Telegraphen-Bataillon Nr. 1

Flieger-truppen

Feld-Achselstücke

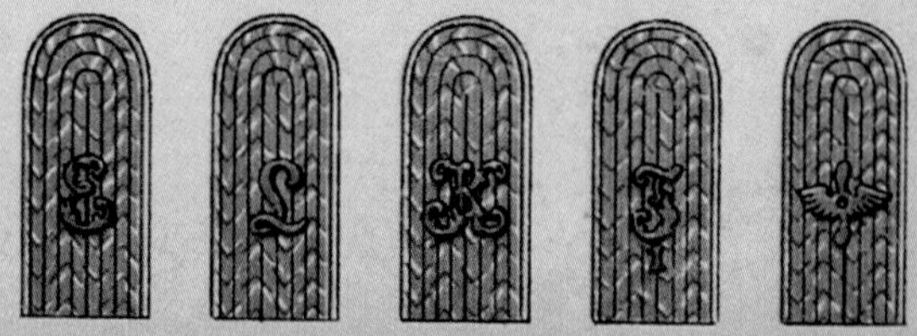

Wie nebenstehend

Train.

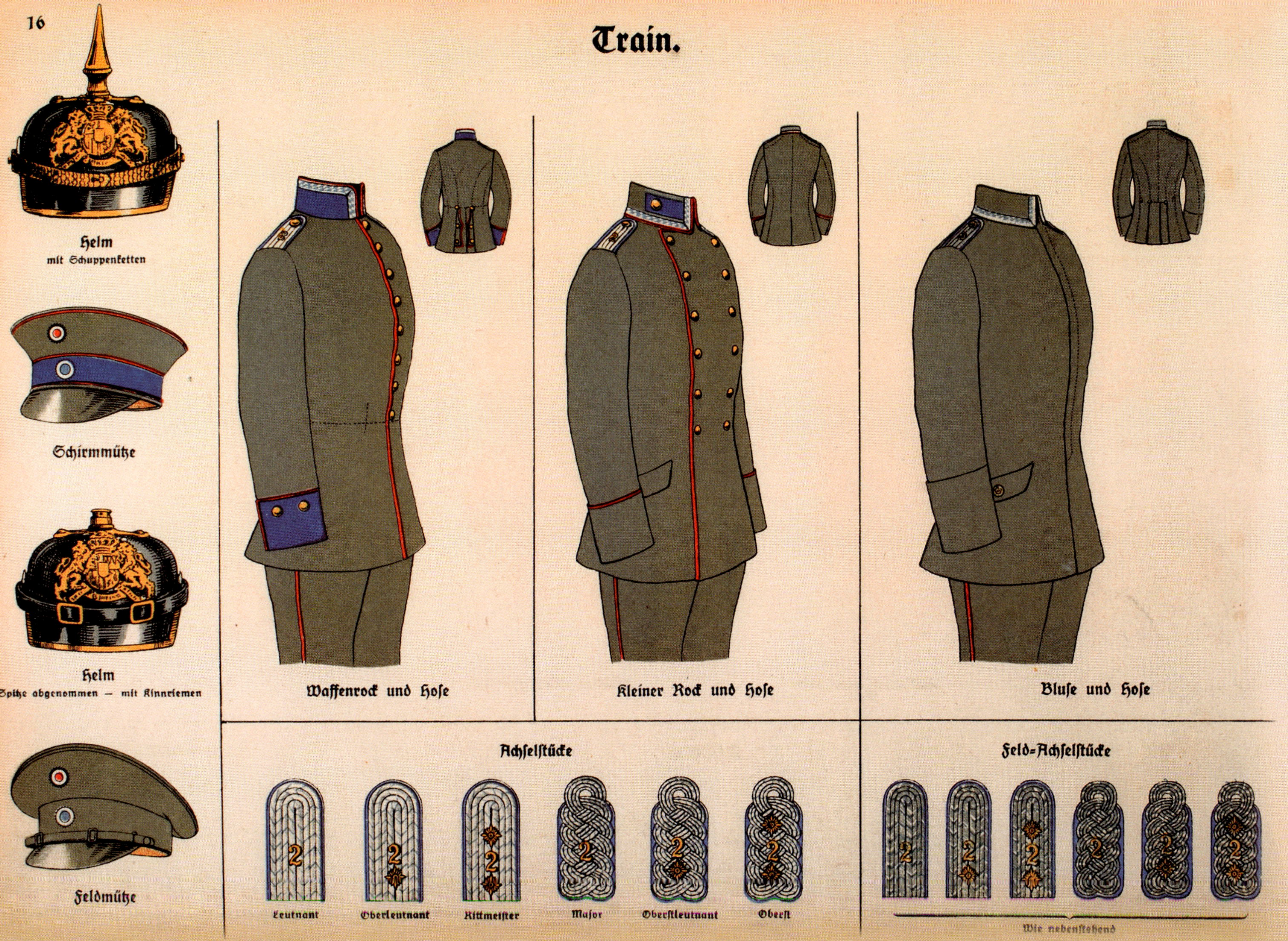
Helm
mit Schuppenketten
Schirmmütze
Helm
– Spitze abgenommen – mit Kinnriemen
Feldmütze
Waffenrock und Hose
Kleiner Rock und Hose
Bluse und Hose
Achselstücke
Feld-Achselstücke
Leutnant
Oberleutnant
Rittmeister
Major
Oberstleutnant
Oberst
Wie nebenstehend

Generale.

Helm mit Schuppenketten (Zum Paradeanzug mit Busch aus weißen und blauen Hahnenfedern)

Schirmmütze

Helm
– Spitze abgenommen. – mit Kinnriemen

Feldmütze

Waffenrock und Hose

Kleiner Rock und Hose

Bluse und Hose

Achselstücke

General-major | General-leutnant | General der Inf., Kav. od. Artillerie | Generaloberst u. General-Feldzeugmeister | Generaloberst m. d. Range eines General-Feldmarschalls | General-Feldmarschall

Feld-Achselstücke

Wie nebenstehend

General-Adjutanten.

Flügel-Adjutanten.

Helm mit Schuppenketten (Zum Paradeanzug mit Busch aus weißem Büffelhaar)

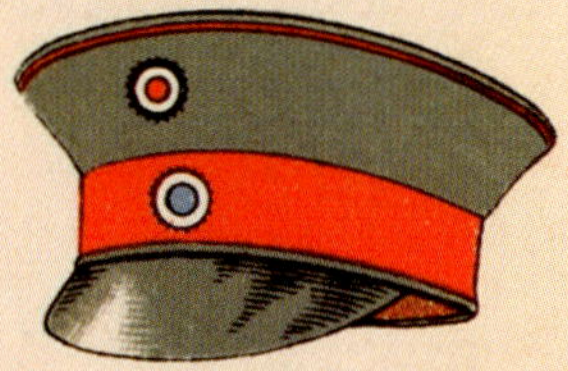

Schirmmütze

Helm – Spitze abgenommen – mit Kinnriemen

Feldmütze

Waffenrock und Hose

Kleiner Rock und Hose

Bluse und Hose

Achselstücke

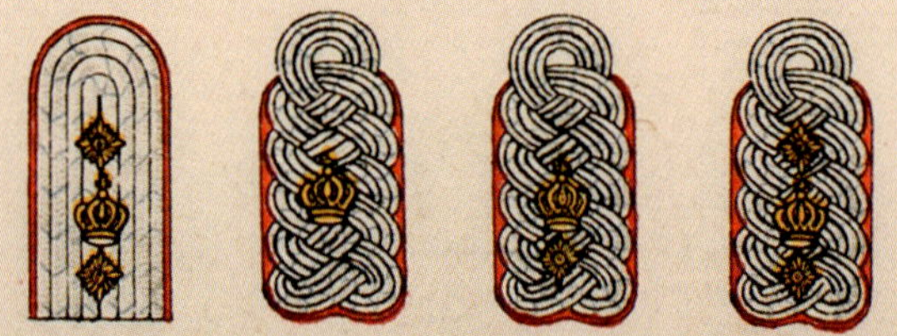

Hauptmann od. Rittmeister — Major — Oberstleutnant — Oberst

Feld=Achselstücke

Wie nebenstehend

Kriegsministerium.

Helm mit Schuppenketten
(Zum Paradeanzug mit Busch
aus weißem Büffelhaar)

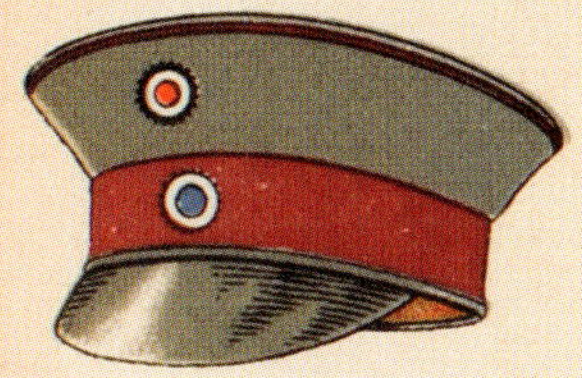

Schirmmütze

Helm
– Spitze abgenommen – mit Kinnriemen

Feldmütze

Waffenrock und Hose

Kleiner Rock und Hose

Bluse und Hose

Achselstücke

Hauptmann — Major — Oberstleutnant — Oberst

Feld-Achselstücke

Wie nebenstehend

Generalstab.

Helm mit Schuppenketten
(Zum Paradeanzug mit Busch
aus weißem Büffelhaar)

Schirmmütze

Helm
– Spitze abgenommen – mit Kinnriemen

Feldmütze

Waffenrock und Hose

Kleiner Rock und Hose

Bluse und Hose

Achselstücke

Hauptmann — Major — Oberstleutnant — Oberst

Feld-Achselstücke

Wie nebenstehend

Gendarmerie-Offiziere.

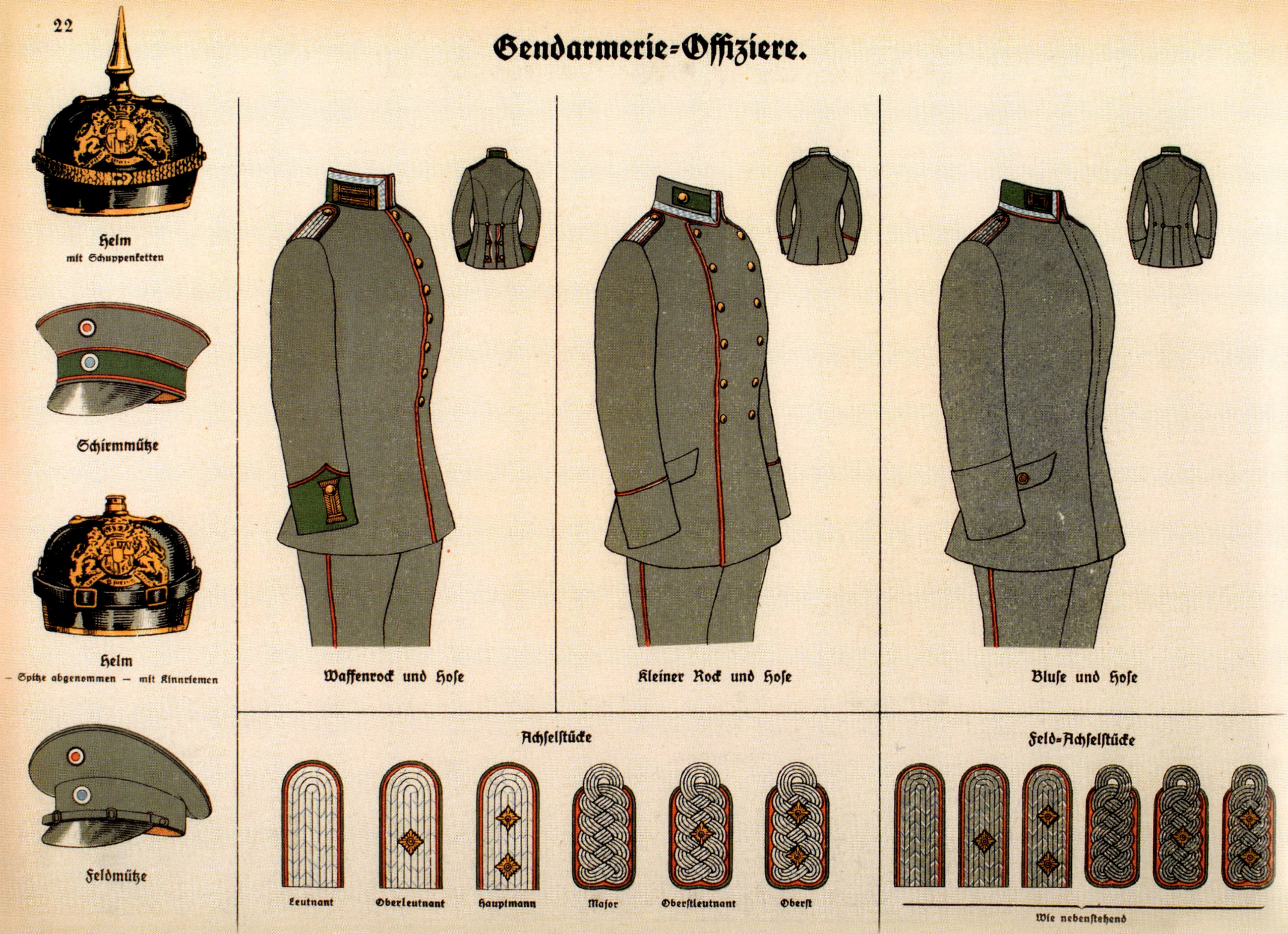

Bezirkskommandos und Bekleidungsämter.

Helm
mit Schuppenketten

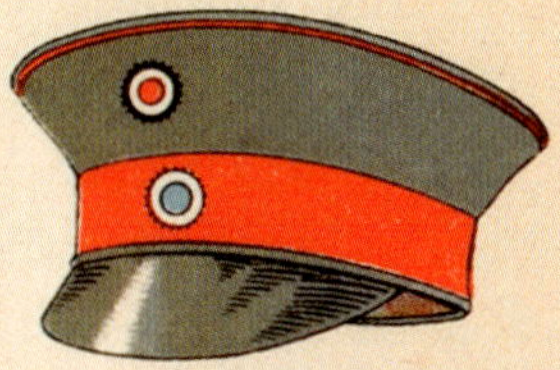

Schirmmütze

Feldmütze

Waffenrock und Hose

Kleiner Rock und Hose

Bluse und Hose

Achselstücke

für Offiziere der Bezirkskommandos

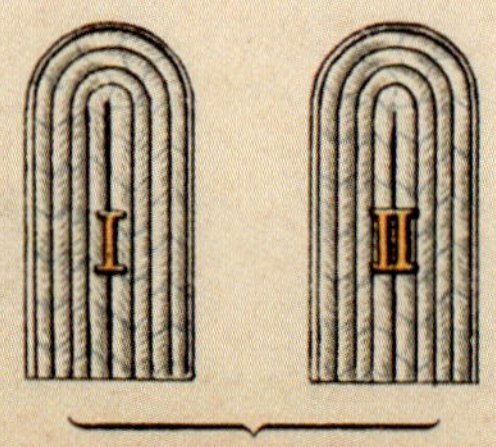

für Offiziere der Bekleidungs-Ämter

Feld-Achselstücke

Wie nebenstehend

Zeug- und Feuerwerks-Offiziere.

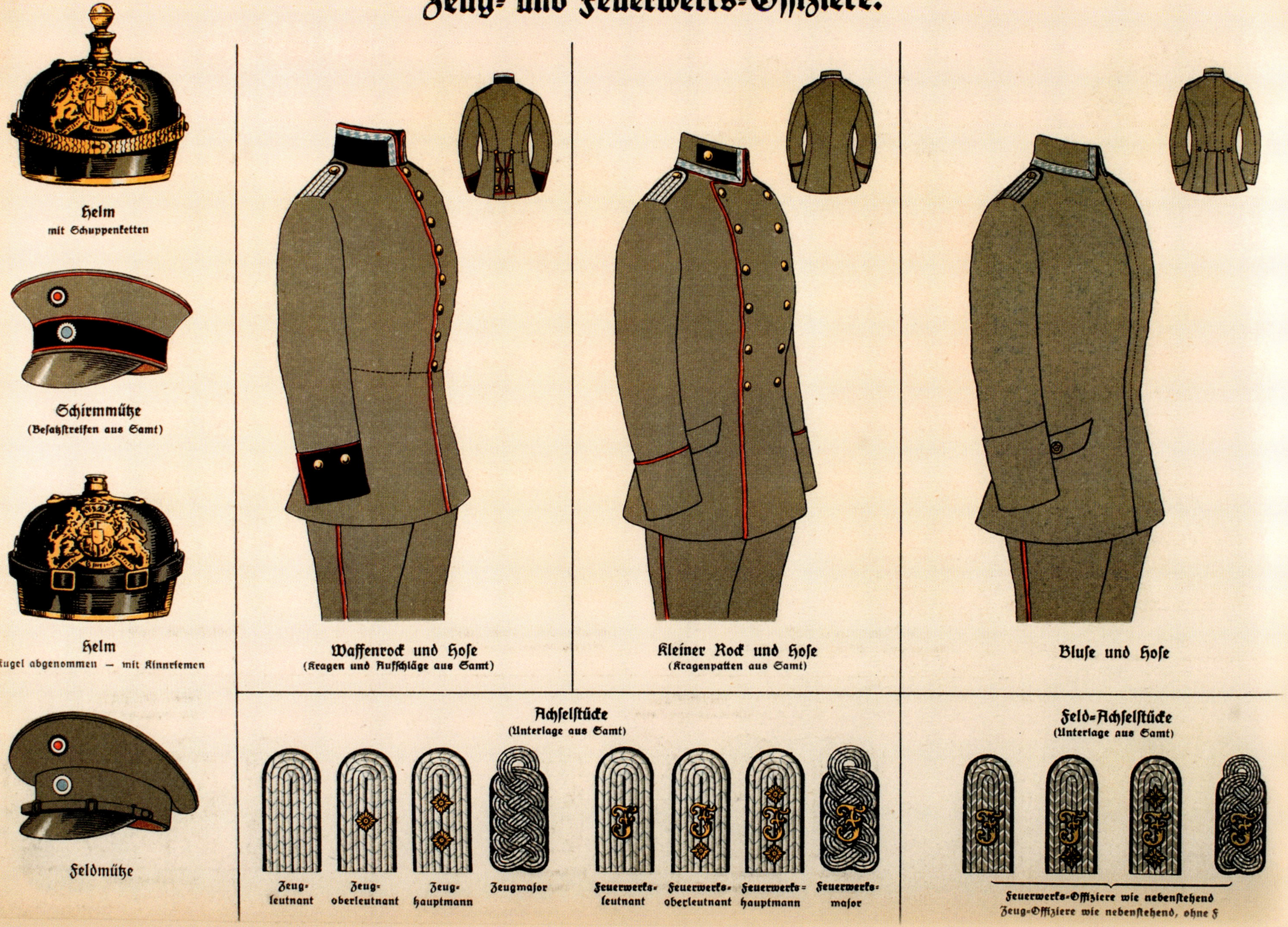

Festungsbau-Offiziere.

Helm
mit Schuppenketten

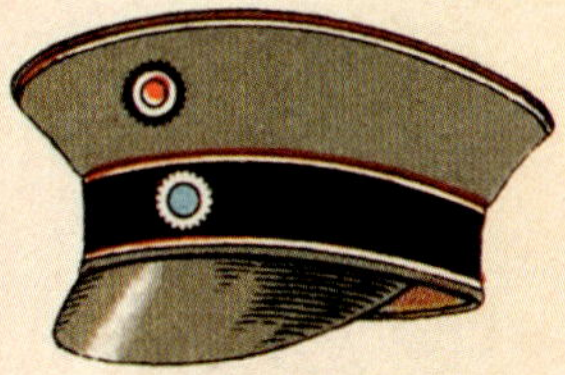

Schirmmütze
(Besatzstreifen aus Samt)

Helm
– Spitze abgenommen – mit Kinnriemen

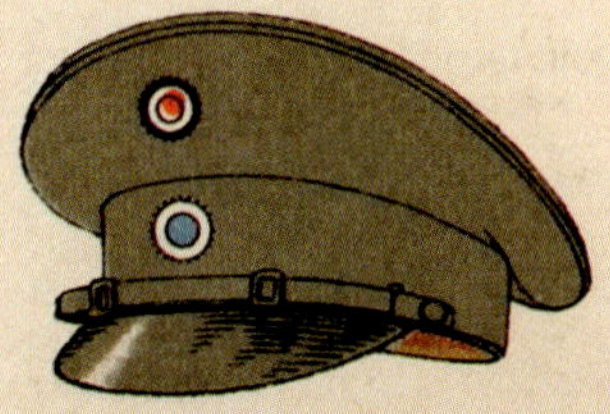

Feldmütze

Waffenrock und Hose
(Kragen und Aufschläge aus Samt)

Kleiner Rock und Hose
(Kragenpatten aus Samt)

Bluse und Hose

Achselstücke
(Unterlage aus Samt)

Festungsbau-leutnant — Festungsbau-oberleutnant — Festungsbau-hauptmann — Festungsbau-major

Feld-Achselstücke
(Unterlage aus Samt)

Wie nebenstehend

Sanitäts-Offiziere im Generalsrang.

Helm mit Schuppenketten
(Zum Paradeanzug mit Busch aus weißen und blauen Hahnenfedern)

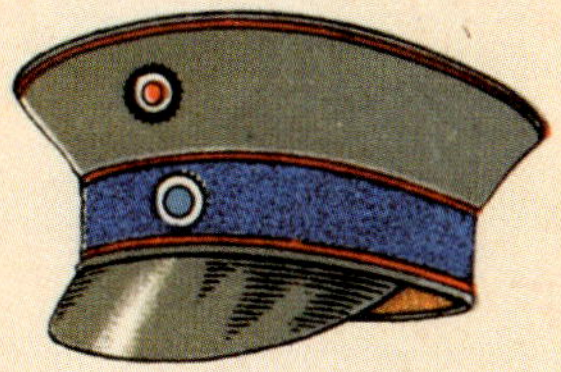

Schirmmütze

Helm
– Spitze abgenommen – mit Kinnriemen

Feldmütze

Waffenrock und Hose

Kleiner Rock und Hose

Bluse und Hose

Achselstücke
(Unterlage aus Samt)

Ober-Generalarzt

Generalstabsarzt der Armee

Generalstabsarzt der Armee mit dem Range eines Generalleutnants

Feld-Achselstücke
(Unterlage aus Samt)

Wie nebenstehend

Sonstige Sanitätsoffiziere.

Helm
mit Schuppenketten

Schirmmütze

Helm
– Spitze abgenommen – mit Kinnriemen

Feldmütze

Waffenrock und Hose

Kleiner Rock und Hose

Bluse und Hose

Achselstücke
(Unterlage aus Samt)

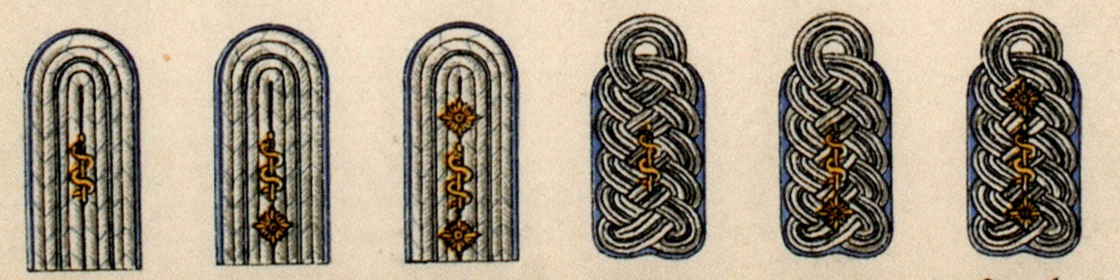

Feld-Achselstücke
(Unterlage aus Samt)

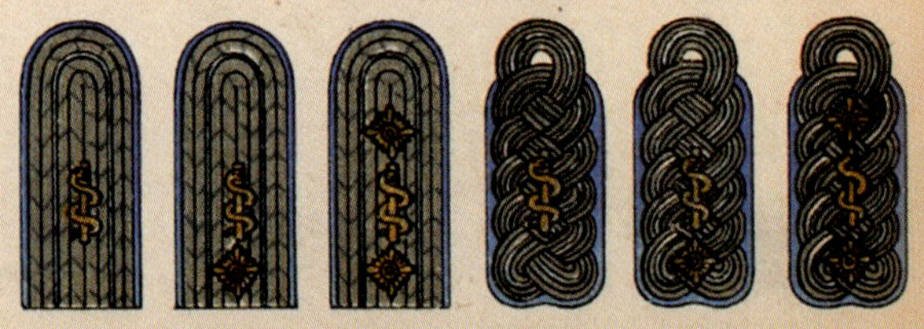

Wie nebenstehend

Veterinär-Offiziere.

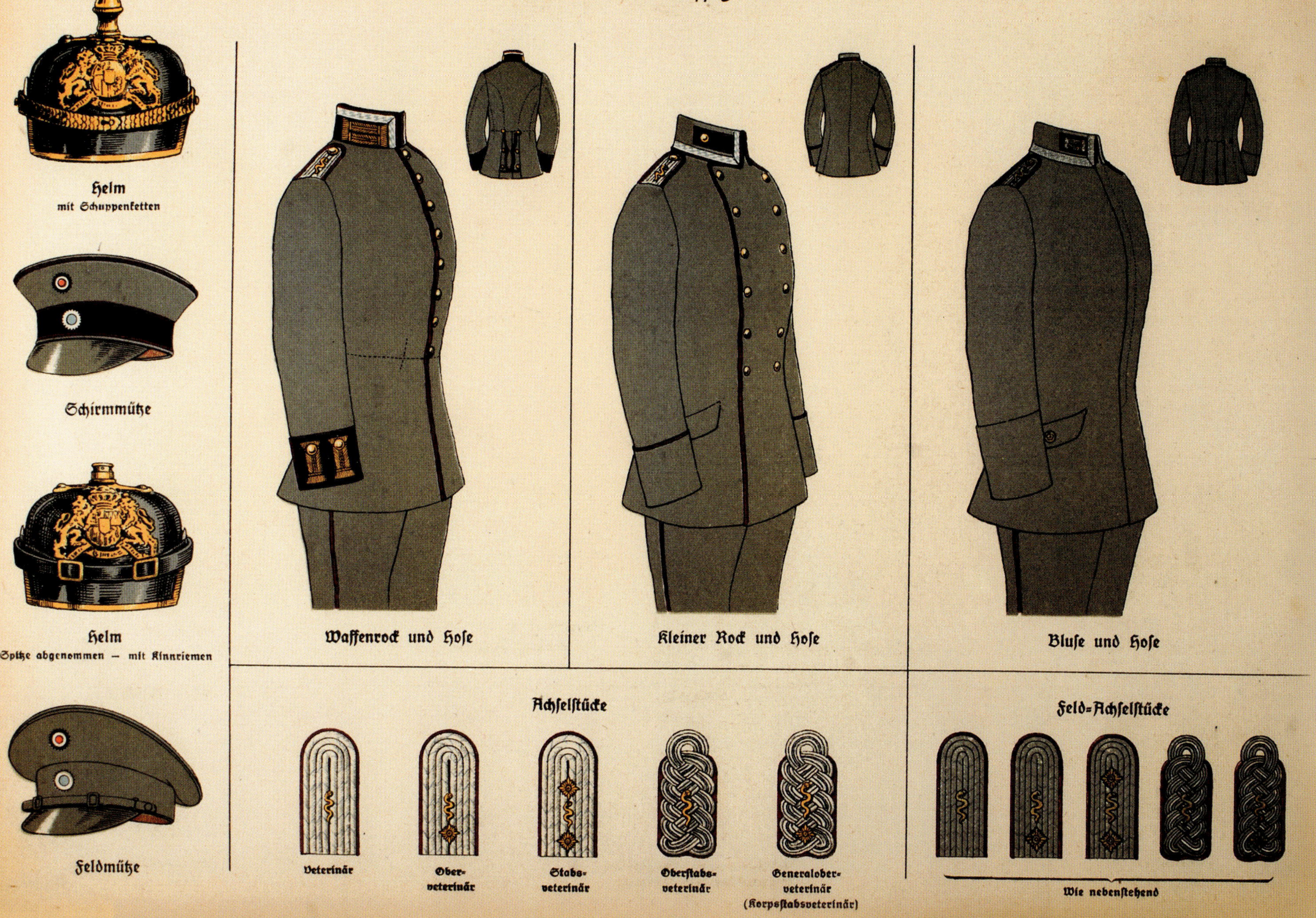

Kriegsministerium.

Vortragende Räte der I. Rangklasse.

Helm mit Schuppenketten
(Zum Paradeanzug mit Busch aus weißen und blauen Hahnenfedern)

Schirmmütze
(Besatzstreifen aus Samt)

Helm
— Spitze abgenommen — mit Kinnriemen

Feldmütze

Waffenrock und Hose
(Kragen und Aufschläge aus Sammt)

Kleiner Rock und Hose
(Kragenpatten aus Samt)

Bluse und Hose

Achselstücke

Wirklicher Geheimer Oberkriegsrat,
Wirklicher Geheimer Oberbaurat

Feld=Achselstücke

Wie nebenstehend

Kriegsministerium.

Vortragende Räte der II. und III. Rangklasse.

Helm
mit Schuppenketten

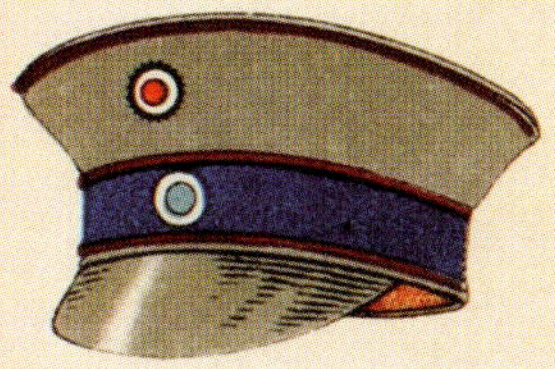

Schirmmütze
(Besatzstreifen aus Samt)

Helm
— Spitze abgenommen — mit Kinnriemen

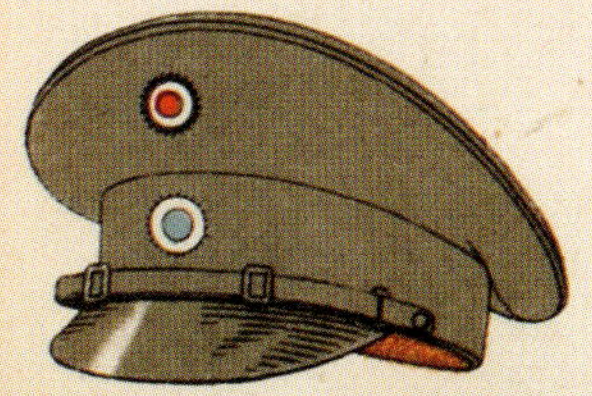

Feldmütze

Waffenrock und Hose
(Kragen und Aufschläge aus Samt)

Kleiner Rock und Hose
(Kragenpatten aus Samt)

Bluse und Hose

Achselstücke

Geheimer Kriegsrat,
Geheimer Baurat

Wirklicher Geheimer Kriegsrat,
Wirklicher Geheimer Baurat

Feld-Achselstücke

Wie nebenstehend

Kriegsministerium.

Geheime expedierende Sekretäre, Geheime Registratoren und Geheimer Kanzleivorsteher.

Helm
mit Schuppenketten

Schirmmütze
(Besatzstreifen aus Samt)

Helm
– Spitze abgenommen – mit Kinnriemen

Feldmütze

Waffenrock und Hose
(Kragen und Aufschläge aus Samt)

Kleiner Rock und Hose
(Kragenpatten aus Samt)

Bluse und Hose

Achselstücke
(Unterlage aus Samt)

Geh. exp. Sekretär,
Geh. Registrator,
Geh. Kanzleivorsteher

als Rechnungsrat
oder
Kanzleirat

als Geheimer Rechnungsrat
oder
Geheimer Kanzleirat

Feld-Achselstücke
(Unterlage aus Samt)

Wie nebenstehend

Kriegsministerium.

Kalkulatoren, Bausekretäre und Kanzleisekretäre.

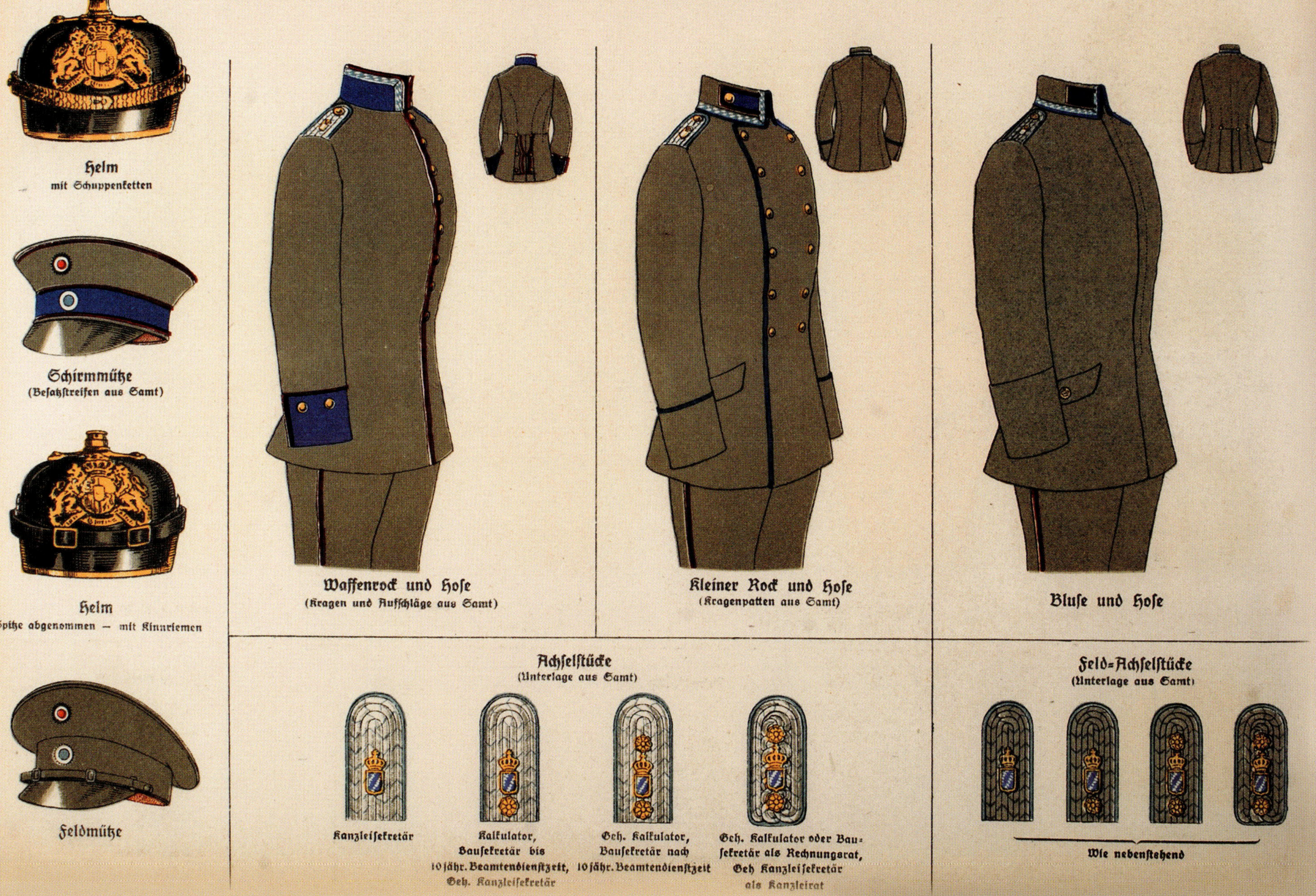

Intendantur.

Militär-Intendanten der I. Rangklasse.

Helm mit Schuppenketten
(Zum Paradeanzug mit Busch aus weißen und blauen Hahnenfedern)

Schirmmütze
(Besatzstreifen aus Samt)

Helm
– Spitze abgenommen – mit Kinnriemen

Feldmütze

Waffenrock und Hose
(Kragen und Aufschläge aus Samt)

Kleiner Rock und Hose
(Kragenpatten aus Samt)

Bluse und Hose

Achselstücke

Wirklicher Geheimer Oberkriegsrat

Feld-Achselstücke

Wie nebenstehend

Intendantur.

Militär-Intendanten (Oberintendanturräte) der II. u. III. Rangklasse, Oberintendanturräte, Intendanturräte und Intendantur-Assessoren.

Helm
mit Schuppenketten

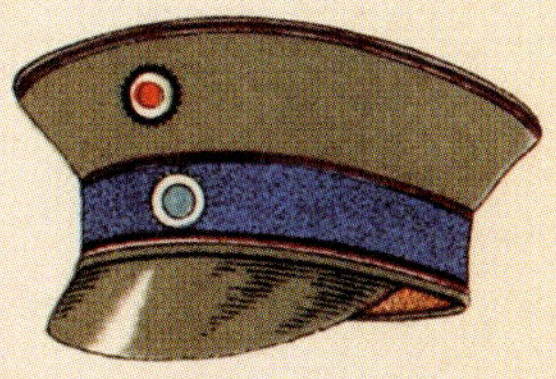

Schirmmütze
(Besatzstreifen aus Samt)

Helm
– Spitze abgenommen – mit Kinnriemen

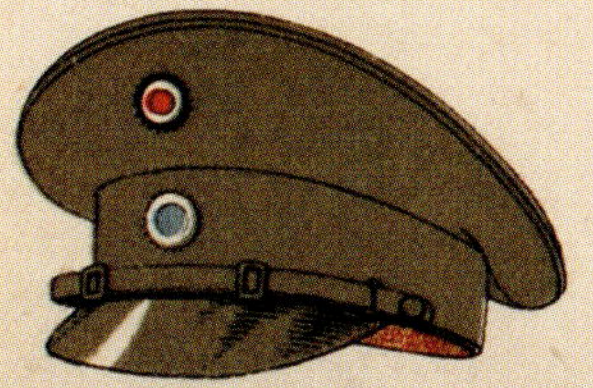

Feldmütze

Waffenrock und Hose
(Kragen und Aufschläge aus Samt)

Kleiner Rock und Hose
(Kragenpatten aus Samt)

Bluse und Hose

Achselstücke

Intendantur-Assessor — Intendantur-rat — Ober-intendanturrat — Militär-Intendant: III. Rangklasse, Geh. Kriegsrat — II. Rangklasse, Wirkl. Geh. Kriegsrat

Feld-Achselstücke

Wie nebenstehend

Intendantur.

Oberintendantursekretäre und Oberintendanturregistratoren, Intendantursekretäre, Intendanturregistratoren, Intendanturdiätäre.

Helm
mit Schuppenketten

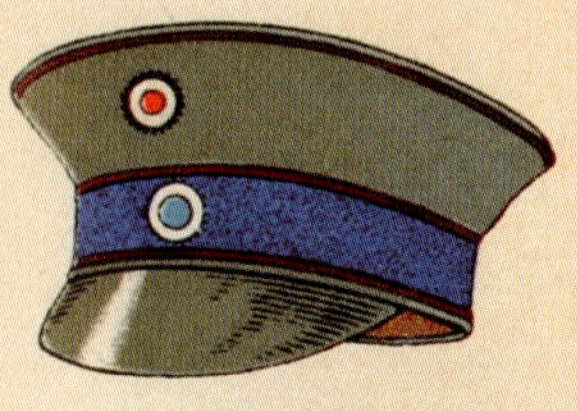

Schirmmütze
(Besatzstreifen aus Samt)

Helm
— Spitze abgenommen — mit Kinnriemen

Feldmütze

Waffenrock und Hose
(Kragen und Aufschläge aus Samt)

Kleiner Rock und Hose
(Kragenpatten aus Samt)

Bluse und Hose

Achselstücke
(Unterlage aus Samt)

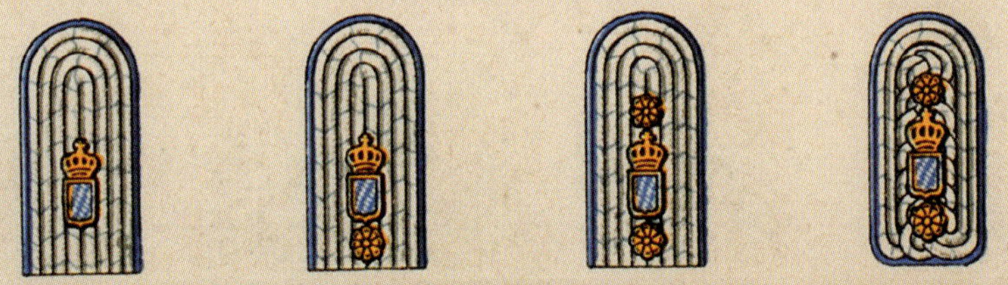

Intendanturdiätär — Intendantursekretär, Intendanturregistrator — Oberintendantursekretär, Oberintendanturregistrator — Oberintendantursekretär Oberintendanturregistrator als Rechnungsrat

Feld-Achselstücke
(Unterlage aus Samt)

Wie nebenstehend

Militär-Justizverwaltung.

Oberkriegsgerichtsräte und Kriegsgerichtsräte.

Helm
mit Schuppenketten

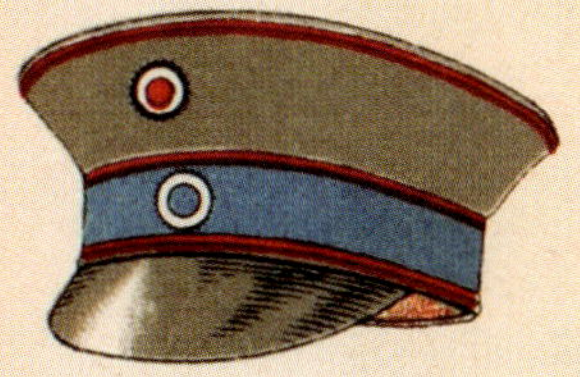

Schirmmütze
(Besatzstreifen aus Samt)

Helm
– Spitze abgenommen – mit Kinnriemen

Feldmütze

Waffenrock und Hose
(Kragen und Aufschläge aus Samt)

Kleiner Rock und Hose
(Kragenpatten aus Samt)

Bluse und Hose

Achselstücke

Kriegsgerichtsrat
der V. Rangklasse

Oberkriegsgerichtsrat
und Kriegsgerichtsrat
der IV. Rangklasse

Oberkriegsgerichtsrat
der III. Rangklasse

Feld-Achselstücke

Wie nebenstehend

Militär-Justizverwaltung.

Oberkriegsgerichtssekretäre, Kriegsgerichtssekretäre, Militär-Gerichtsassistenten.

Helm
mit Schuppenketten

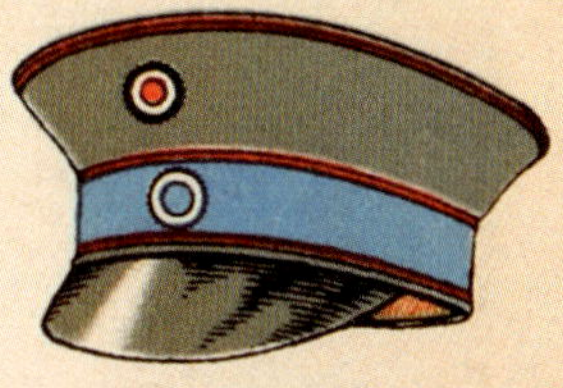

Schirmmütze

Helm
– Spitze abgenommen – mit Kinnriemen

Feldmütze

Waffenrock und Hose

Kleiner Rock und Hose

Bluse und Hose

Achselstücke

Militärgerichts-Assistent

Kriegsgerichts-sekretär

Oberkriegs-gerichtssekretär

Oberkriegsgerichts-sekretär als Rechnungsrat

Feld-Achselstücke

Wie nebenstehend

Militärbaubeamte.

Intendantur- und Bauräte, Militär-Bauamtmänner, Intendantur- und Bauassessoren.

Helm
mit Schuppenketten

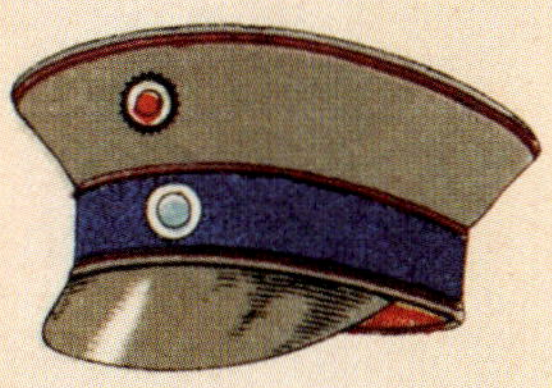

Schirmmütze
(Besatzstreifen aus Samt)

Helm
— Spitze abgenommen — mit Kinnriemen

Feldmütze

Waffenrock und Hose
(Kragen und Aufschläge aus Samt)

Kleiner Rock und Hose
(Kragenpatten aus Samt)

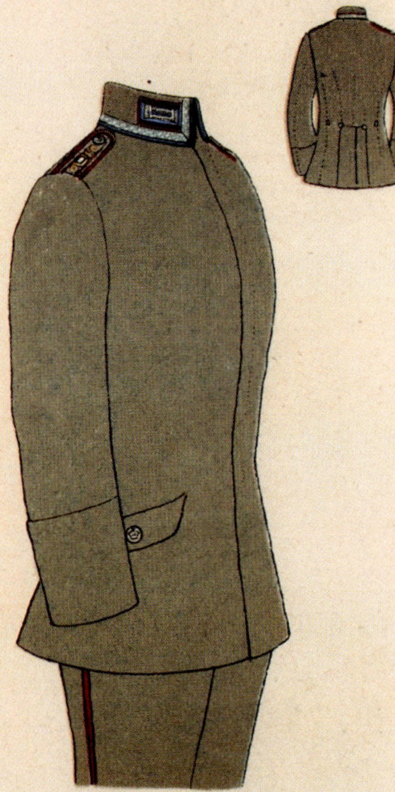

Bluse und Hose

Achselstücke

Militär-Bauamtmann, Intendantur- u. Bauassessor

Intendantur- u. Baurat, Militär-Bauamtmann als Baurat

Intendantur- u. Baurat mit dem Titel und Rang eines Geheimen Baurats

Feld-Achselstücke

Wie nebenstehend

Militärbaubeamte.

Oberintendanturbausekretäre, Intendanturbausekretäre, Intendanturbaukalkulatoren.

Helm
mit Schuppenketten

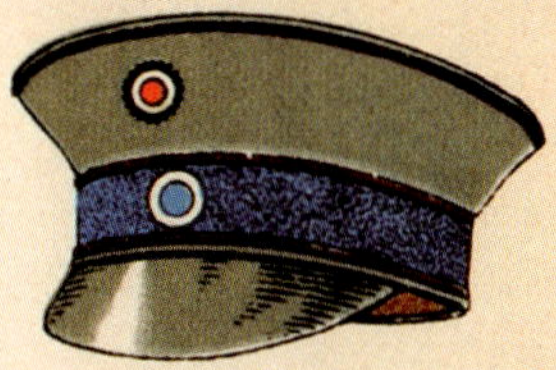

Schirmmütze
(Besatzstreifen aus Samt)

Helm
– Spitze abgenommen – mit Kinnriemen

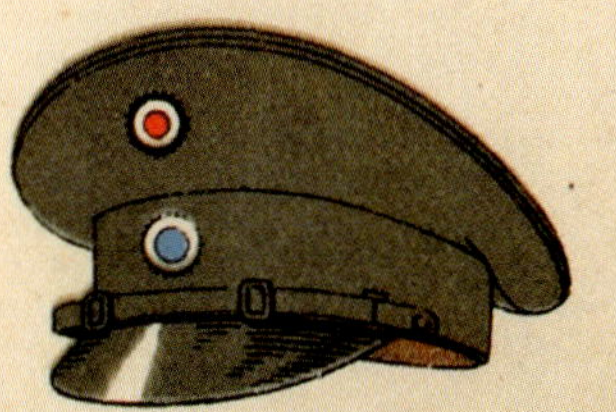

Feldmütze

Waffenrock und Hose
(Kragen und Aufschläge aus Samt)

Kleiner Rock und Hose
(Kragenpatten aus Samt)

Bluse und Hose

Achselstücke
(Unterlage aus Samt)

Intendanturbausekretär, Intendanturbaukalkulator

Oberintendanturbausekretär nach 10jähr. Dienstzeit als etatsm. Beamter

Oberintendanturbausekretär als Rechnungsrat

Feld-Achselstücke
(Unterlage aus Samt)

Wie nebenstehend

Militärbaubeamte.

Obermilitärbausekretäre, Obermilitärbauregistratoren, Militärbausekretäre und Militärbauregistratoren.

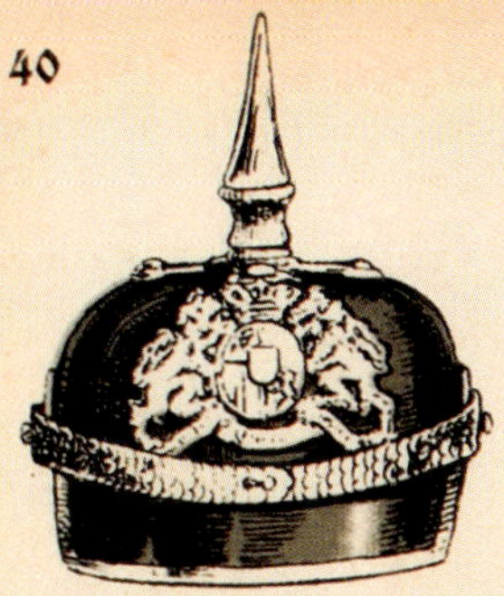

Helm
mit Schuppenketten

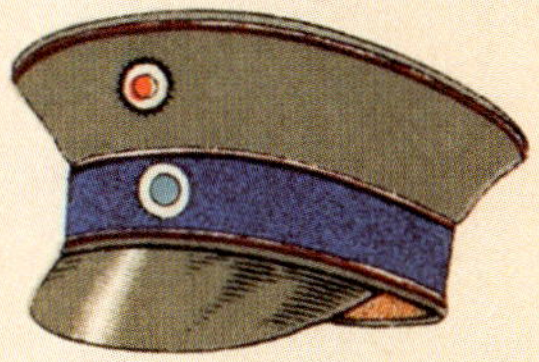

Schirmmütze

Helm
– Spitze abgenommen – mit Kinnriemen

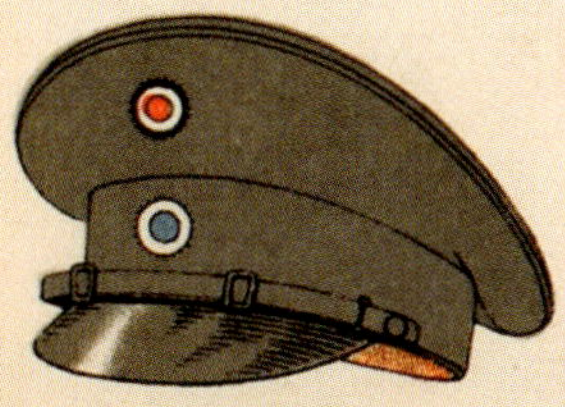

Feldmütze

Waffenrock und Hose

Kleiner Rock und Hose

Bluse und Hose

Achselstücke

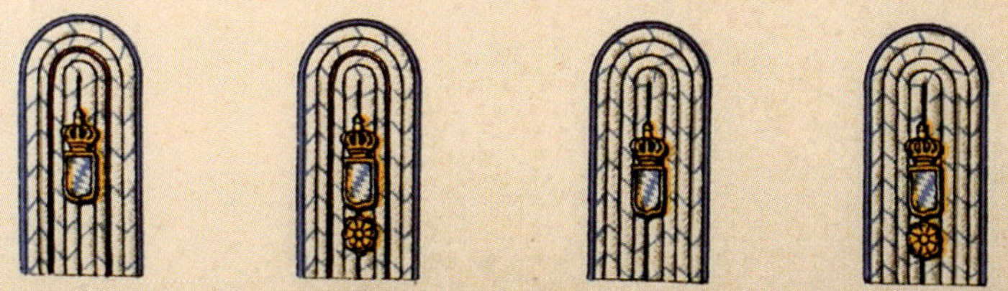

Militärbausekretär und Obermilitärbausekretär mit einem Stellendienstalter bis zu 6 Jahren / von mehr als 6 Jahren

Militärbauregistrator und Obermilitärbauregistrator mit einem Stellendienstalter bis zu 6 Jahren / von mehr als 6 Jahren

Feld-Achselstücke

Wie nebenstehend

Militär-Apotheker.

Oberapotheker.

Helm
mit Schuppenketten

Schirmmütze
(Besatzstreifen aus Samt)

Helm
– Spitze abgenommen – mit Kinnriemen

Feldmütze

Waffenrock und Hose
(Kragen und Aufschläge aus Samt)

Kleiner Rock und Hose
(Kragenpatten aus Samt)

Bluse und Hose

Achselstücke

Oberapotheker

Oberapotheker,
die die Übung A mit Erfolg abgeleistet haben oder
mit einem Rangdienstalter von mehr als 6 Jahren

Feld-Achselstücke

Wie nebenstehend

Zahlmeister, Kassenbeamte, Rendant beim Generalstab, Proviantamts-, Garnisonverw.-, Lazarettverw.-, Bekleidungsamts-Beamte, Beamte der Militär-Bildungsanstalten und der militärischen Strafanstalten auf Oberhaus, der Remonte-Inspektion, Remonte-Depots und -Anstalt.

(Helmbeschlag und Knöpfe: Zahlmeister versilbert, die übrigen voraufgeführten Beamten vergoldet).

Helm
mit Schuppenketten

Schirmmütze

Helm
– Spitze abgenommen – mit Kinnriemen

Feldmütze

Waffenrock und Hose

Kleiner Rock und Hose

Bluse und Hose

(Achselstücke siehe Tafel 45)

Achselstücke zu Tafel 44.

	Inspektor mit einem Stellendienstalter von 6 Jahren und darunter	Zahlmeister, Inspektor mit einem Stellendienstalter von mehr als 6 Jahren	Kriegs- und Pensions-Zahlmeister, Kontrolleur d. Gen.-Mil.-Kasse, Kassier d. Mil.-Pens.-Kasse, Oberbuchhalter, Oberzahlmeister, Rendant, Proviantmeister	als Rechnungsrat	als Geheimer Rechnungsrat
Zahlmeister					
Kassenbeamte					
Rendant beim Generalstab					
Bekleidungsamtbeamte					
Proviantamtsbeamte					

		Inspektor mit einem Stellendienstalter von 6 Jahren und darunter	Inspektor mit einem Stellendienstalter von mehr als 6 Jahren	Oberinspektor, Rendant, Administrator	als Rechnungs- oder Kanzleirat	als Geheimer Rechnungsrat
Garnisonverwaltungsbeamte						
Lazarettverwaltungsbeamte						
Beamte der Militär-Bildungsanstalten und der militärischen Strafanstalten						
Beamte der Remonte-Inspektion, der Remonte-Depots und der Remonte-Anstalt	Rat der Remonte-Depotverwaltung, Administratoren der Remonte-Depots, Remonte-Depots-Inspektoren					
	Kanzleisekretäre und Registratoren					

Feldachselstücke wie Achselstücke, jedoch schmäler (allgemein 4,5 cm breit), ohne Steifeinlage, Schnüre und Abzeichen matt

Verkehrstruppen.

Werkstättenvorsteher bei der Kraftfahrkompagnie.

Helm
mit Schuppenketten

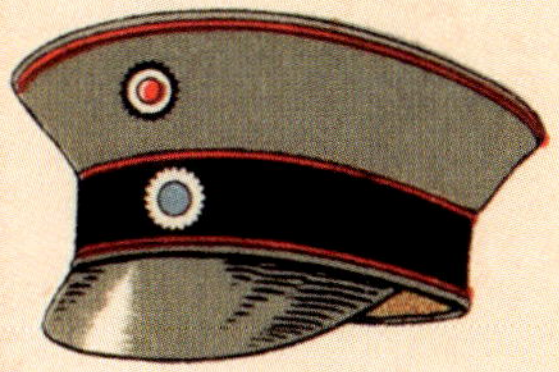

Schirmmütze

Helm
– Spitze abgenommen – mit Kinnriemen

Feldmütze

Waffenrock und Hose

Kleiner Rock und Hose

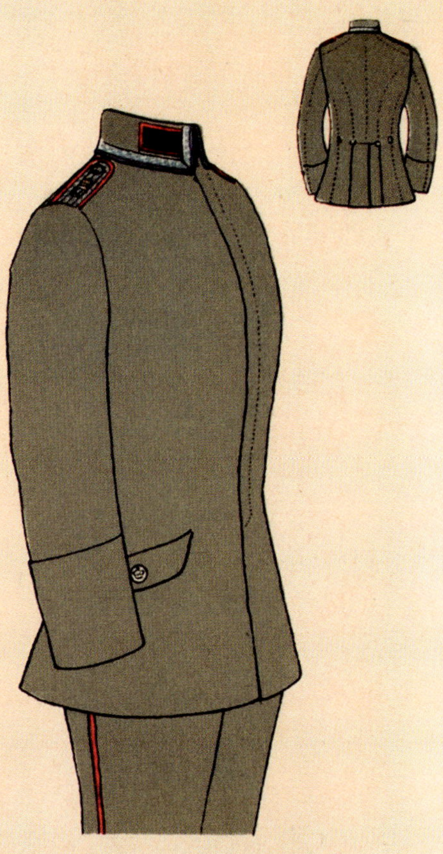

Bluse und Hose

Achselstücke

Werkstättenvorsteher

Feld-Achselstücke

Wie nebenstehend

II.

Uniformen für Mannschaften.

Inhaltsverzeichnis:

Infanterie.

Infanterie-Leib-Regiment.

Helm
mit Kinnriemen

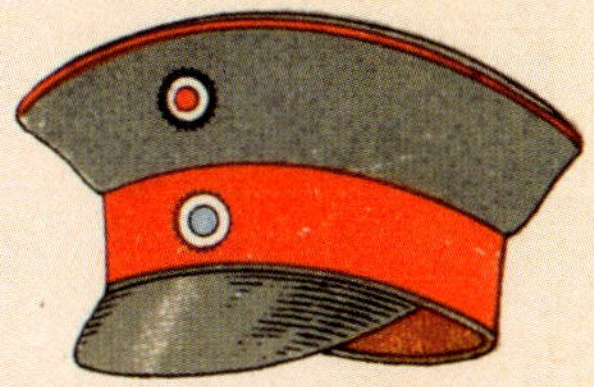

Schirmmütze

Helm
– Spitze abgenommen – mit Kinnriemen

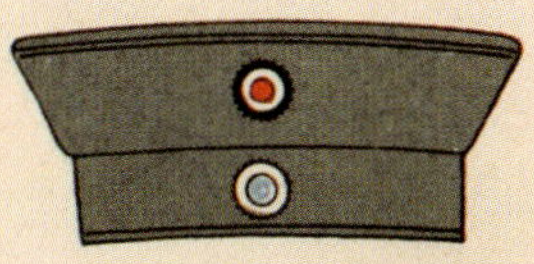

Feldmütze

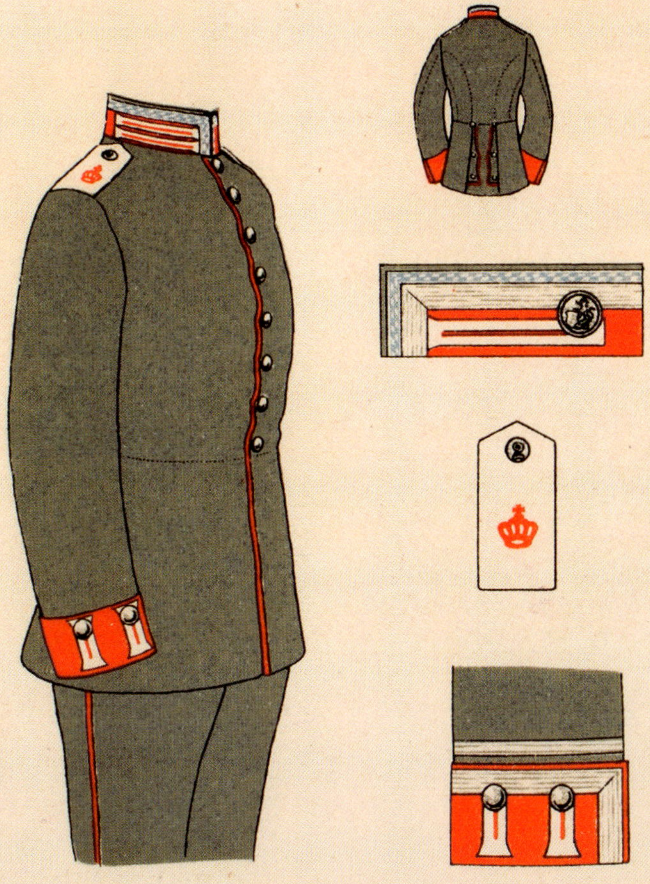

Waffenrock und Hose

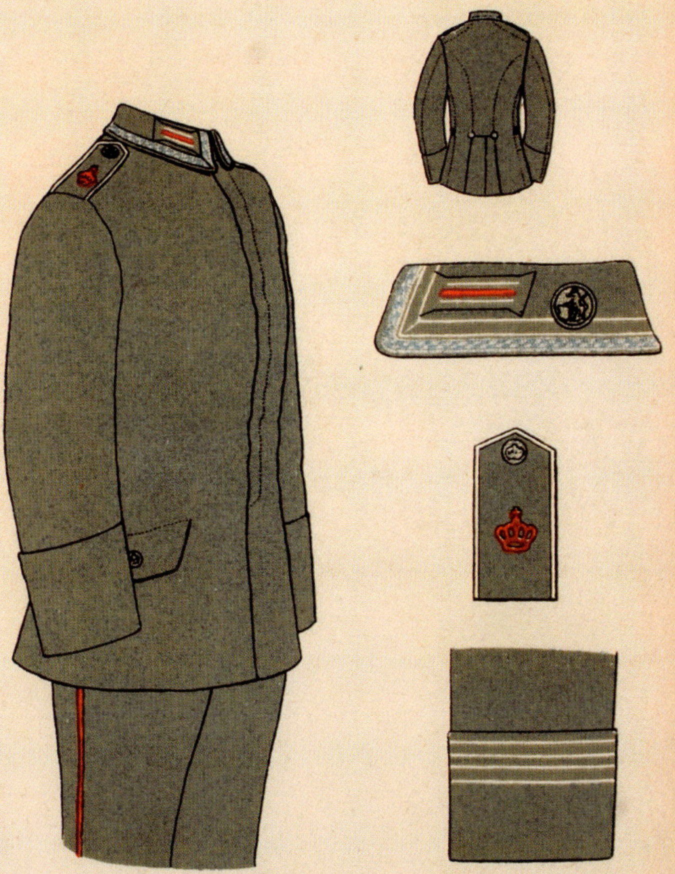

Bluse und Hose

Infanterie.

Sämtliche übrigen Infanterie-Regimenter.

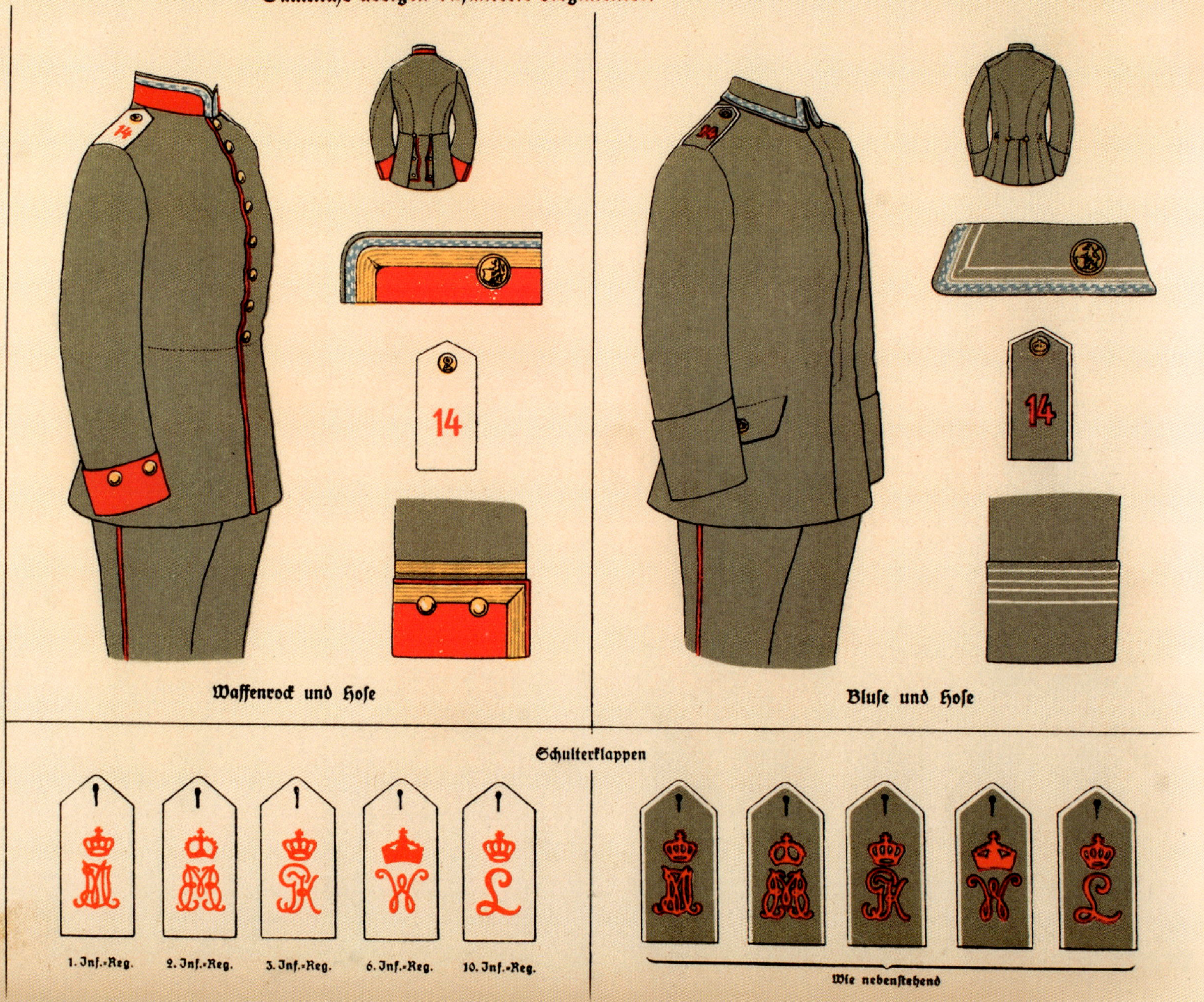

Unteroffizierschulen.

Helm
mit Kinnriemen

Schirmmütze

Helm
– Spitze abgenommen – mit Kinnriemen

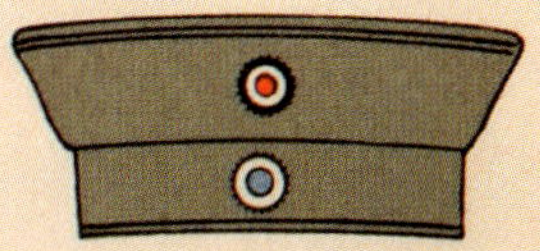

Feldmütze

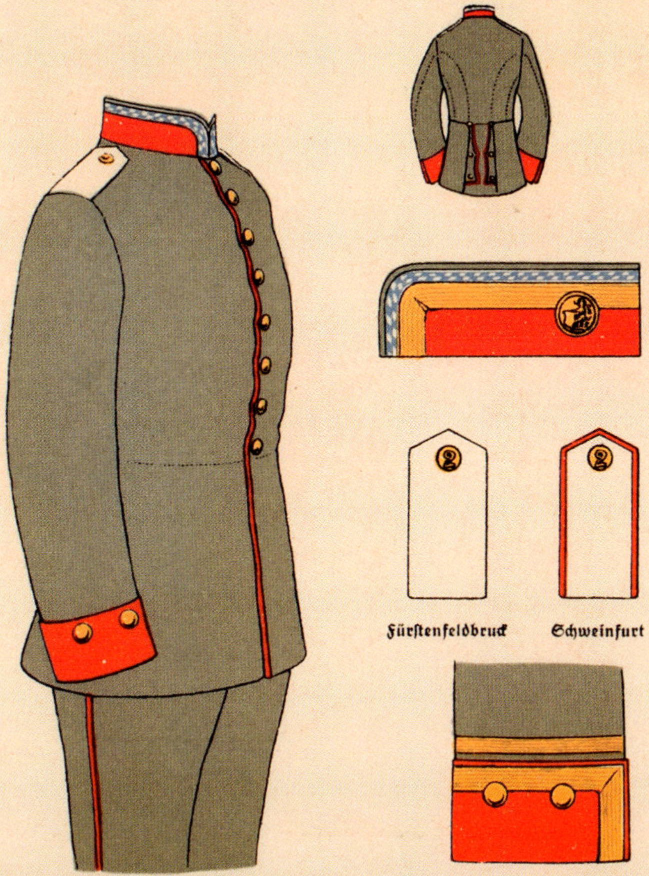

Waffenrock und Hose

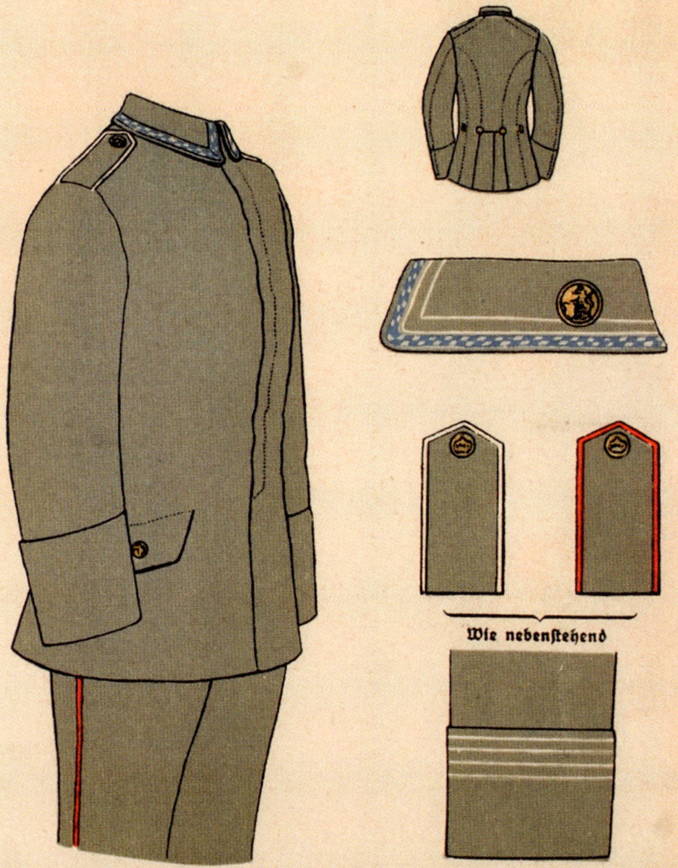

Bluse und Hose

Bezirkskommandos u. Handwerker-Abteilungen der Bekleidungsämter.

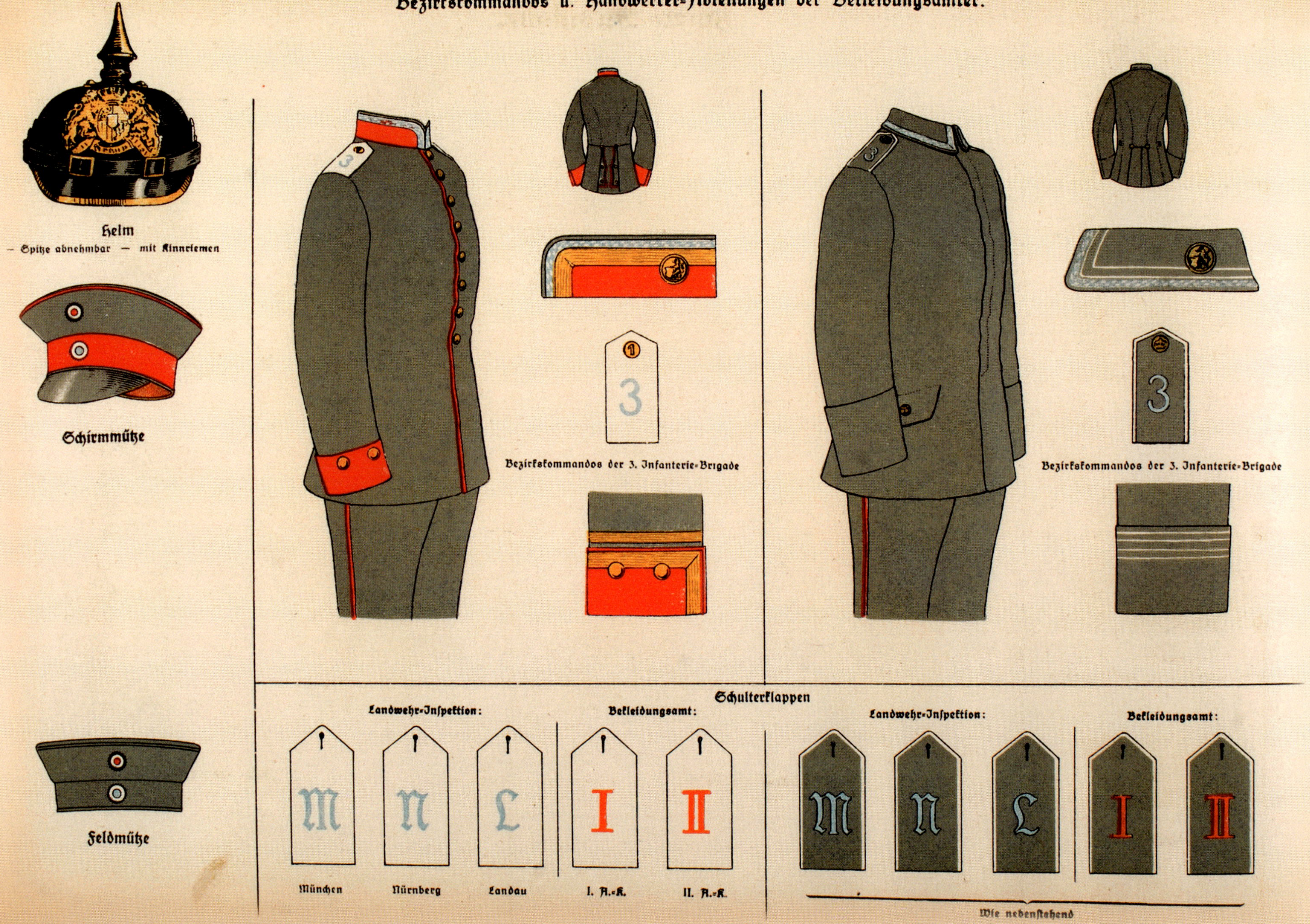

Jäger-Bataillone.

Tschako
mit Kinnriemen

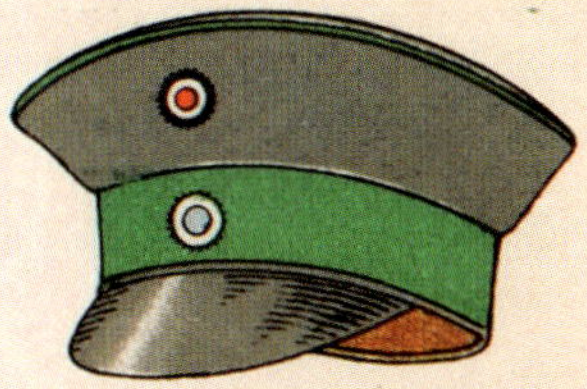

Schirmmütze

Tschako
— Feldzeichen abgenommen — mit Kinnriemen

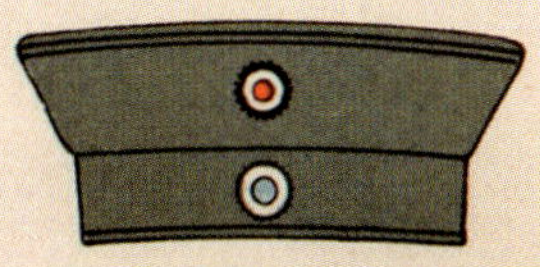

Feldmütze

Waffenrock und Hose

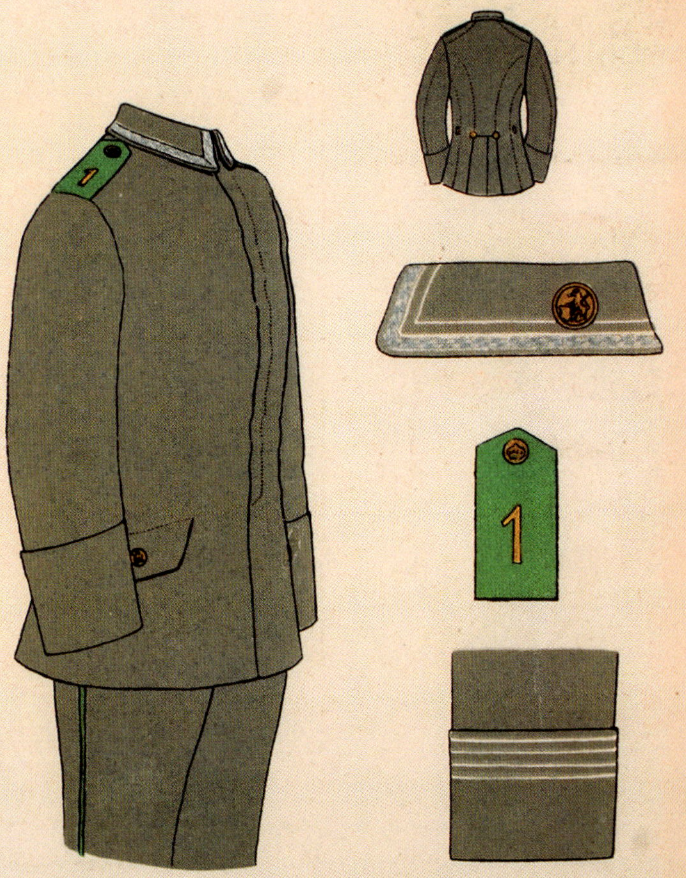

Bluse und Hose

Kavallerie.

1. Schweres Reiter-Regiment.

Helm
mit Kinnriemen

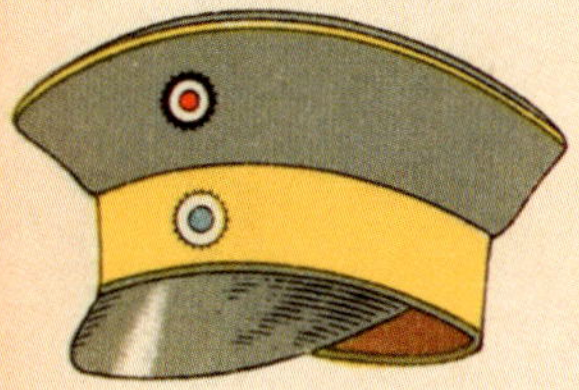

Schirmmütze

Helm
– Spitze abgenommen – mit Kinnriemen

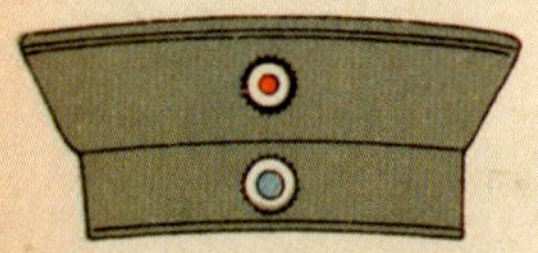

Feldmütze

Waffenrock und Hose

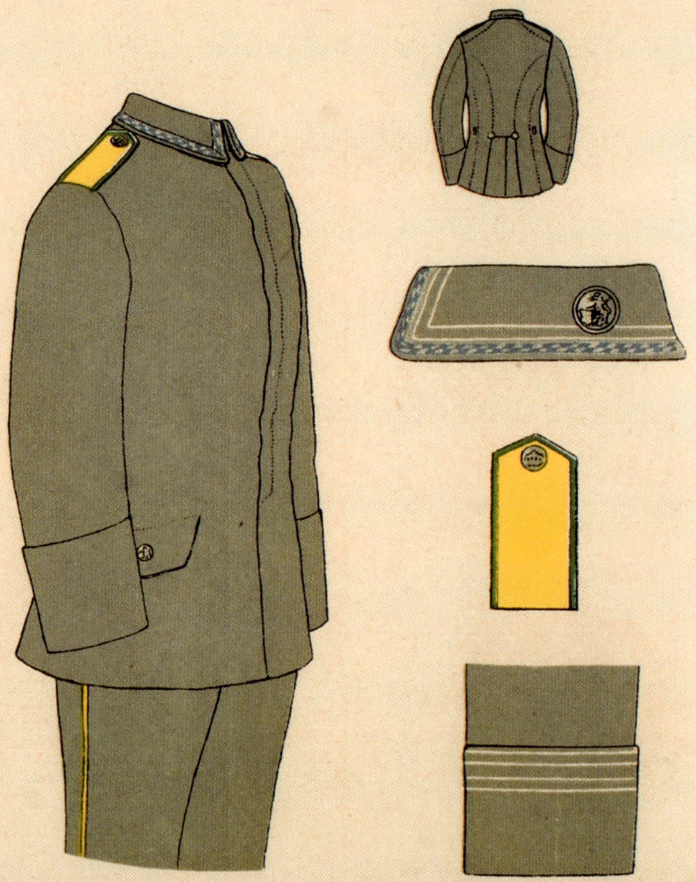

Bluse und Hose

Kavallerie.

2. Schweres Reiter-Regiment.

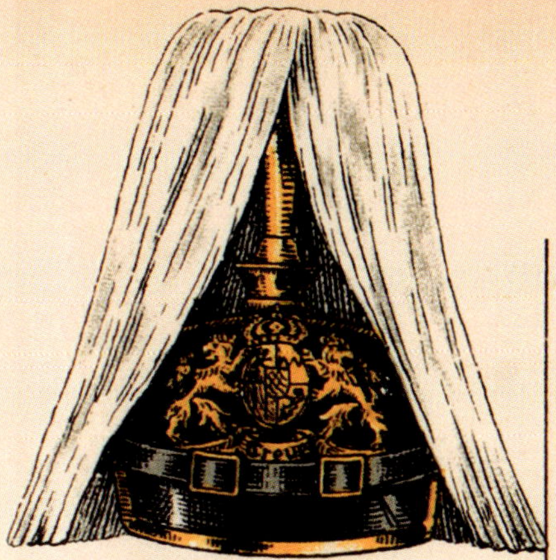

Helm mit Kinnriemen
und mit weißem Haarbusch

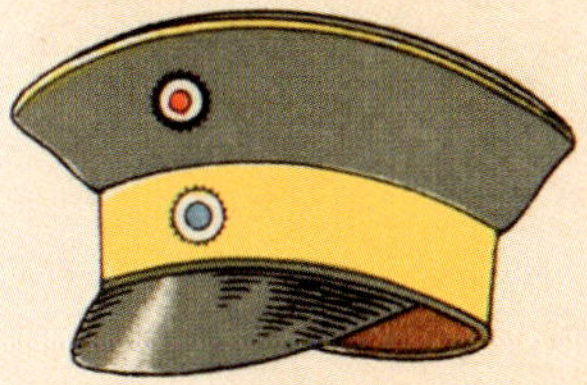

Schirmmütze

Helm
– Spitze abgenommen – mit Kinnriemen

Feldmütze

Waffenrock (mit Paraderabatte) **und Hose**

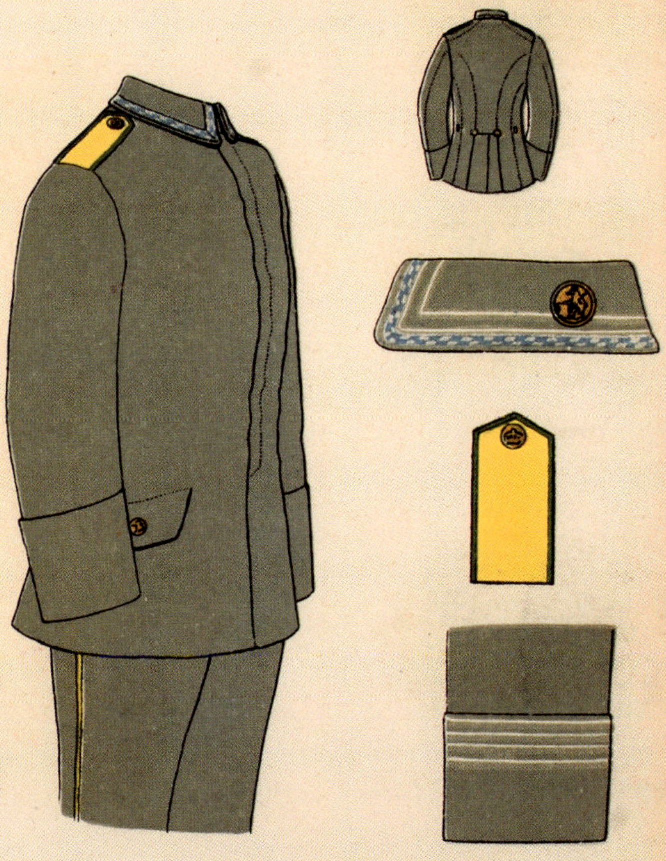

Bluse und Hose

Kavallerie.

1. Ulanen-Regiment.

Tschapka
mit Kinnriemen

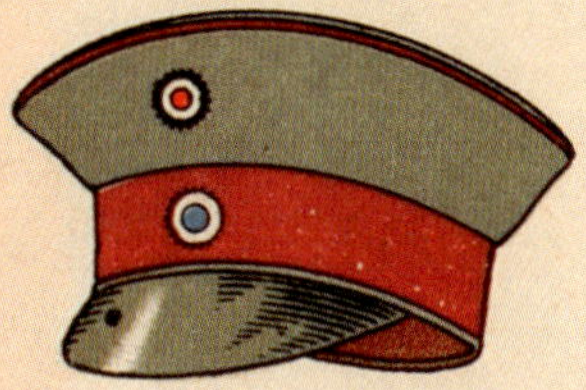

Schirmmütze

Tschapka
— Deckel abgenommen — mit Kinnriemen

Feldmütze

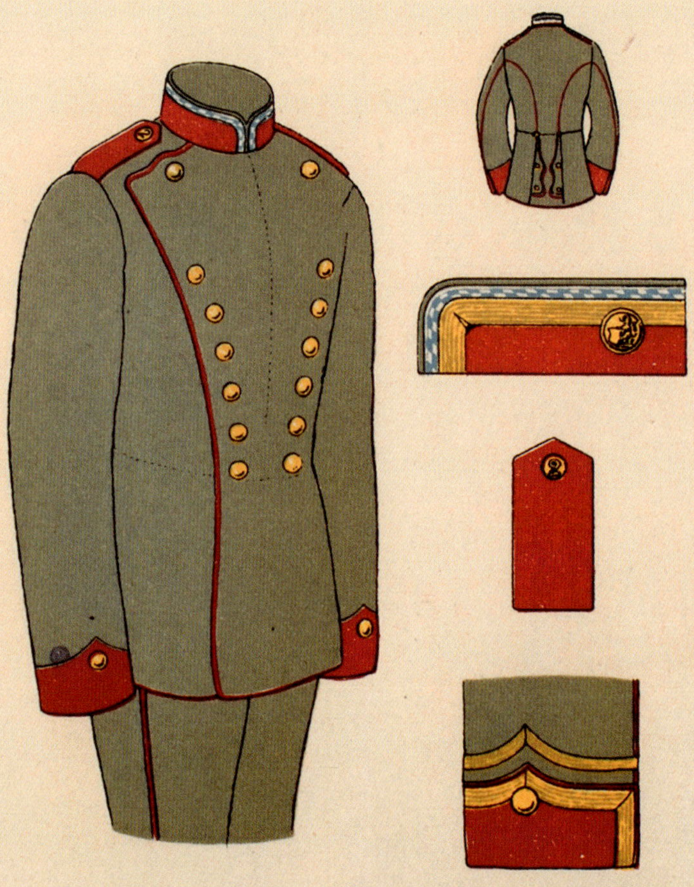

Waffenrock und Hose

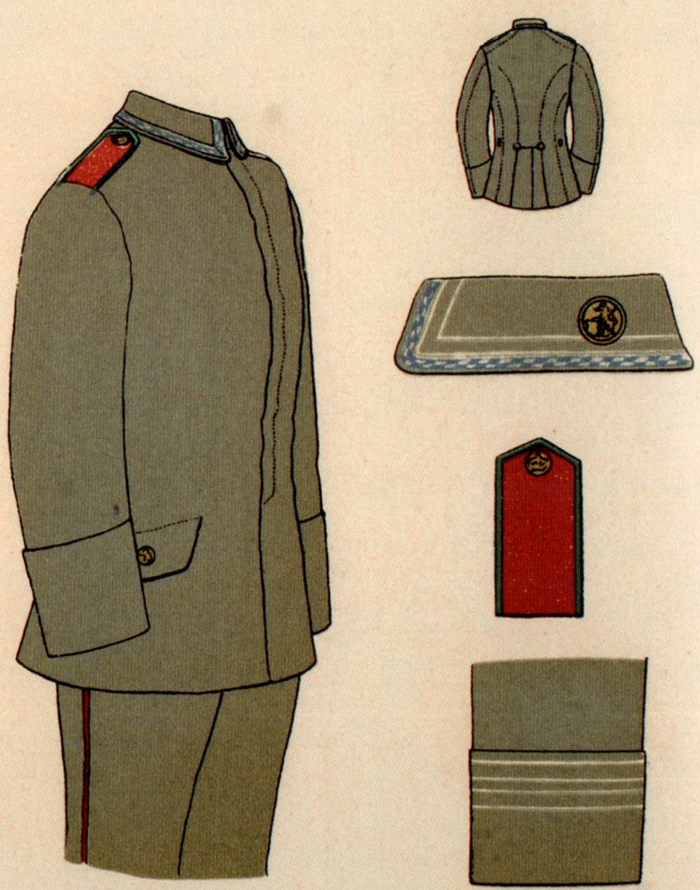

Bluse und Hose

Kavallerie.

2. Ulanen-Regiment.

Tschapka mit Kinnriemen und mit weißem Haarbusch

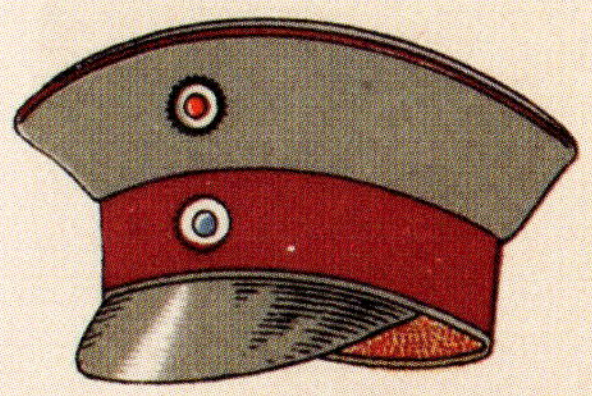

Schirmmütze

Tschapka
— Deckel abgenommen — mit Kinnriemen

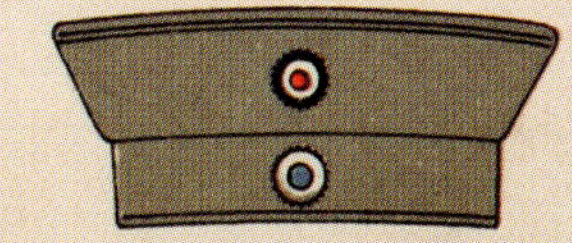

Feldmütze

Waffenrock (mit Paraderabatte) und Hose

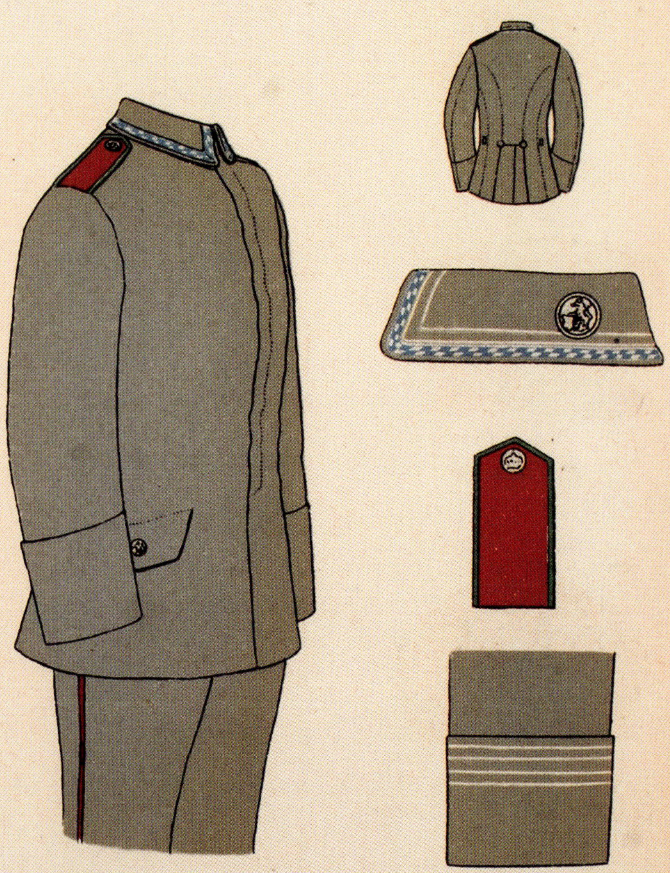

Bluse und Hose

Kavallerie.

1. Chevaulegers-Regiment.

Helm
mit Kinnriemen

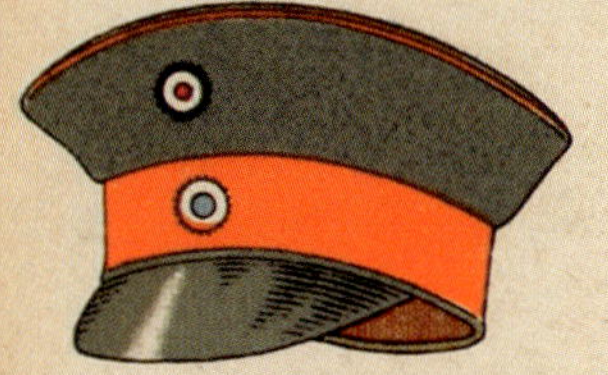

Schirmmütze

Helm
– Spitze abgenommen – mit Kinnriemen

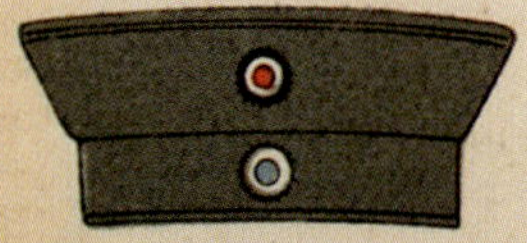

Feldmütze

Waffenrock und Hose

Bluse und Hose

Kavallerie.

2. Chevaulegers-Regiment.

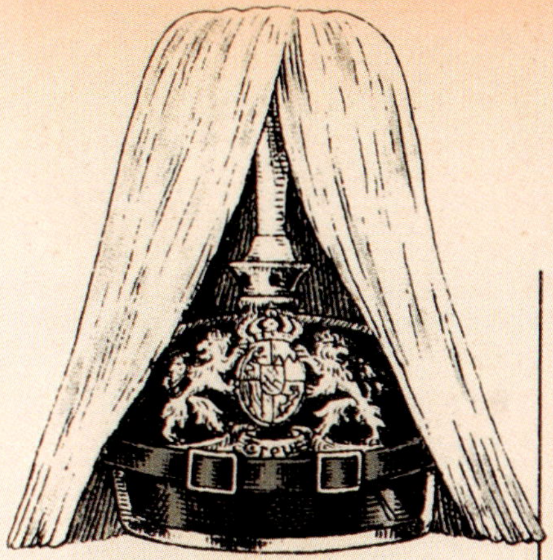

Helm mit Kinnriemen und mit weißem Haarbusch

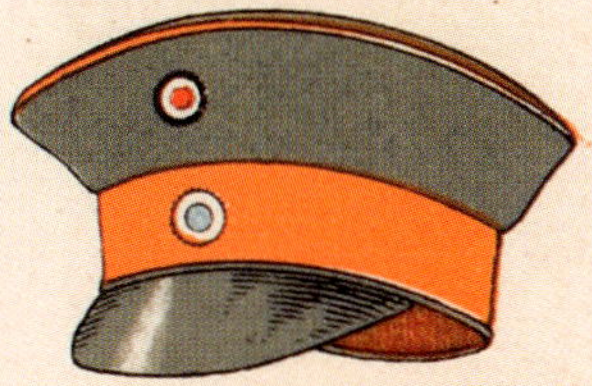

Schirmmütze

Helm
— Spitze abgenommen — mit Kinnriemen

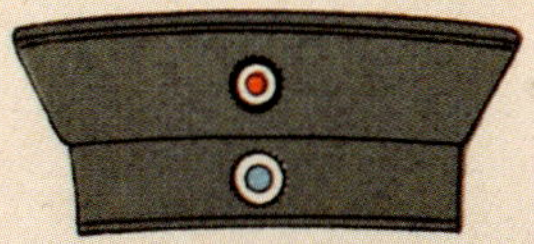

Feldmütze

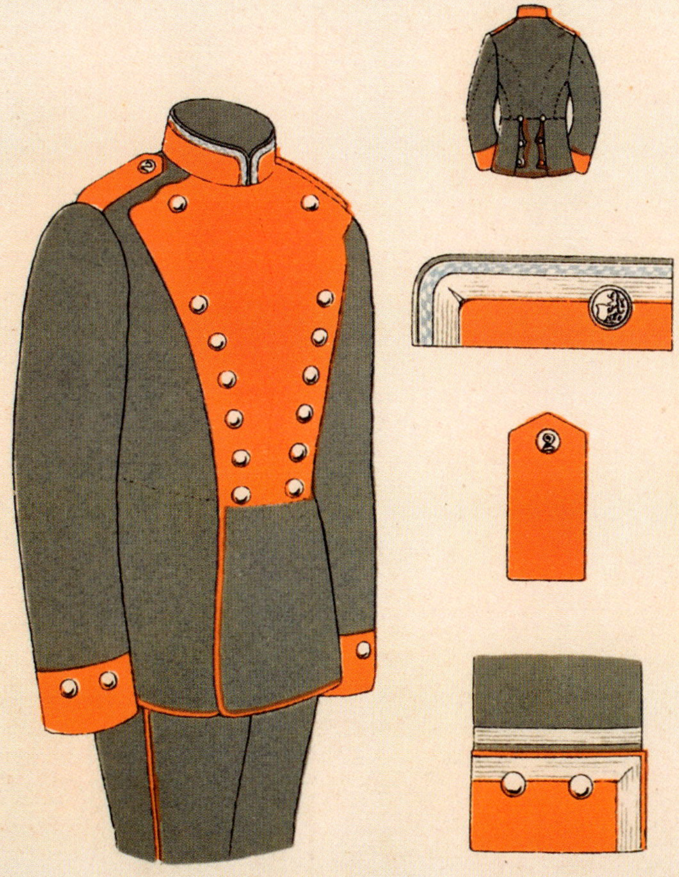

Waffenrock (mit Paraderabatte) **und Hose**

Bluse und Hose

Kavallerie.

3. Chevaulegers-Regiment.

Helm
mit Kinnriemen

Schirmmütze

Helm
– Spitze abgenommen – mit Kinnriemen

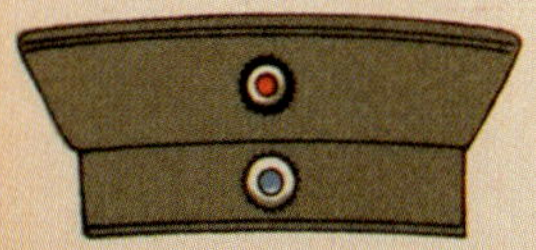

Feldmütze

Waffenrock und Hose

Bluse und Hose

Kavallerie.

6. Chevaulegers-Regiment.

Helm mit Kinnriemen und mit weißem Haarbusch

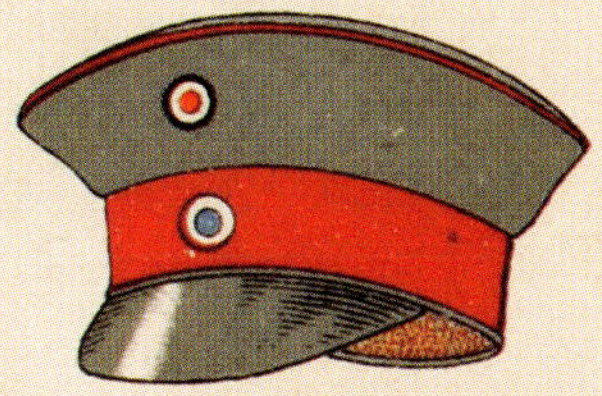

Schirmmütze

Helm
– Spitze abgenommen – mit Kinnriemen

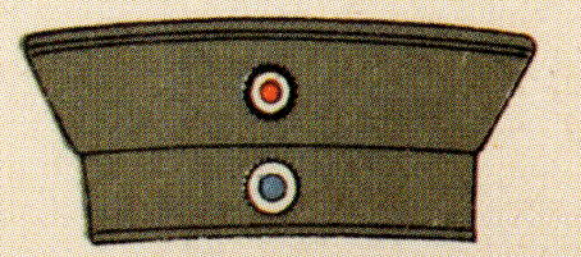

Feldmütze

Waffenrock (mit Paraderabatte) und Hose

Bluse und Hose

Kavallerie.

4. Chevaulegers-Regiment.

Helm
mit Kinnriemen

Schirmmütze

Helm
Spitze abgenommen — mit Kinnriemen

Feldmütze

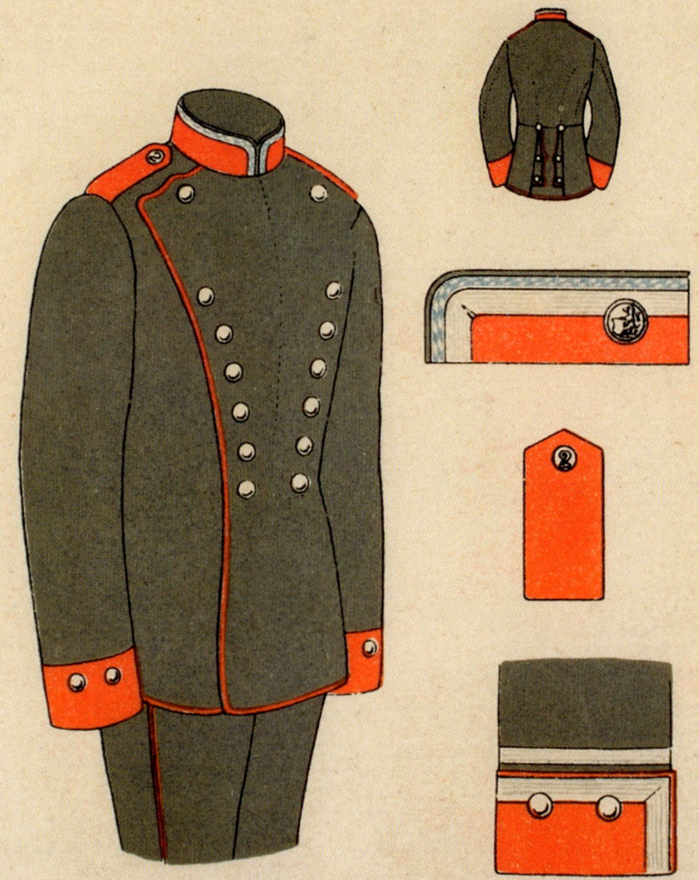

Waffenrock und Hose

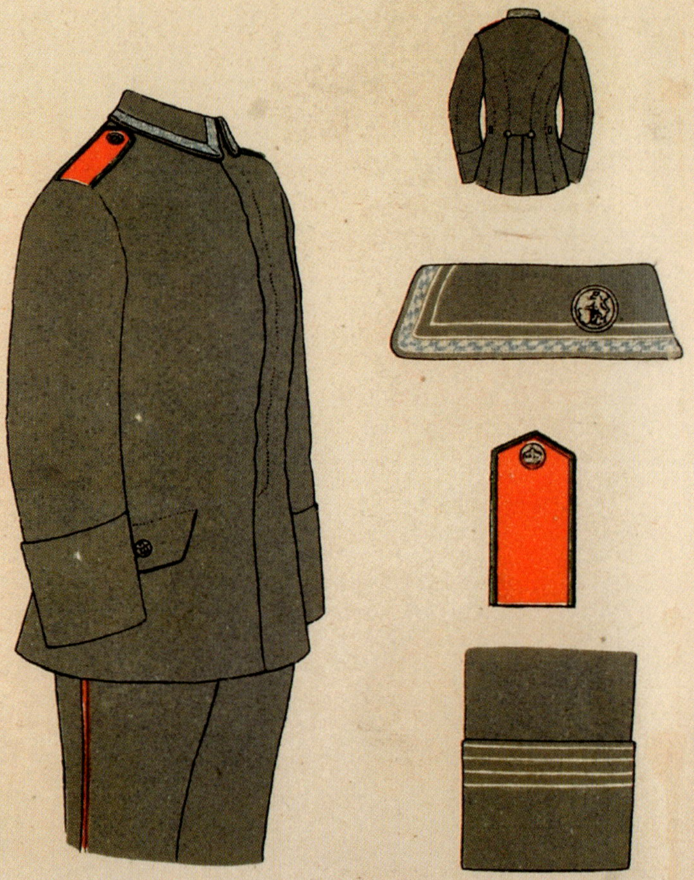

Bluse und Hose

Kavallerie.

5. Chevaulegers-Regiment.

Helm mit Kinnriemen
und mit weißem Haarbusch

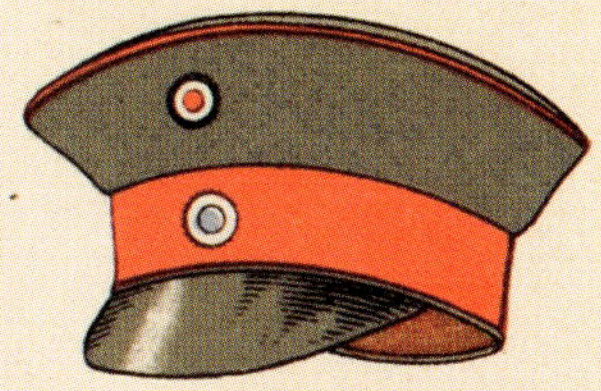

Schirmmütze

Helm
– Spitze abgenommen – mit Kinnriemen

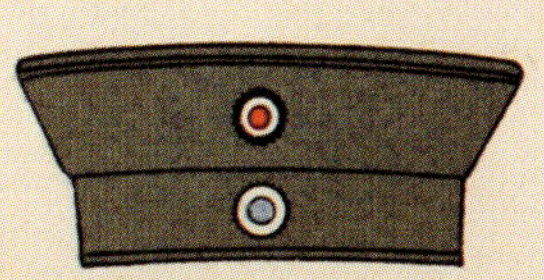

Feldmütze

Waffenrock (mit Paraderabatte) **und Hose**

Bluse und Hose

Kavallerie.

7. Chevaulegers-Regiment.

Helm
mit Kinnriemen

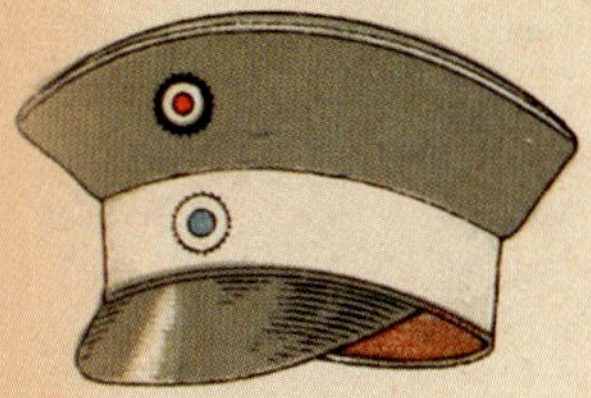

Schirmmütze

Helm
— Spitze abgenommen — mit Kinnriemen

Feldmütze

Waffenrock und Hose

Bluse und Hose

Kavallerie.

8. Chevaulegers-Regiment.

Helm mit Kinnriemen
und mit weißem Haarbusch

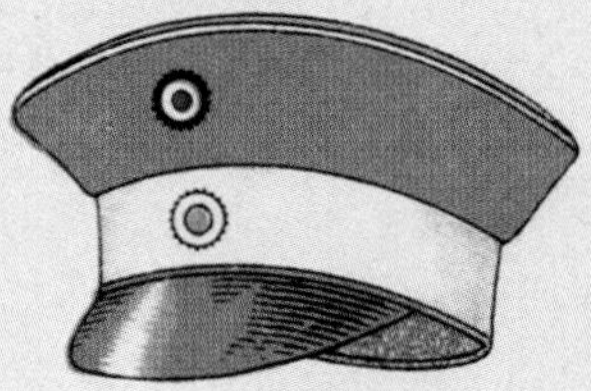

Schirmmütze

Helm
– Spitze abgenommen – mit Kinnriemen

Feldmütze

Waffenrock (mit Paraderabatte) **und Hose**

Bluse und Hose

Feldartillerie.

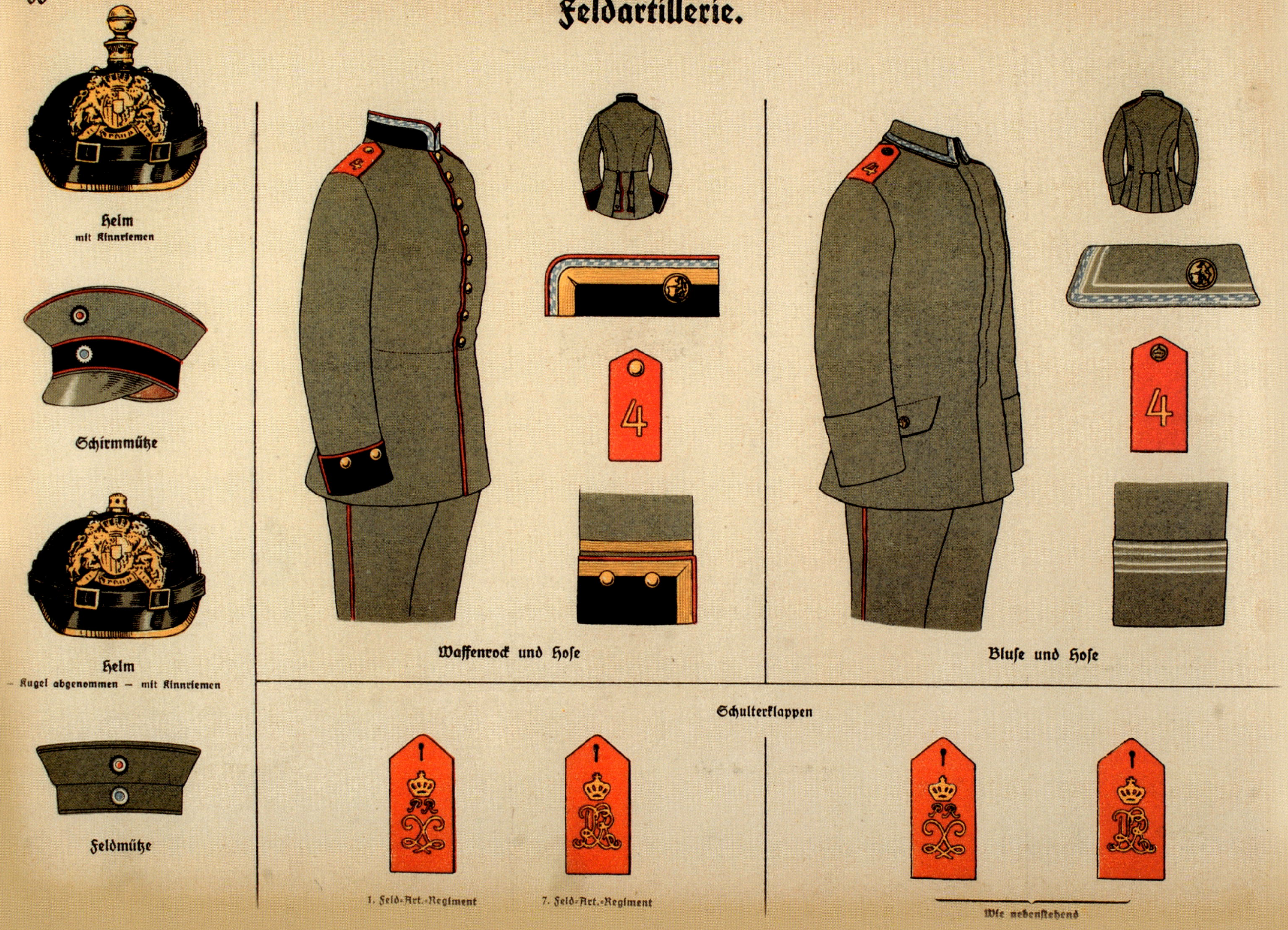

Fußartillerie.

Helm
mit Kinnriemen

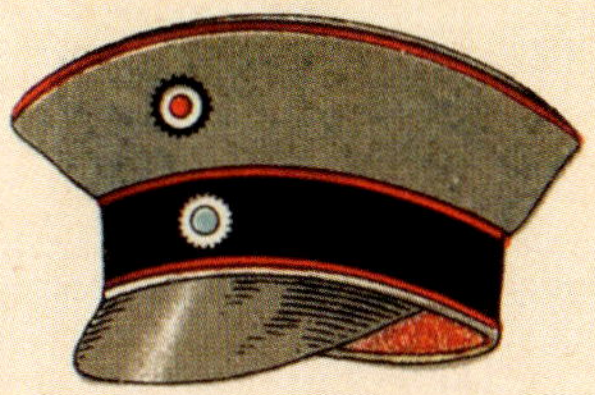

Schirmmütze

Helm
— Kugel abgenommen — mit Kinnriemen

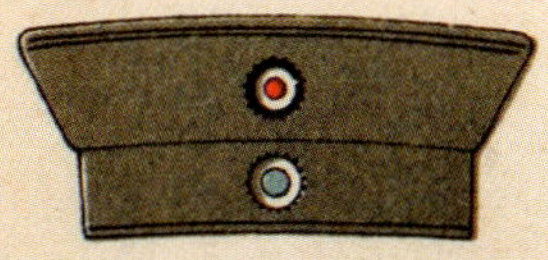

Feldmütze

Waffenrock und Hose

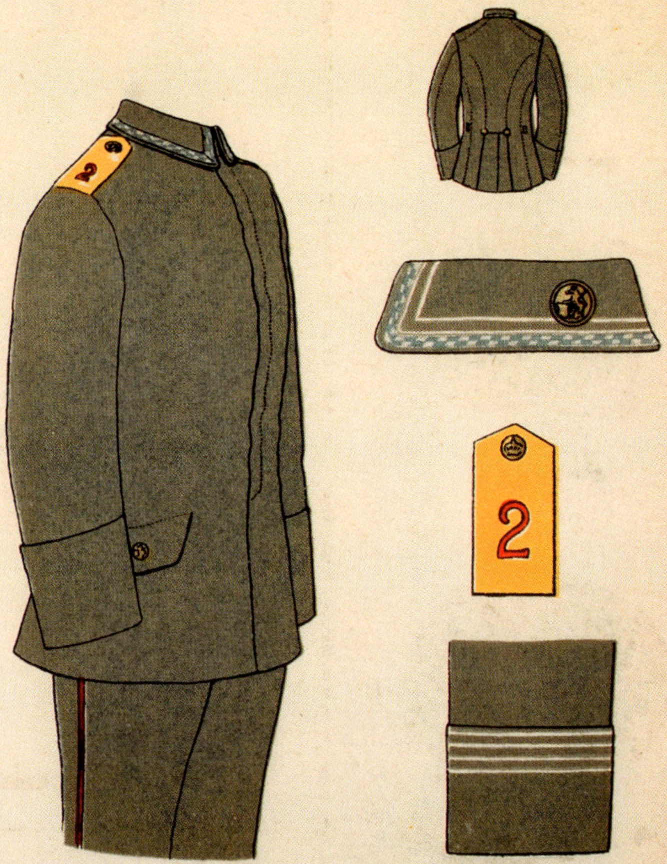

Bluse und Hose

Pionier-Bataillone.

Helm
mit Kinnriemen

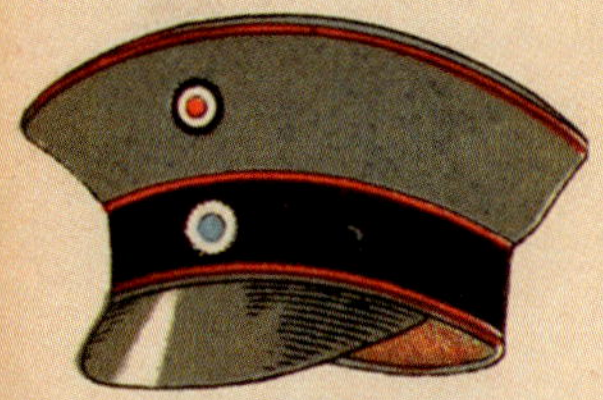

Schirmmütze

Helm
– Spitze abgenommen – mit Kinnriemen

Feldmütze

Waffenrock und Hose

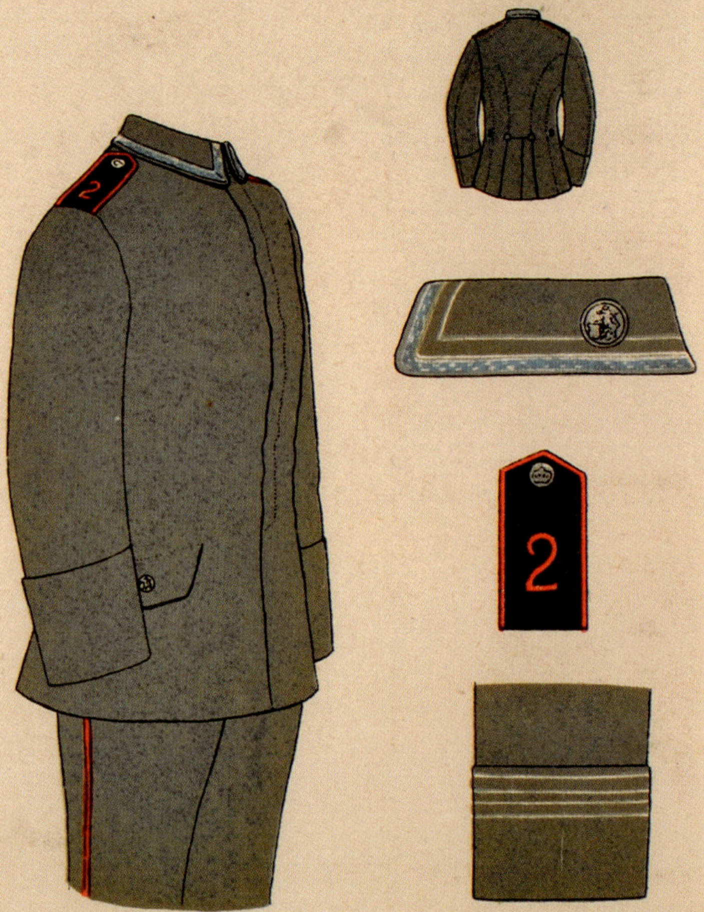

Bluse und Hose

Verkehrstruppen.

Eisenbahn-, Luftschiffer-, Kraftfahr-, Telegraphen- und Flieger-Truppen.

Tschako
mit Kinnriemen

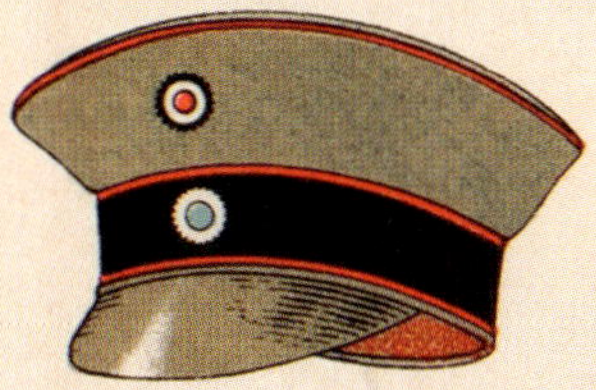

Schirmmütze

Tschako
– Feldzeichen abgenommen – mit Kinnriemen

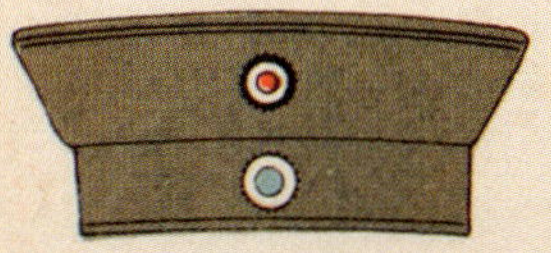

Feldmütze

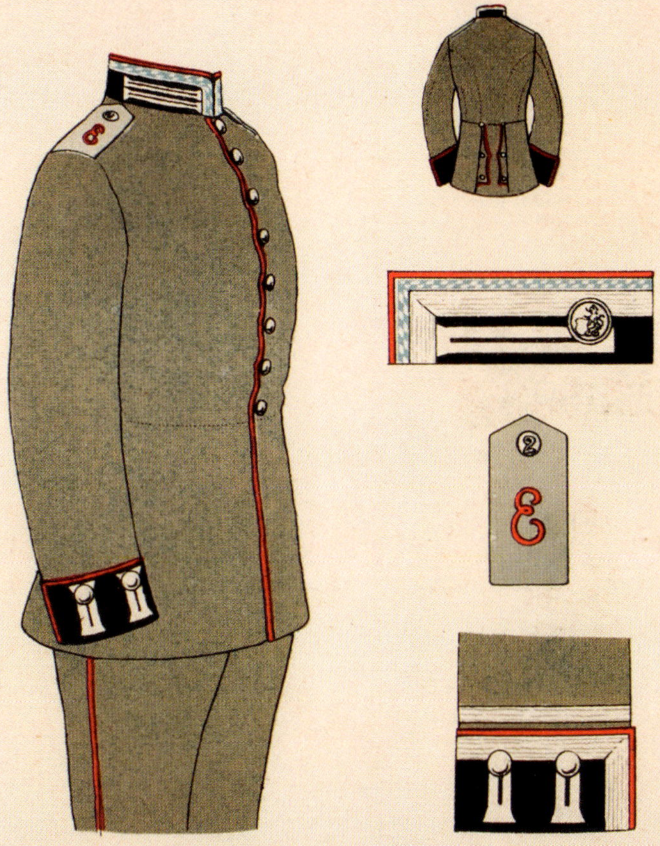

Waffenrock und Hose

Bluse und Hose

Schulterklappen

Eisenbahn-Bataillon | Luftschiffer-Kompagnie | Kraftfahr-Kompagnie | Telegraphen-Bataillon Nr. 1 | Flieger-Bataillon

Wie nebenstehend

Train.

Train=Abteilungen.

Helm
mit Kinnriemen

Schirmmütze

Helm
– Spitze abgenommen – mit Kinnriemen

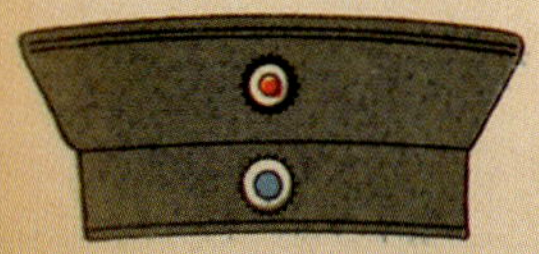

Feldmütze

Waffenrock und Hose

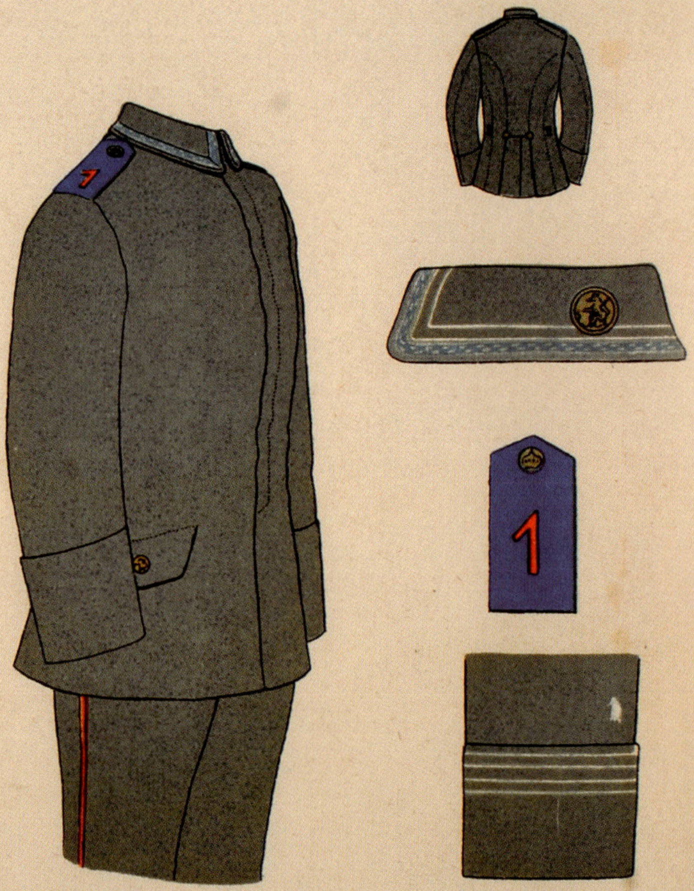

Bluse und Hose

Train.

Krankenträger.

Dienstmütze
(Feldmütze mit Schirm und Kinnriemen)

Feldmütze

Haben keinen Waffenrock.

Bluse und Hose

Train.

Militärkrankenwärter, Köche, Apothekenhandwerker.

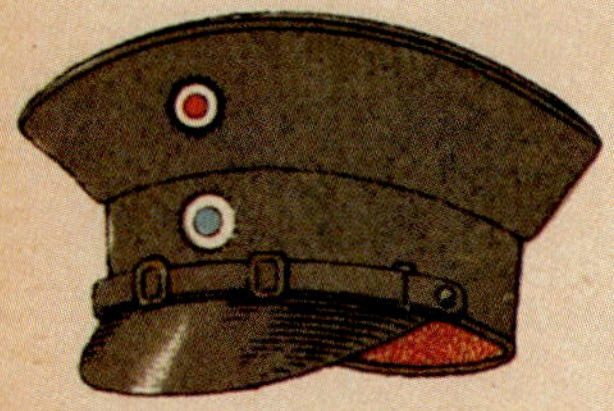

Dienstmütze
Feldmütze mit Schirm und Kinnriemen

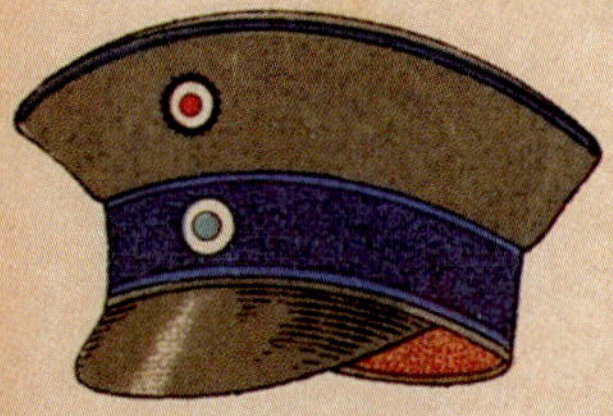

1
Schirmmütze

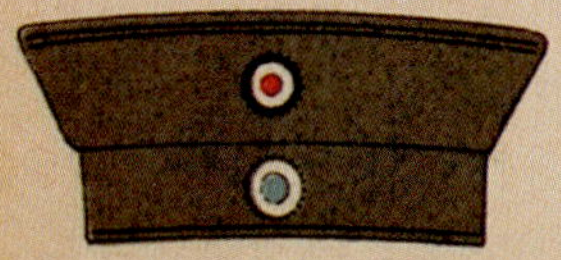

Feldmütze

Waffenrock und Hose
(Waffenrock tragen nur Militärkrankenwärter in den Garnisonlazaretten)

Bluse und Hose